Better Homes and Gardens®
Step·by·Step
MICROWAVE
COOK BOOK

© Copyright 1987 by Meredith Corporation, Des Moines, Iowa.
All Rights Reserved. Printed in the United States of America.
First Edition. Fourth Printing, 1988.
Library of Congress Catalog Card Number: 86-62166
ISBN: 0-696-01500-5

BETTER HOMES AND GARDENS® BOOKS

Editor: Gerald M. Knox
Art Director: Ernest Shelton
Managing Editor: David A. Kirchner
Editorial Project Managers: James D. Blume, Marsha Jahns,
    Rosanne Weber Mattson, Mary Helen Schiltz

Department Head, Cook Books: Sharyl Heiken
Associate Department Heads: Sandra Granseth,
    Rosemary C. Hutchinson, Elizabeth Woolever
Senior Food Editors: Julia Malloy, Marcia Stanley, Joyce Trollope
Associate Food Editors: Linda Henry, Mary Major, Diana McMillen,
    Mary Jo Plutt, Maureen Powers, Martha Schiel,
    Linda Foley Woodrum
Test Kitchen: Director, Sharon Stilwell;
    Photo Studio Director, Janet Pittman;
    Home Economists: Lynn Blanchard, Jean Brekke, Kay Cargill,
    Marilyn Cornelius, Jennifer Darling, Maryellyn Krantz,
    Lynelle Munn, Dianna Nolin, Marge Steenson

Associate Art Directors: Linda Ford Vermie, Neoma Alt West,
    Randall Yontz
Assistant Art Directors: Lynda Haupert, Harijs Priekulis,
    Tom Wegner
Senior Graphic Designers: Jack Murphy, Stan Sams,
    Darla Whipple-Frain
Graphic Designers: Mike Burns, Sally Cooper, W. Blake Welch,
    Brian Wignall
Art Production: Director, John Berg; Associate, Joe Heuer;
    Office Manager, Emma Rediger

President, Book Group: Fred Stines
Vice President, General Manager: Jeramy Lanigan
Vice President, Retail Marketing: Jamie Martin
Vice President, Administrative Services: Rick Rundall

BETTER HOMES AND GARDENS® MAGAZINE
President, Magazine Group: James A. Autry
Vice President, Editorial Director: Doris Eby
Executive Director, Editorial Services: Duane L. Gregg
Food and Nutrition Editor: Nancy Byal

MEREDITH CORPORATE OFFICERS
Chairman of the Board: E.T. Meredith III
President: Robert A. Burnett
Executive Vice President: Jack D. Rehm

Step-by-Step Microwave Cook Book
Editors: Mary Major, Julia Malloy, Diana McMillen, Martha Schiel
Editorial Project Manager: James D. Blume
Graphic Designers: Sally Cooper, Neoma Alt West
Electronic Text Processors: Cindy McClanahan, Donna Russell
Contributing Photographers: Mike Dieter, Scott Little
Food Stylists: Therese McDonnell, Janet Pittman
Contributing Illustrator: Kate Brennan Hall
Contributing Home Economist: Karen Fabian

Our seal assures you that every recipe in the *Step-by-Step Microwave Cook Book* has been tested in the Better Homes and Gardens® Test Kitchen. This means that each recipe is practical and reliable, and meets our high standards of taste appeal.

On the front cover:
Clockwise from upper left: *Peanutty Rice-Stuffed Burgers* (see recipe, page 160), *Peach-Walnut Torte* (see recipe, page 75), *Chicken Véronique* (see recipe, page 186), and *Polish Sausage Soup* (see recipe, page 238).

■ Make the leap. ■ Take your microwave beyond the realm of reheating and defrosting and into the timesaving world of microwave cooking. ■ To discover how easy and quick microwave cooking really is, leaf through our *Step-by-Step Microwave Cook Book*. ■ You'll find more than 300 recipes to tempt you, from traditional basics to some just-right-for-today newcomers. ■ And, because we wanted you to have successful results with every one, we took some extra steps in compiling this book. ■ We simplified each recipe as much as possible and tested it in at least three microwave ovens. ■ Then, to guide you, we added helpful information sections, tips, and pictures. ■ Yes, we not only tell you how to cook in your microwave oven, we show you how— with colorful, easy-to-understand photographs. ■ You'll find important cooking steps pictured on the same page as the corresponding recipe. ■ And, because microwave-cooked foods look different from conventionally cooked foods, you'll see photographs that show how your dish should look when it's done. ■ To top it all off, we've packed in extra features, such as reheating and defrosting charts, nutrition analysis for each recipe, information on microwave-cooking techniques and cookware, hints on menu planning and recipe conversion, plus dozens of nifty hints that make microwave cooking fun. ■

MICROWAVE BASICS

The information on the next few pages covers everything you need to know about microwave cooking, from the way your oven works to the best equipment to use. But before you roll up your sleeves, you should know how the wattage of your oven can affect your recipe's cooking time.

Know your oven wattage

All microwave ovens are not alike. One significant difference is their power outputs (or wattages), which affect how fast they cook. Most larger models offer between 600 and 700 watts of cooking power; most compact models yield only 400 to 550 watts. The lower the oven wattage, the slower the rate of cooking.

We based our recipe timings on 600- to 700-watt ovens. When necessary, we also list timings for 400- to 550-watt ovens. To find out more about your oven's output wattage and how it can affect recipe timings, turn to page 9.

Herbed Chicken and Peas
(see recipe, page 190)

Pineapple-Raisin Upside-Down Cake
(see recipe, page 73)

6

All about microwaves

Turn on a flashlight in the dark and you can get an idea of how a microwave oven works. Just like light beams, microwaves travel in straight paths, reflect off metal surfaces, and pass through all but the most opaque materials. Microwaves adapt well to cooking because foods absorb them, the metal microwave oven walls reflect them, and glass, paper, and plastic cooking containers don't block their path to the food.

The way they cook

Microwaves cause food molecules to vibrate and rub against one another. This rubbing produces heat, cooking the food without ever heating the oven. Your gas or electric oven, on the other hand, has to generate enough heat to warm the oven before the food even starts to cook.

As in conventional cooking, foods micro-cook from the outside in. Microwaves, though, can penetrate only ¾ to 2 inches into all sides of the food. That means for thick foods such as roasts, microwaves cook the outer layers but do not reach the center. So, to cook the center, heat has to spread from the outside edges. Make this happen by cooking food on a lower power level or by letting it stand after cooking.

The power of microwaves

In a conventional oven, the cooking time increases as the temperature decreases. In a microwave oven, the cooking time increases as the amount of food increases. For example, four potatoes take more time to micro-cook than one potato.

The reason: Large amounts of food need more microwaves than small amounts, but because the number of microwaves in an oven

Microwaves penetrate from the edges. The roast above is brown on the outside but remains uncooked in the center.

always remains the same, large amounts receive no more microwaves per minute than small amounts. Since the larger amount isn't absorbing any more microwaves per minute, it needs more time to cook.

Likewise, areas of food hit by more microwaves than others will cook faster. If your oven has a spot where food always bubbles first, that area is called a hot spot. We'll teach you to work around hot spots for even cooking.

Microwaves are safe

Your microwave oven is about the safest appliance in your kitchen. A properly maintained microwave, in fact, is safe enough for children to use, because, unlike the range-top or conventional oven, the microwave oven has no hot elements for kids to touch.

If you're concerned about leaking microwaves, lay your fears aside. The federal government requires that each oven meet strict emission standards before it leaves its manufacturer. The door, the most likely place for leakage to occur, has a seal, screen, and double lock that shuts the oven off instantly when you open the door. If your microwave oven door doesn't close properly or if there is any damage to the hinge, latch, or seal, have the oven checked by a qualified service person.

Nor should you worry about the safety of micro-cooked food. Just like the flashlight beam, microwaves and their effects vanish once the switch is off.

To make sure you are cleaning, operating, and maintaining your microwave oven properly and safely, read the manufacturer's suggestions in your oven manual.

Owner's Manual

WHAT WATT ?

Your microwave oven

The key to successful microwave cooking is understanding how your microwave oven operates. All microwave ovens are not created equal. If you learn why your oven cooks at a rate different from other ovens, you'll be able to compensate for the variation.

The basic oven
All microwave ovens are metal-lined boxes that house a microwave-generating tube called a magnetron. These boxes all have doors with double safety locks to prevent microwaves from leaking, and air vents to allow steam, but not microwaves, to escape. The similarities, however, end there.

What about watts?
The higher the output wattage of your microwave oven, the faster it cooks on high power. As we mentioned on page 6, most larger models offer between 600 and 700 watts of cooking power and cook faster than the smaller models that often yield only 400 to 550 watts. Look in your owner's manual or on your oven to find the power output. If you can't find the wattage listed in either place, measure it yourself, following the tip at far right.

Wattage and timings
For this book, we measured the power output of each of the two dozen microwave ovens in our Test Kitchen. Then we tested every recipe in at least three ovens. That way, we knew we could give you an accurate time range for your oven at home.

The time ranges within our recipes are based on the timings for 600- to 700-watt ovens. Unless we tell you otherwise, these timings will work for 400- to 550-watt ovens as well. Where timings or power levels differ for 400- to 550-watt ovens, we list them separately at the bottoms of the recipes, as shown at left. If your oven has more than 700 watts of output, expect your timings to be shorter than ours.

If the dish fits
Whether your oven is on your counter, under your cupboards, or over your range, it has to be large enough to cook the amount of food you need. And the size of oven cavities varies widely.

Learn which dishes will fit into your oven and check recipes to be sure the required dishes won't be too large. (If you own an oven with a built-in turntable, choose dishes that are small enough that they won't bump into the oven's walls as they turn.) When appropriate, we list smaller dish options for ovens with small cavities, as shown at left.

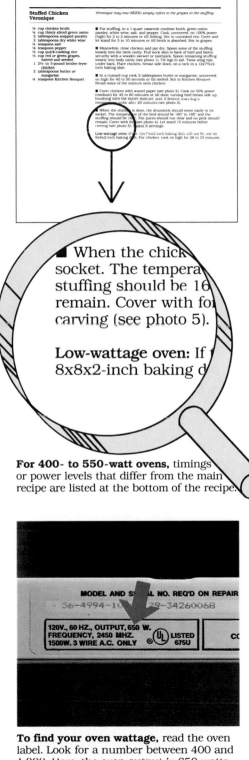

For 400- to 550-watt ovens, timings or power levels that differ from the main recipe are listed at the bottom of the recipe.

To find your oven wattage, read the oven label. Look for a number between 400 and 1,000. Here, the oven output is 650 watts. The power from the outlet is 1,500 watts.

Finding your oven's output wattage: If you can't find the wattage in your owner's manual or on the oven label, here's a simple way to figure it out. (This test won't work if you live at a higher altitude.)

In a 2-cup measure, heat 1 cup tap water (about 70°), uncovered, on 100% power (high). If the water boils in less than 3 minutes, your oven probably has 600 watts or more of output. If the water takes longer than 3 minutes to boil, your oven may have a power output of fewer than 600 watts.

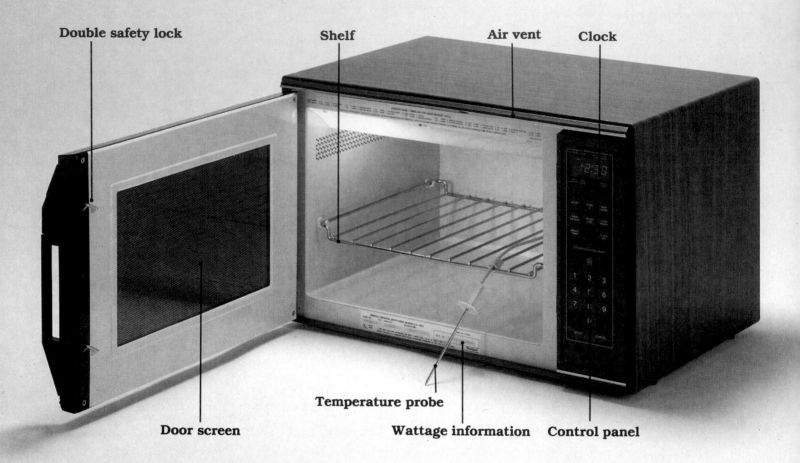

Double safety lock

Shelf

Air vent

Clock

Door screen

Temperature probe

Wattage information

Control panel

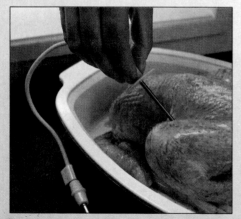

With a probe, foods cook to a preset temperature. To ensure even cooking, test in a few spots with a regular thermometer.

Make sure your dishes will fit inside your oven before starting a recipe. Then check to see if the dishes can be turned easily.

To simplify setting dial controls, our time ranges are in half-minute increments.

At the controls

Control panels differ from oven to oven. Solid-state touch panels with digital readouts are the most accurate, because you can set your oven to the exact second of cooking time. Dials and slide controls are a little less accurate but adequately serve most purposes. They also are easier for some people to use.

We kept our time ranges to half-minute increments to make setting dial controls easy.

Power plays

Ovens offer anywhere from one to ten power levels. How to select the best power level for a specific food is one of the most often asked microwave-cooking questions. To learn more about power levels, turn to page 12.

Automatic cooking sensors

All microwave ovens cook by time, but some also respond to other programmed information, such as temperature, weight, or humidity. This book primarily relies on cooking by time and visual appearance, but we do include temperatures where cooking with a temperature probe would help.

If you have a probe, you can cook liquids, meats, and poultry to preset temperatures. Since the temperature of the food may vary in spots, use the probe only as a guide and check for doneness in several places with a thermometer.

If your oven is specially equipped, you may be able to defrost or cook by weight, or by a humidity or infrared sensor. If so, consult your owner's manual to learn when and how to make the best use of these features.

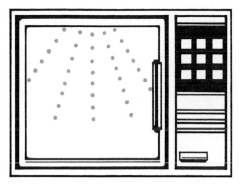

Stirrer fans or antennas scatter microwaves in some ovens. In others, turntables move through the microwaves.

Spreading microwaves evenly

The way microwaves flow from the magnetron into the oven cavity affects how evenly foods cook. To scatter the microwaves and help foods cook more evenly, many ovens have stirrer fans in their tops (as shown above), bottoms, or sides. One brand has a rotating antenna. Still others offer built-in turntables to move foods through a band of microwaves.

If your oven has a stirrer fan or antenna, you'll need to turn dishes occasionally. If you have a built-in turntable, set food slightly off center so the middle will cook, too.

One-step, two-step cooking

Your oven may allow you to program two, three, or even four cooking steps at once. It may even beep before moving on to the next stage. This feature is handy if you want a reminder to rearrange the food or change power levels.

Cook's not in

If you're planning to be away from the kitchen close to mealtime, see if you can program your oven to start in your absence. Just make sure the food won't sit in the oven so long that it will be unsafe to eat. As a rule, don't let meat and dairy products stand longer than one hour at room temperature.

Since the microwave is so fast anyway, it may be just as easy to start cooking after you get home. Then you won't need to worry about preprogramming your oven or food safety.

Dinner's ready but you're not

Once a food is cooked, your oven may be able to keep it warm on 5% or 10% power until you're ready to eat. That's great, but keep in mind that some foods can overcook if left too long on the keep-warm setting.

On the shelf

An oven shelf makes cooking several dishes at the same time easier, especially with small amounts of food. But if you're cooking large amounts or using a number of dishes at once, a conventional oven might be just as quick as your microwave.

Be prepared, too, to switch the foods during cooking; those on the top shelf might cook faster than those on the bottom. You may also want to add faster-cooking items later so everything will be done at the same time. Consult your owner's manual for specific directions.

Some like it brown

If you have a browning unit in your oven, you can brown baked goods and meats. But remember that the preheating required by these browning units can cut the timesaving advantage of microwave cooking. Browning units also rule out the use of most plastic cookware and some plastic cooking utensils.

Power levels

We regulate the rate of cooking in a conventional oven by turning the temperature control. Microwave ovens, on the other hand, can only be on or off, so we must rely on power levels to control the rate of cooking. Some microwave ovens offer only high power; others offer as many as ten power levels.

Power in a microwave oven refers to the amount of time the oven is generating microwaves. The higher the power level, the longer the oven is on and the faster the food cooks. On 100% power, the oven is generating microwaves 100% of the time; on 50% power, it is doing so only half of the time.

When to use which power level

The proper power levels are specified in every recipe in this book. But, if you're ever in doubt about a food, the guidelines and pictures at right and opposite will help you select the correct level.

Lower powers work best for delicate foods such as baked goods, because they allow time between bursts of power for the heat to penetrate evenly.

Sometimes you may need to use several power levels within the same recipe. You can do this either with a cooking program (if your oven has this feature) or by manually resetting the power.

Power levels in this book

In this book we rely primarily on 100% (high), 50% (medium), and 30% (medium-low) power levels. We occasionally call for 70% (medium-high) and 10% (low).

High or 100% power works well for poultry parts, vegetables, liquids, sauces, ground meats, fish, and fruits.

Medium-high or 70% power is perfect for stewing less-tender meats and reheating casseroles and cooked meats.

Medium or 50% power is great for baking breads or cakes and cooking whole birds or large cuts of meat.

By any other name

If expressing the powers in percentages sounds unfamiliar to you, don't worry. Manufacturers name power levels differently, but most of their terms mean about the same thing. Some oven makers use numbers (10, 9, 8, 7, etc.), where 10 is 100%. Others use words (high, medium, low), where high or full is 100%. Still others rely on cooking terms (cook, roast, bake, defrost), where cook is 100%.

In our recipes, we refer to the percentage and the word description of the power level you should use; for example, 100% power (high). If you're unsure, use the chart, opposite, to compare your oven's system of naming power levels to ours.

The power behind the name

Sometimes the percentage of power assigned to a name may differ from oven to oven. Medium on one oven, for instance, may actually mean 60% power rather than 50%.

So, even though the chart is a good guideline for most purposes, if you're baking delicate mixtures, you may want to determine exactly how much power each power level represents on your oven. Check your owner's manual first. If it doesn't list the power level for each name, check the tip in the colored box, opposite. It tells you how to figure out the power percentage yourself.

Medium-low or 30% power is best for evenly defrosting fish and other frozen foods and cooking some cuts of pork.

Low or 10% power is handy for allowing yeast-bread dough to rise quickly without cooking. (See the tip on page 56.)

The defrost power setting

The defrost setting on most ovens generally means 30% power. On this lower power level, food thaws without cooking.

You should always defrost a food completely before beginning to micro-cook it. Otherwise, the microwaves will cook the thawed parts before the frozen parts. You will find more detailed information

on defrosting in charts at the end of most recipe chapters and on page 277.

The keep-warm power setting

Even though manufacturers often bill it as a deluxe feature, the keep-warm setting is nothing more than 5% or 10% power. By exposing food to periodic bursts of microwaves, this setting keeps food warm without much further cooking, although overcooking is possible.

Low-wattage ovens

Notice that the chart below rates power levels for 600- to 700-watt ovens. If you have a 700-watt oven, high power is 700 watts, but if you own a 500-watt oven, high power is 500 watts. As you might expect, if both ovens are set on high, a 700-watt oven will cook foods faster than a 500-watt oven.

In addition, many low-wattage ovens offer only two power levels: high and 30% (low or defrost). When necessary, we list special low-wattage power levels and timings with our recipes (see page 9). If your low-wattage oven does have more than two power levels, try the power levels and timings in the main recipe first.

Finding your oven's power levels

If your owner's manual doesn't mention the percentage of power assigned to each power level, you can roughly determine it in one of two ways.

First, if you can hear your oven's power-on and power-off cycles, compare the time the oven is on to the time it is off. When the on time equals the off time, you have 50% power. When the oven is on one-tenth of the time, you have 10% power.

For a more accurate method of determining power levels, fill two identical cups each with 1 cup of water. Make sure the water is the same temperature in both cups. Cook 1 cup of water on 100% power and record the time it takes to boil.

Cook the other cup of water on the power level you want to test. If the water takes twice as long to boil as on 100%, you have 50% power. If it takes ten times as long, you have 10% power.

Microwave power settings for 600- to 700-watt ovens

Percent		Number		Word rank		Cooking term
100%	=	10	=	High	=	Cook
70%	=	7	=	Medium-High	=	Roast
50%	=	5	=	Medium	=	Simmer
30%	=	3	=	Medium-Low	=	Defrost
10%	=	1	=	Low	=	Warm

Microwave-safe materials

If you have glass, plastic, wood, clay, china, pottery, or paper products in your kitchen, you may already own microwave cookware. Take stock of your current equipment to see if it meets your microwave needs. If you find you need to build your supply, look for durable, easy-to-clean, multi-purpose materials.

Glass

Glass is ideal for microwave cooking because it's attractive and versatile. Clear glass lets you see through it to check doneness.

Use glass that's labeled as heat resistant or oven tempered. It's generally thicker and heavier than table glassware and can easily withstand extreme changes in temperature. (You can take it from the freezer to the microwave to the dining table without worrying about it breaking.)

To prevent accidents, avoid cracked dishes or dishes that have been dropped. Microwaves can focus on a crack or weak spot and cause a dish to shatter. If you're unsure about a particular glass or ceramic dish, try the microwave dish test, opposite.

Ceramics

Pottery, porcelain, china, and stone cookware are generally safe for the microwave, but check them with the dish test, opposite, just to be sure.

Glass ceramic dishes are suited to all types of micro-cooking. Centuraware and Pyroceram, however, will not withstand microwaves because their glaze gets too hot.

Glass, ceramic, and glass ceramic dishes all offer the added advantage of adapting to conventional-oven baking, too.

Plastics

The dos and don'ts of using plastic cookware in microwave ovens can be confusing. There are some plastics that work perfectly in the microwave, including specially developed materials that can withstand temperatures of up to 400° or 600°.

You'll also discover many plastics that will melt with simple reheating and defrosting. Plastic foam, plastic packaging, and melamine, for example, are not microwave safe. What's more, plastics can melt if the ingredients inside get too hot, as is the case with high-fat, high-sugar mixtures. Foods such as butter, candies, syrup, and high-fat meat dishes should not be cooked in some plastics.

Another plastic product frequently used in microwave cooking is clear plastic wrap. Use plastic wrap with care—as a cover, not as a wrapping. The wrap could melt if it touches extremely hot foods.

With so many different plastics available, it's hard to know which are best for the microwave. Eliminate any confusion by following manufacturer's directions. If you do not see a label indicating microwave safety, assume the container or plastic wrap is not safe for the microwave and do not use it. And if you notice a plastic utensil melting or emitting a bad odor, immediately remove it from the microwave oven and do not eat food from it.

Clear, heat-resistant glass lets you see through it to check doneness. It also withstands extreme temperature changes.

Pottery, stoneware, porcelain, and china are usually safe for microwave cooking, but try the dish test, opposite, to be sure.

Some special cookware plastics withstand temperatures of up to 600°, which means they'll work in your conventional oven, too.

Paper

Paper products generally work well in the microwave. Waxed paper is handy because it prevents spattering without trapping steam. Paper plates, napkins, and towels offer easy-cleanup convenience.

To be safe, use paper products in your microwave for no more than ten minutes, and avoid using towels made from recycled paper, which can catch fire. Also be careful with high-fat and high-sugar foods, because cooking them in paper can start a fire, too.

Choose undyed paper products, because the dyes on colored paper can leak onto the food. Look for products that are labeled as microwave safe, then follow the manufacturer's instructions.

Wood and straw

Use wood and straw products only for short-term heating and cooking. With longer cooking, the microwaves can dry and chip or crack the finish on these dishes.

Paper plates, napkins, and towels absorb fat from bacon. Look for undyed paper products labeled as microwave safe.

Metal

For the most part, metal and foil reflect microwaves, preventing food near them from cooking.

Metal works in your favor if you want to protect (shield) parts of foods from overcooking. First, check your owner's manual to see if your manufacturer recommends using metal in your model. If so, use only small amounts of foil in proportion to the food; otherwise, microwaves will bounce around the oven cavity, possibly causing sparks (arcing).

Some special microwave cookware pieces, such as browning dishes, use metal to their advantage. The microwaves heat the metal parts of these dishes, turning them into hot cooking surfaces.

If you're using metal in your oven, prevent arcing by keeping metal from touching metal, including the oven walls. Avoid using twist ties, which have metal under the paper. And be aware that the trims or glazes of some glassware, china, and pottery occasionally contain metal. Because this trim can heat and break or crack the dish, don't use these dishes for micro-cooking.

Wood and straw should be used only for very brief heating or cooking, such as in warming bread.

Metal is a part of many microwave browning dishes. The hot metal surface browns and cooks the food.

Microwave cookware

When you're choosing cookware, look for shapes that are suited to microwave cooking and sizes that fit the amounts you usually prepare. If you can find cookware that's also useful for conventional baking or for cooking a variety of foods, great! Then narrow your selection to dishes that are easy to clean and store.

Sizing it up
The dish's size is important for two reasons. First, it should fit into your oven. If you have a turntable, the dish shouldn't hit the oven's walls as it turns.

Second, the size of the dish should match the amount of food. If your dish is too large, your food may take longer to cook. If it's too small, your food may bubble over. Because micro-cooked foods do bubble up, choose a slightly larger dish than what you would use for conventional cooking.

Even the depth of a dish can affect cooking time. Piled or stacked foods make more efficient use of microwaves. Nuts toast faster and more evenly in a glass measure than when spread out.

Shaping up
The shape of your container affects how evenly foods cook. Foods in the corners of rectangular dishes, for example, sometimes overcook because microwaves enter from two sides and give the foods a double dose. That's why it's best to use round shapes for cakes, custards, and other microwave-baked foods. A ring-shaped dish is even better because it eliminates the center, where food often is hard to cook.

Cover it up
Look for dishes with microwave-safe covers to save on plastic wrap. (See page 22 for more on covering.)

Stocking a microwave kitchen
Now that you know what to look for in microwave cookware, it's time to stock your kitchen. Here's a list of basic cookware you may already have and some specially designed cookware you may want for micro-cooking favorite foods.

Basic Cookware	Special Cookware
A. 1-, 1½-, and 2-quart casseroles	**A.** 12-inch-round browning dish*
B. 9-inch pie plate	**B.** Egg poacher and cake dish
C. 6- and 10-ounce custard cups	**C.** Muffin pan
D. 8x1½-inch round baking dish	**D.** Rectangular browning dish
E. 12-inch-round platter*	**E.** Steamer/colander
F. 10x6x2-inch baking dish	**F.** Teapot and cup
G. 8x8x2-inch baking dish	**G.** 9-cup fluted tube pan
H. 12x7½x2-inch baking dish*	**H.** Freestanding turntable*
I. 1-, 2-, and 4-cup measures	**I.** Popcorn popper*
J. Individual casserole	**J.** 6-cup ring mold
	K. Bacon/meat racks
*Dish may not fit into an oven with a small cavity.	*Dish may not fit into an oven with a small cavity.

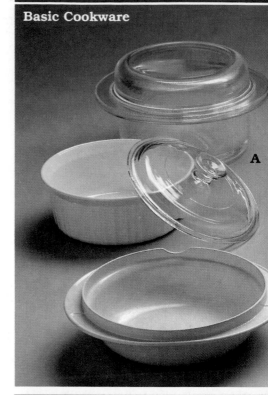

Basic Cookware

Special Cookware

Factors affecting cooking time

In microwave cooking, the judgments you make about cooking time determine whether your dish turns out to be a delicacy or a disaster.

For success, follow the recipes and timings in this book closely. Always check for doneness at the minimum cooking time, and add more time if necessary.

Many factors can affect your timing for a recipe: your outlet's power output, your oven's output wattage, the power level you use, and the food you're cooking.

Power source
Make sure you're getting the maximum power from your oven. If possible, plug it into an outlet on a separate circuit from your other appliances.

If you notice your oven cooks slower at certain times, you may be operating it during peak power periods, when the outlet cannot feed maximum power into the oven. During these times, compensate for the decrease in power by cooking foods longer.

Oven wattage
Different oven models vary in their power outputs. Our recipe timings are for ovens with 600 to 700 watts of power. When the timings differ for ovens with fewer than 600 watts, we list them. Ovens with more than 700 watts may cook faster. To find out about wattage and your oven's cooking power, turn to pages 6 and 9.

Power level
In conventional cooking, as you decrease the oven temperature, you increase the cooking time. In microwave cooking, as you decrease the power level, you increase the cooking time.

Foods micro-cooked on a lower power level, such as medium or medium-low, take longer because they're exposed to microwaves only part of the time. For more information on power levels, turn to pages 12 and 13.

What you cook affects how long it takes
Think about the food you want to cook. Is it in small or large pieces? Is it thick or thin? Is it dense or porous? Does it contain much fat or sugar? Is it moist or dry? Is it frozen, chilled, or at room temperature? All of these factors can change the cooking time. That's why it's important to follow the ingredients and directions exactly as written in our recipes.

The amount of food
The food that gets the most microwaves is the food that cooks the fastest. So, because your oven produces the same number of microwaves whether you're cooking large or small amounts, less food cooks in less time. One cup of cheese sauce will cook faster than two cups, because one cup receives twice as many microwaves.

Because quantity affects the timing so much, we recommend that you use the ingredient amounts listed in our recipes.

The size of the food
Thinner foods cook faster than thicker foods because microwaves penetrate up to only 2 inches from the surface. To cook a thick pot roast, microwave-generated heat must slowly travel from the edges to the center. Burgers, on the other hand, cook quickly because microwaves penetrate throughout.

Likewise, smaller pieces cook faster than larger pieces. A sliced carrot cooks in less time than a whole carrot. For best results, follow our recipe directions for sizes and cuts.

The food's composition
Microwaves penetrate porous foods more easily than dense foods. Light and airy muffins cook faster than denser potatoes.

Similarly, sugars and fats attract microwaves and heat faster than liquids, starches, and proteins. For that reason, you can expect a cup of maple syrup to heat faster than a cup of coffee, and the fat in meat to sizzle and spatter before the meat is cooked (it's a good idea to trim fat when you can).

Moisture also attracts microwaves, acting as a heat conductor. That's why juicy, fresh corn kernels heat quickly and evenly, but a batch of popcorn can contain both burned and unpopped kernels.

The starting temperature of food
Just as in conventional cooking, the initial temperature of the food affects the microwave cooking time. A frozen block of fish, for example, takes longer to cook than its chilled counterpart. In a microwave oven, though, the effect is more pronounced.

Small amounts cook faster. One cup of cheese sauce cooks faster than two cups, because it absorbs double the microwaves.

Sugars attract microwaves better than liquids, so maple syrup will heat quicker than an equal amount of coffee.

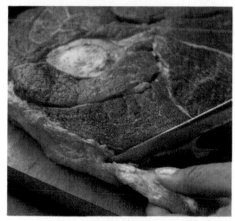

Fat attracts microwaves, so trim as much of it as you can. Otherwise, it will spatter and burn before the meat is cooked.

Porous foods cook more easily than dense foods. Since muffins are more porous than potatoes, they'll cook sooner.

Colder foods take longer to cook. A block of frozen fish will take more time than chilled fresh fish.

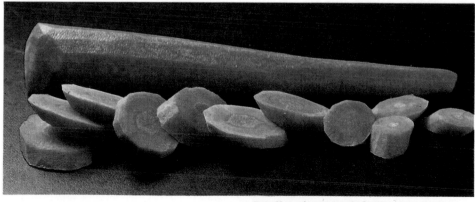

Smaller pieces cook faster than larger pieces. A sliced carrot cooks in less time than a whole carrot.

Moisture attracts microwaves. That's why a fresh ear of corn cooks better in the microwave than drier popcorn kernels.

Techniques for even cooking

Foods often cook unevenly in the microwave oven. The edges of foods cook before the centers, small pieces cook faster than large pieces, and high-fat, high-sugar, or less-dense parts of foods cook sooner than other areas. What's more, some ovens have hot spots. In spite of all this, you can still cook foods evenly if you try the following techniques.

Finding the hot spots

Every oven has an individual microwave pattern. Some areas may be bombarded by more microwaves than others and heat faster. These hot spots generally mean uneven cooking.

To minimize the unevenness, find out if your oven has hot spots. Watch different foods as they cook. If you consistently see one area of food bubbling before the rest, you probably have a hot spot. (The edges, though, will always bubble before the center.)

Avoid placing food in the hot spot when you can. If that's not possible, try changing the shape of the dish, shielding the food, or

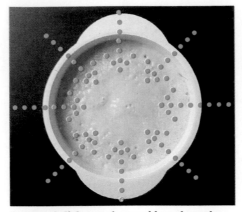

In round dishes, cakes and breads cook evenly because microwaves enter equally from all edges.

rearranging the pieces to make sure the food does not stay in the hot spot too long.

Don't be square

When you're cooking breads, cakes, or custards, choose round or ring-shaped dishes rather than square or rectangular ones. Rectangular dishes have corners where microwaves enter from two sides, doubling their strength. The result is overcooked food.

To shield, cover the corners of rectangular dishes with foil. Corners need protection because they get a double microwave dose.

Round dishes, of course, have no corners. And ring-shaped dishes eliminate both the corners and the center, meaning the edges won't overcook while you wait for the food in the center to finish. A few types of foods, such as brownies, need to be cooked in square or rectangular dishes. When that's the case, we ask you to protect the food in the dish's corners by shielding it.

Foods in hot spots bubble first because they get more microwaves than foods in other areas.

Shielding

Shielding microwaves with foil prevents cooked parts from heating further while other parts finish. Before you try shielding, check your owner's manual to see if you can use foil in your oven. (If you can't, expect foods in corners to overcook.)

To shield square or rectangular dishes, cover the corners with foil. During cooking, cover any areas that are heating faster than others. Use small amounts of foil relative to the amount of food, and, to prevent sparks, be sure the foil doesn't touch other metal.

Even sizes and shapes

Another way to avoid uneven cooking is to make sure the food is as evenly shaped and sized as possible. Also try to cut or fold the food so it is the same thickness throughout.

If pieces are thicker at one end, arrange the food so the thicker portions are near the edges. With the thicker portions cooking quickly on the edges and the thinner portions cooking slowly in the center, all parts of the food should be done at the same time.

Parts that are high in fat or sugar also may cook faster than other parts. That means the fat on a piece of meat or a jelly filling in a bread might heat faster than the meat or bread itself. Keep an eye out in case you need to move or shield these parts during cooking.

Keep in mind, too, that a large bone can act as a shield to the meat next to it, preventing adequate cooking. If the bone is easy to remove, take it out. Otherwise, compensate by arranging the food carefully so the bone is near the center of the dish.

Pieces that are uniform in size and shape cook at the same rate. If meatballs are uneven, the small ones will overcook before the large meatballs are done.

To cook uneven shapes, place thicker portions toward the edges of the dish and thinner portions toward the center.

Shield thin areas to prevent overcooking. For whole birds, that usually means the drumsticks and wing tips.

Large bones can keep the meat next to them from cooking. If a bone is easy to remove, cut it out.

Make sure foods are the same thickness. Fold under the thin parts of fish fillets so those portions won't cook too fast.

Covering up

How do you know when to cover foods during microwave cooking? As a rule of thumb, cover any food in the microwave that you would cover during conventional cooking. Cover foods that spatter or those that cook more evenly in a steamy atmosphere. Leave sauces or delicate mixtures that require frequent stirring uncovered.

Which covers should you use?

■ *Dish lids* or *vented microwave-safe clear plastic wrap* create a tight seal, holding the steam inside so it evenly surrounds the food. Tight covers work especially well with casseroles and steamed, boiled, or braised foods, such as vegetables, fruit, fish, skinned poultry, and ground meat.

Before using a dish with a lid, check to see if the dish and lid are microwave safe (see the dish test on page 15). Or, for plastic wrap, make sure it's recommended for microwave cooking. Vent the wrap by turning back one corner to allow steam to escape.

Even with venting, steam can build. So remove lids or plastic carefully, making sure the steam escapes away from you.

■ *Undyed paper towels* are handy as a cover when you're cooking bacon or reheating breads, rolls, and items with a crisp crust. The paper absorbs grease and moisture, allows steam to escape, and prevents fat from spattering. Avoid colored paper towels because harmful dyes may leak onto the food.

■ *Waxed paper* allows enough steam to escape so the food doesn't stew. Use it for foods that spatter and meats that don't need tenderizing, such as poultry.

Dish lids or plastic wrap hold steam and are great for vegetables, casseroles, fruit, fish, skinned poultry, and ground meat.

Vent microwave-safe wrap by turning back a corner. This cuts steam pressure, but still allows steam to build.

Microwave-safe paper towels are perfect for cooking bacon. They prevent spattering by absorbing grease and moisture.

Waxed paper keeps spattering to a minimum without steaming the food. It helps poultry develop a brown skin.

Stirring, turning, and rearranging

Moving foods during cooking ensures that all parts cook evenly. To do this, you can stir mixtures, rearrange small pieces, turn large pieces over, or turn the dish.

■ *Stirring* from the edges to the center brings heat from the fast-cooking edges to the slow-heating center. You can stir sauces, soups, liquids, and some casseroles.

■ Pieces of food that are cooking unevenly may need to be *rearranged*. Place less-cooked portions close to the edges.

■ The bottoms of foods often cook faster than the tops. Whenever you see this happening, simply *turn over* large pieces.

■ For those foods that don't lend themselves to stirring, rearranging, or flipping, *turn the dish* halfway around partway through the cooking time. That way, the microwaves will hit and cook different areas.

When you open the oven to move the food or turn the dish, cooking stops and the food loses heat. So after stirring, turning, or rearranging foods, quickly shut the door and resume cooking.

Standing time

Just as in conventional cooking, many microwave-cooked foods continue to cook after you remove them from the oven. Generally speaking, foods that require *standing time* after conventional cooking require it after microwave cooking, too. This standing time allows the heat to move from the edges to the center, ensuring that the food is evenly cooked. Large quantities need more standing time than small amounts.

Remove foods that need to stand, such as cakes, breads, custards, and layered casseroles, from the microwave oven when the edges are perfectly done but the centers are slightly underdone. (If you cook until the centers are done, the edges will overcook.) Let the foods stand on a wire rack until their centers look done.

Testing for doneness

Knowing when foods are done is one of the hardest skills to master in microwave cooking, because micro-cooked foods look different from conventionally cooked ones. Judging doneness is even trickier when some parts of the food may be done while others are not.

Begin by learning to use all of the techniques on these and the previous pages. And, as you prepare our recipes, use our photographs to help you judge doneness by sight. Remember to check several places to make sure there are no underdone spots. If you follow our advice, you can count on your recipes being evenly and perfectly done every time.

Stir casseroles to spread the heat from the hot edges to the cooler center.

Rearrange foods that can't be stirred so they'll heat evenly. Turn less-cooked parts that were toward the inside to the outside.

Turn the dish halfway around if you can't rearrange the food. Put colored tape on the dish to mark your turns, if you like.

Turn over large pieces like burgers if you notice they're cooking faster on the bottom than on top.

Let foods stand after cooking so the heat can spread. Muffins are slightly wet when fresh from the oven, but dry on standing.

Micro-cooked foods look different from conventionally cooked ones. Cakes don't brown so need another doneness test.

APPETIZERS AND SNACKS

Keep your next party hopping with microwave appetizers. Your microwave oven will help you keep hot food at your guests' fingertips, yet allow you to spend a minimum of time in the kitchen. You can also slow down the pre-party rush by making your recipes ahead, then heating them in the microwave at party time.

Adaptable appetizers
This chapter offers everything from party nibbles to elegant first courses, including popcorn, snack mixes, nachos, hot dips, stuffed meatballs, and seafood appetizers.

The selection reflects the kinds of snack foods that adapt well to microwave cooking. For the most part, that means recipes that don't need to brown or crisp. So, when you're looking for microwave appetizer recipes, follow our lead and choose moist foods with natural color. Stay away from recipes that require deep-fat frying or oven-baking for crispness.

Snack mixes are surprising exceptions to this won't-get-crisp rule. You'll find that even though our snack mixes are soft when you remove them from the oven, they crisp as they cool.

Smart microwave techniques
When it comes to bite-size snacks, be careful how you slice them. Cut portions into uniform shapes and sizes for even cooking.

Also pay attention to how you arrange the food. Foods in the center of the plate generally cook slower than those near the edges. If possible, place small pieces in a circular pattern on the plate, leaving the center open. If you have to fill the entire plate to make everything fit, switch the center pieces with the edge pieces halfway through the cooking time.

Hot Cheese Dip
(see recipe, page 37)

Deviled Meatballs
(see recipe, page 28)

A little at a time

Serve every plate of hors d'oeuvres fresh and hot by cooking small batches throughout your party. In addition to being fresher, small amounts also take less time and cook more evenly than large amounts. For example, we found that the Shrimp-Stuffed Mushrooms in this chapter heated more evenly when we cooked half of the recipe at a time.

Warming up

Don't worry about foods cooling on the serving table. You can rewarm them in your microwave. You'll find reheating hints scattered throughout this section. Be sure to check foods often so they won't overcook and toughen.

Double-duty cookware

One of the bonuses of making appetizers in your microwave oven is less cleanup; you often can cook and serve in the same container. Where possible, we've called for containers you may already have. The only extra equipment you might need are a large round platter and a special microwave popcorn popper.

Holiday Party Mix
(see recipe, page 40)

**Cider and Ginger
Pork Kabobs**
(see recipe, page 29)

25

Shaping filled meatballs

Choose-a-Filling Meatballs

Delicious surprises hide inside these bite-size morsels.

1 beaten egg
½ cup soft bread crumbs
2 tablespoons finely chopped onion
1 tablespoon snipped parsley
1 clove garlic, minced
¼ teaspoon salt
⅛ teaspoon pepper
½ pound ground beef *or* lamb
Desired filling*
Snipped parsley (optional)

■ In a medium mixing bowl stir together egg, crumbs, onion, 1 tablespoon parsley, garlic, salt, and pepper. Add meat and mix well. Divide meat into 20 portions (see photo 1). Shape each portion around desired filling, using *1 piece* or *½ teaspoon* filling for *each* meatball (see photo 2). Seal filling inside.

■ Arrange meatballs in an 8x8x2-inch baking dish. Cover with waxed paper. Cook on 100% power (high) for 4 to 6 minutes or till no pink remains, rearranging and turning meatballs over once (see photo 3). Drain off fat (see photo 4). Sprinkle with additional snipped parsley, if desired. Serve with toothpicks. Reheat as necessary (see tip, below). Makes 20 meatballs (5 servings).

---

*Filling options: Halved water chestnuts, pimiento-stuffed olives, ½-inch cheese cubes, walnut *or* pecan halves, seasoned croutons, pickle relish, prepared horseradish, chopped chutney, *or* canned green chili peppers, rinsed and chopped.

TIP Reheating Meatballs

Whether you're warming meatballs that have cooled on the buffet table, or some you've chilled or frozen, your microwave makes reheating a breeze. For cooled 1½-inch meatballs, heat 8 to 10 meatballs, uncovered, on 100% power (high) for 1 to 2 minutes. Heat 18 to 20 cooled meatballs for 2 to 3 minutes.

For chilled cooked meatballs, heat 18 to 20, uncovered, on high for 3 to 4 minutes, rearranging once. For frozen meatballs, heat 18 to 20 on high for 5 to 6 minutes, rearranging twice.

1

Meatballs should be the same size so they will all cook at the same rate. For even-size meatballs, pat the meat mixture into a 5x4-inch rectangle. Using a sharp knife, cut the rectangle into 1-inch squares.

2

To fill the meatballs, pat each portion flat and wrap it around the desired filling, as shown. Make sure the meat completely surrounds the filling to prevent leakage during cooking.

3

Halfway through the cooking time, turn each meatball over. The dish's heat and the accumulating juices cook the meatball bottoms faster than the tops. At the same time, switch the center with the edge meatballs. Microwaves penetrate from the sides, so meatballs along the edges cook faster than those in the center.

4

After cooking, drain the meatballs briefly on paper towels and pour off the juices. If you notice more juices than you're used to, don't worry; liquid doesn't evaporate as much in microwave cooking as it does in conventional cooking.

Deviled Meatballs

Meatballs with a devil of a zing. (Pictured on pages 24–25.)

1 beaten egg
¾ cup soft bread crumbs
    (1 slice)
¼ cup apple cider *or* juice
2 tablespoons finely chopped
    onion
¼ teaspoon salt
1 pound lean ground beef
¾ cup apple cider *or* juice
1 tablespoon cornstarch
½ cup chili sauce
1 teaspoon Worcestershire
    sauce
½ teaspoon dry mustard

■ In a medium mixing bowl combine egg, bread crumbs, ¼ cup cider or juice, onion, and salt. Add beef. Mix well. Shape into 36 meatballs (see photo 1, page 27). Arrange meatballs on a 12-inch-round platter. Cover with waxed paper. Cook on 100% power (high) for 5 to 7 minutes or till no pink remains, rearranging and turning meatballs over once (see photo 3, page 27). Drain on paper towels (see photo 4, page 27).

■ For sauce, in a 1½-quart casserole combine ¾ cup cider or juice and cornstarch. Stir in chili sauce, Worcestershire sauce, and mustard. Cook, uncovered, on high for 4 to 6 minutes or till thickened and bubbly, stirring every minute till slightly thickened, then every 30 seconds.

■ Add meatballs to sauce, stirring to coat. Cook about 1 minute more or till heated through. Serve with toothpicks. Reheat as necessary (see tip, page 26). Makes 36 meatballs (9 servings).

Low-wattage oven: For *meatballs,* if dish will not fit, use a 10-inch-round plate and cook half at a time on high for 4 to 6 minutes. For *sauce,* cook on high 5 to 8 minutes, stirring after 3 minutes, then every minute.

South-of-the-Border-Style Meatballs

1 beaten egg
1 4-ounce can diced green chili
    peppers, rinsed, seeded,
    and drained
¼ cup finely chopped onion
2 tablespoons fine dry bread
    crumbs
⅛ teaspoon garlic powder
1 pound lean ground beef
½ of an 11-ounce can (⅔ cup)
    condensed cheddar cheese
    soup*
½ of an 8-ounce can (½ cup)
    taco *or* enchilada sauce

■ In a medium mixing bowl combine egg, green chilies, onion, bread crumbs, and garlic powder. Add beef and mix well. Shape into 36 meatballs (see photo 1, page 27). Arrange meatballs on a 12-inch-round platter. Cover loosely with waxed paper. Cook on 100% power (high) for 5 to 7 minutes or till no pink remains, rearranging and turning meatballs over once (see photo 3, page 27). Drain meatballs on paper towels (see photo 4, page 27).

■ For sauce, in a 2-cup measure combine condensed soup and taco or enchilada sauce. Cook, uncovered, on high for 2 to 4 minutes or till mixture is heated through and smooth, stirring twice with a fork. Put meatballs in a bowl. Add sauce. Serve with toothpicks. Reheat as necessary (see tip, page 26). Makes 36 meatballs (9 servings).

Low-wattage oven: For *meatballs,* if the dish will not fit, use a 10-inch-round plate and cook half at a time on high for 4 to 6 minutes. For *sauce,* cook on high for 4 to 6 minutes.

*Note: Make soup with the leftover condensed soup. Add ⅔ cup *milk or water* and cook on high for 2 to 3 minutes or till hot, stirring once.

Cider and Ginger Pork Kabobs

For even cooking, thread the meatballs on the ends of the skewers, with the mushrooms and peppers in the middle. (Pictured on pages 24–25.)

  1 beaten egg
  ¼ cup crushed chow mein
     noodles
  2 tablespoons apple juice *or*
     cider
  1 tablespoon soy sauce
  ½ teaspoon grated gingerroot
  ½ pound ground pork *or* beef
18 small whole fresh
     mushrooms (6 ounces)
  1 medium green *or* red sweet
     pepper, cut into ¾-inch
     squares
  ¼ cup apple juice *or* cider
  1 tablespoon vinegar
  ¼ teaspoon cornstarch

■ In a medium mixing bowl combine egg, crushed noodles, 2 tablespoons apple juice or cider, soy sauce, and gingerroot. Add meat and mix well. Shape into 18 meatballs (see photo 1, page 27).

■ On nine 6-inch-long wooden skewers alternately thread mushrooms and pepper squares. Place *one* meatball on *each* end of *each* skewer. Arrange kabobs in a 12x7½x2-inch baking dish. Set aside.

■ For glaze, in a 1-cup measure stir together ¼ cup apple juice or cider, vinegar, and cornstarch. Cook, uncovered, on 100% power (high) for 1 to 2 minutes or till mixture is thickened and bubbly, stirring every 30 seconds. Set glaze aside.

■ Cover kabobs with vented clear plastic wrap. Cook on high for 5 to 7 minutes or till no pink remains in meat, rearranging and turning kabobs over and brushing with glaze once during cooking. Transfer to a serving platter. Brush with glaze before serving. Makes 9 servings.

Low-wattage oven: For *kabobs,* if the dish will not fit, use an 8x8x2-inch baking dish and cook half at a time on high for 4 to 6 minutes.

Barbecue-Style Ham Bites

  1 cup frozen small whole
     onions
  1 8-ounce can tomato sauce
  ¼ cup orange marmalade *or*
     plum jelly
  2 teaspoons cornstarch
  2 teaspoons Worcestershire
     sauce
  ⅛ teaspoon ground cloves
     Several dashes bottled hot
     pepper sauce
  1 pound fully cooked ham, cut
     into ¾-inch cubes, *or* one
     16-ounce package
     frankfurters, sliced into
     quarters crosswise

■ In a 1½-quart casserole cook onions, covered, on 100% power (high) for 2 to 3 minutes or till thawed; drain. Stir together tomato sauce, marmalade or jelly, cornstarch, Worcestershire sauce, cloves, and hot pepper sauce. Stir into onions. Cook, uncovered, for 5 to 7 minutes or till bubbly, stirring every minute.

■ Add meat to onion mixture. Stir gently to coat. Cook, covered, on high till meat is heated through (5 to 7 minutes for ham and 3 to 5 minutes for frankfurters), stirring twice. Serve with toothpicks. Reheat as necessary (see tip, below). Makes 8 to 10 servings.

> ### TIP   Reheating Appetizers
>
> When warm appetizers cool on the serving table, pop them back into your microwave oven to reheat. As a rule of thumb, reheat on 100% power (high), checking every 30 seconds and rearranging or stirring as necessary.

Glazed Sausage Links

A spicy sweet-and-sour pineapple glaze adds gusto to these tiny links.

1   8¼-ounce can pineapple
    chunks
¼   cup vinegar
3   tablespoons honey
2   tablespoons soy sauce
1   tablespoon cornstarch
1   teaspoon finely shredded
    orange peel
¼   teaspoon ground ginger
⅛   teaspoon garlic powder
    Dash ground red pepper
2   5½-ounce packages small
    smoked sausage links

■ For sauce, drain pineapple, reserving syrup. Add enough water to syrup to equal ½ cup. In a 1½-quart casserole combine the syrup mixture, vinegar, honey, soy sauce, cornstarch, orange peel, ginger, garlic powder, and red pepper. Cook, uncovered, on 100% power (high) for 3 to 5 minutes or till thickened and bubbly, stirring every minute.

■ Stir in the sausages. Cook, uncovered, for 1½ to 3 minutes. Stir in the pineapple. Cook for 2½ to 4 minutes more or till heated through. Serve with toothpicks. Keep warm during serving. Makes 12 servings.

Low-wattage oven: For *sauce,* cook on high for 7 to 9 minutes.

Taco Chicken Nuggets

Serve these with taco or enchilada sauce.

2   whole large chicken breasts
    (about 2 pounds total),
    skinned, boned, and halved
    lengthwise
¼   cup cornmeal
½   of a 1¼-ounce envelope
    (about 2½ tablespoons)
    taco seasoning mix

■ Cut chicken into 1-inch pieces. In a bag combine cornmeal and taco mix. Add chicken pieces, a few at a time. Shake to coat, then place in a 12x7½x2-inch baking dish. Cover with a paper towel. Cook on 100% power (high) for 5 to 7 minutes or till done, rearranging once. Serve with toothpicks. Reheat as needed (see tip, page 29). Makes 12 servings.

Low-wattage oven: If the dish will not fit, use an 8x8x2-inch dish and cook half at a time on high for 3 to 6 minutes.

TIP **Bacon-Wrapped Nibbles**

Wrap bacon around a filling for a quick snack. Just cut 4 slices of *bacon* in half crosswise. Place between paper towels on a plate. Cook on 100% power (high) for 2 to 3 minutes or till bacon begins to brown but is still pliable, turning once. Wrap bacon around desired filling. Fasten with a wooden toothpick. Arrange on a plate lined with paper towels, leaving center of plate open. Cover with a paper towel and cook on high for 1½ to 2½ minutes or till done, turning plate once. Makes 8.

Filling options: 2 chicken livers, quartered; 8 frozen fried-potato nuggets, thawed; 8 fresh or frozen shelled medium shrimp, thawed and deveined; 8 water chestnuts.

Five-Spice Chicken Wingettes

We've made five-spice powder from ginger, cinnamon, aniseed, fennel, and cloves. You can substitute ¾ teaspoon purchased five-spice powder.

¾ cup dry sherry
¼ cup soy sauce
2 cloves garlic, minced
½ teaspoon ground ginger
⅛ teaspoon ground cinnamon
⅛ teaspoon aniseed, crushed
⅛ teaspoon fennel seed
  Dash ground cloves
  Dash ground red pepper *or*
    black pepper
1½ pounds chicken wings

■ For marinade, in a large mixing bowl combine sherry, soy sauce, garlic, ginger, cinnamon, aniseed, fennel, cloves, and pepper. Set aside.

■ Rinse chicken. Pat dry. Remove wing tips. Reserve for stock or other use. Cut each wing at joint to make 2 sections (see photo 1). Add chicken pieces to marinade. Cover and marinate 3 to 24 hours in the refrigerator.

■ Drain chicken. Arrange chicken pieces in a 12x7½x2-inch baking dish with meaty portions toward the edge of the dish (see photo 2). Cover with waxed paper. Cook on 100% power (high) for 8 to 10 minutes or till no pink remains, giving the dish a half-turn once. Serve warm. Reheat as necessary (see tip, page 29). Makes 16 to 18 servings.

Low-wattage oven: If the dish will not fit, use an 8x8x2-inch baking dish and cook half at a time on high for 4 to 6 minutes.

1

For easy-to-pick-up appetizers, cut chicken wings into wingettes. Begin by removing the wing tip. (Save the tips for making stock.) Then, using a sharp boning knife, cut the remaining piece in two at the joint, as shown.

2

To get the most even cooking, arrange the chicken wingettes in the baking dish so the meatiest portions face the outside.

Citrus Shrimp

Citrus Shrimp

Serve this enticing first course in coquilles, as shown opposite.

12 ounces fresh *or* frozen
    shelled shrimp *or* scallops
 2 tablespoons sliced pitted
    ripe olives
 2 tablespoons thinly sliced
    green onion
 2 cloves garlic, minced
 2 tablespoons dry white wine
 ½ teaspoon finely shredded
    lemon peel
 1 tablespoon lemon juice
 ½ teaspoon snipped fresh basil
    Snipped fresh parsley

■ Thaw shrimp or scallops, if frozen (see chart, page 123). Peel and devein shrimp, or cut large scallops in half (see photo 1 or 2, page 119). In a 1½-quart casserole combine olives, green onion, garlic, wine, lemon peel, lemon juice, basil, ⅛ teaspoon *salt,* and ⅛ teaspoon *pepper.* Add shrimp or scallops.

■ Cook, covered, on 100% power (high) for 2 to 4 minutes or till shrimp turn pink or scallops are opaque, stirring every minute. Use a slotted spoon to serve. Sprinkle with parsley. If desired, garnish with lemon slices. Makes 6 servings.

Scallops with Butter

Each flavored butter gives a new twist to this dippable seafood.

12 ounces fresh *or* frozen
    scallops *or* shelled shrimp
 2 tablespoons water
 ¼ cup butter *or* margarine

■ Thaw seafood, if frozen (see chart, page 123). Cut large scallops in half, or peel and devein shrimp (see photo 1 or 2, page 119). In a 1½-quart casserole combine seafood and water. Cook, covered, on 100% power (high) 2 to 4 minutes or till scallops are opaque or shrimp turn pink. Drain. In a 1-cup measure cook butter, uncovered, 45 to 60 seconds or till melted and hot. To serve, dip seafood into butter. Serves 6.

> **Herb Butter:** Prepare Buttery Scallops as above, *except* add 1 tablespoon snipped *parsley* and ½ teaspoon dried *dillweed, basil, tarragon, or oregano,* crushed, to butter before cooking.
>
> **Garlic Butter:** Prepare Buttery Scallops as above, *except* add 2 cloves *garlic,* minced, to butter before cooking.
>
> **Peppery Butter:** Prepare Buttery Scallops as above, *except* add ½ teaspoon bottled *hot pepper sauce* to butter before cooking.
>
> **Onion-Mustard Butter:** Prepare Buttery Scallops as above, *except* add 2 tablespoons finely chopped *green onion* and 1 teaspoon *prepared mustard* to butter before cooking.
>
> **Citrus-Ginger Butter:** Prepare Buttery Scallops as above, *except* add ½ teaspoon finely shredded *orange, lemon, or lime peel;* 1 tablespoon *orange, lemon, or lime juice;* and ⅛ teaspoon ground *ginger* to butter before cooking.

Arranging bite-size snacks

Shrimp-Stuffed Mushrooms

Cook one plateful for your party's early arrivals and one for latecomers.

20 large fresh mushrooms
(with caps 2 to 2½ inches
in diameter)
1 3-ounce package cream
cheese, softened
¼ cup finely chopped celery
2 tablespoons finely chopped
green onion *or* snipped
chives
½ teaspoon Worcestershire
sauce
Dash garlic powder
Dash bottled hot pepper
sauce
1 4½-ounce can tiny shrimp,
drained and rinsed
Grated Romano *or* Parmesan
cheese

■ Clean mushrooms and remove stems (see photo 1). Reserve stems for use in a soup or other recipe within 2 days. Arrange *half* of the mushroom caps, stem sides up, on a 10-inch-round plate, leaving the center open.

■ Cover with vented clear plastic wrap. Cook on 100% power (high) for 2 to 3 minutes or till almost tender and just starting to water out, giving the plate a half-turn once. Invert caps on paper towels to drain. Repeat with remaining mushroom caps.

■ For filling, in a medium mixing bowl stir together softened cream cheese, celery, green onion or chives, Worcestershire sauce, garlic powder, and hot pepper sauce. Fold in shrimp (see photo 2).

■ Spoon *1 rounded teaspoon* filling into *each* mushroom cap (see photo 3). Arrange half of the stuffed mushrooms on the plate, leaving the center open. Sprinkle with Romano or Parmesan cheese. Cook, uncovered, on high for 2½ to 3½ minutes or till heated through, giving the plate a half-turn once (see photo 4). Repeat with remaining mushrooms. Makes 10 servings.

TIP Softening Cream Cheese

Forget to take the cream cheese out to soften? Don't worry, just follow these fast directions:
   Unwrap the chilled cream cheese and put it into a microwave-safe mixing bowl. Heat, uncovered, on 100% power (high) till softened. Allow 15 to 30 seconds for one 3-ounce package or 45 to 60 seconds for one 8-ounce package.

1

Choose mushrooms that are as uniform in size as possible. To remove the stems, simply bend them back slightly and pull gently. Then arrange half of the empty mushroom caps, stem sides up, in a circle on the plate, leaving the center open. Save the mushroom stems to use in a soup or sauce.

2

For the cream cheese to combine easily with the other ingredients, it first must be softened in a microwave-safe mixing bowl. The cream cheese should be soft enough that the shrimp does not break up when gently stirred in.

3

Fill each mushroom cap with a rounded teaspoon of the shrimp mixture. With the filling on one spoon, use the back of a second spoon to push the filling into the caps, as shown.

4

Microwave energy may be stronger in certain spots of your oven, so, to obtain even doneness, you must move your foods at least once during cooking. Without removing the plate from the oven, simply give it a half-turn. The mushrooms that were in the back will now be in the front.

Pizza Nachos

Cook and serve on the same platter, rinsing between batches.

½ pound bulk Italian sausage
1 medium onion, chopped
   (½ cup)
¼ cup chopped green pepper
1 3-ounce can sliced
   mushrooms, drained
⅛ teaspoon pepper
   Few dashes bottled hot
   pepper sauce
5 cups tortilla chips
2 cups shredded mozzarella,
   cheddar, *or* Monterey Jack
   cheese (8 ounces)

■ For topping, in a 1½-quart casserole combine sausage, onion, and green pepper. Cook, covered, on 100% power (high) for 4 to 6 minutes or till meat is brown and vegetables are tender, stirring once. Drain. Stir in mushrooms, pepper, and pepper sauce. Cook, covered, for 1 minute.

■ Arrange *2½ cups* tortilla chips in a layer on a 12-inch-round platter. Spoon *half* of the topping evenly over chips. Top with *half* of the cheese (see photo, below). Cook, uncovered, on high for 1½ to 2½ minutes or till melted, giving the dish a half-turn once. Serve nachos warm. Repeat. Makes 12 to 16 servings.

Low-wattage oven: For *chips and topping,* if the dish will not fit in your oven, use a 10-inch-round plate.

Quick Nachos: Prepare Pizza Nachos as above, *except* omit meat topping. Top *each* platter of chips and cheese with ¼ cup *taco sauce* and 1 to 2 tablespoons canned *green chili peppers,* chopped, *or* pitted *ripe olives,* sliced.

Spoon the hot meat topping over the tortilla chips. Then sprinkle on your choice of shredded cheese and micro-cook. The cheese will melt quickly, so watch closely and check at the minimum time to make sure it does not overcook and toughen.

Layered Fiesta Spread

Dig into colorful layers of Mexican flavors.

1 pound ground beef
½ cup chopped onion
1 teaspoon chili powder
1 16-ounce can refried beans
1 6-ounce container frozen
    avocado dip, thawed
2 cups shredded cheddar
    cheese (8 ounces)
    Dairy sour cream
    Tortilla *or* corn chips

■ In a 10-inch pie plate combine beef and onion. Cover with waxed paper. Cook on 100% power (high) for 5 to 8 minutes or till meat is no longer pink and onion is tender, stirring once. Drain off fat. Stir in chili powder, then refried beans. Cook, covered, for 4 to 6 minutes or till heated through, stirring once. Stir again.

■ Spread avocado dip over meat mixture. Cook, uncovered, on high for 3 to 4 minutes or till avocado dip is hot, giving the dish a half-turn once. Top with shredded cheese. Cook, uncovered, for 1 to 2 minutes or till cheese is softened, giving the dish a half-turn once. Dollop sour cream over cheese. Serve with tortilla or corn chips. Makes 8 to 10 servings.

Hot Cheese Dip

Pictured on pages 24–25.

¼ cup finely chopped onion
1 tablespoon butter *or*
    margarine
1 teaspoon cornstarch
¼ teaspoon pepper
¾ cup milk
1 tablespoon Worcestershire
    sauce
2 cups shredded American
    cheese (8 ounces)
1 3-ounce package cream
    cheese, softened
1 tablespoon snipped parsley
    Assorted unsalted crackers,
    chips, *or* vegetable
    dippers, *or* all three

■ In a 1½-quart casserole combine onion and butter or margarine. Cook, covered, on 100% power (high) for 1½ to 2½ minutes or till onion is tender, stirring once. Stir in cornstarch and pepper. Add milk and Worcestershire sauce. Cook, uncovered, for 2 to 4½ minutes or till slightly thickened and bubbly, stirring every minute (mixture will appear curdled). Stir in American cheese, cream cheese, and parsley. Cook, uncovered, on high for 3 to 4 minutes or till cheese is melted and mixture is heated through, stirring every minute.

■ Keep dip warm in a fondue pot over fondue burner, or reheat in casserole, as necessary, on 50% power (medium) for 2 to 3 minutes. Serve with crackers, chips, or vegetables. Makes 2 cups (8 servings).

Beer and Cheese Dip: Prepare Hot Cheese Dip as above, *except* substitute ¾ cup *beer* for the milk.

Chili con Queso Dip: Prepare Hot Cheese Dip as above, *except* substitute 1 cup shredded *Monterey Jack cheese* for 1 cup of the American cheese. Add one 4-ounce can *green chili peppers,* rinsed, seeded, and chopped, and several dashes bottled *hot pepper sauce* with the cheeses. Continue as directed above. Before serving, stir in 1 medium *tomato,* peeled, seeded, and finely chopped.

Herbed Swiss Dip: Prepare Hot Cheese Dip as above, *except* add ½ teaspoon *caraway seed or* crushed dried *tarragon* to the onion mixture. Substitute ¾ cup *dry white wine or beer* for the milk, and 2 cups shredded process *Swiss cheese* for the American cheese.

Thickening a hot dip

Creamy Vegetable Dip

1 9- *or* 10-ounce package
   frozen chopped broccoli,
   chopped spinach, *or*
   artichoke hearts
⅓ cup water
1 8-ounce carton dairy sour
   cream
⅓ cup milk
¼ cup cucumber, garlic, *or*
   blue cheese salad dressing
2 tablespoons all-purpose
   flour
¼ teaspoon dried thyme,
   crushed
⅛ teaspoon celery salt
   Assorted chips, crackers,
   breadsticks, *or*
   vegetable dippers

■ In a 1½-quart casserole combine desired vegetable and water. Cook, covered, on 100% power (high) for 6 to 8 minutes or till tender, stirring once to break up vegetables (see photo 1). *Do not drain.*

■ Meanwhile, in a blender container combine sour cream, milk, salad dressing, flour, thyme, and celery salt. Cover and blend till smooth.

■ Add *undrained* vegetables to blender container (see photo 2). Cover and blend till smooth. Return mixture to casserole. Cook, uncovered, on high for 5 to 7 minutes or till thickened and bubbly, stirring every minute till slightly thickened, then every 30 seconds (see photo 3). Cook, uncovered, for 1 minute more.

■ Serve with chips, crackers, breadsticks, or vegetable dippers (see photo 4). If dip cools, reheat in the uncovered casserole on high for 1 to 2 minutes or till hot, stirring every 30 seconds. If necessary, add a little milk to thin. Makes 3½ cups dip (18 servings).

TIP Serving Hot Dips in Cheese Shells

A chunk of cheese makes a great edible serving dish for hot vegetable, seafood, cheese, or chili dips. You'll need a 2-pound round or block of natural cheese cut about 3 inches thick. Try cheddar, Colby, Edam, fontina, Gouda, Monterey Jack, or provolone cheese.

Remove the wax coating or rind, if the cheese has one. If the cheese is rounded, cut a thin slice from the top and invert the cheese so it stands on the cut surface. Using a grapefruit knife and spoon, hollow out the cheese round or block, leaving a shell about ½ inch thick. Save cheese from center and top for another use.

Place the cheese shell in a 1-quart casserole or 8x4x2-inch loaf dish. Spoon the hot dip into the shell. Cook, uncovered, on 100% power (high) for 3 to 4 minutes or till the sides of the cheese soften and conform to the edges of the casserole or loaf dish (the cheese should be soft enough for spreading or dipping). Give the dish a half-turn every minute of cooking.

1 Stir the vegetables once about halfway through the cooking time to break the frozen block into smaller pieces, as shown. Small pieces defrost faster and more evenly than large pieces. At the same time, move any slow-thawing pieces to the edges.

2 Add the hot, undrained vegetables to the sour cream mixture in the blender container, as shown. Cover and blend till the mixture is smooth. The heat from the vegetables will raise the temperature of the dip and shorten the cooking time.

3 Return the dip to the casserole. Cook, uncovered, for 5 to 7 minutes or till thickened and bubbly, as shown, stirring every minute till slightly thickened, then every 30 seconds, so the dip will not boil over. Stir from the center to the edges of the mixture to distribute the heat evenly.

4 Great dippers for hot dips are: crackers, breadsticks, chips, and an assortment of vegetables, including pea pods, sweet red or green pepper strips, cherry tomatoes, broccoli or cauliflower flowerets, carrot or celery sticks, mushrooms, radishes, and zucchini or cucumber slices.

If the dip thickens and cools on standing, stir in a little milk to thin it, then reheat.

Oriental Snack Mix

For directions on toasting nuts, see the tip on page 281.

1 5-ounce can (3 cups) chow
   mein noodles
3 cups bite-size shredded
   wheat biscuits
1 cup toasted whole almonds
¼ cup cooking oil
3 tablespoons soy sauce
¼ teaspoon garlic powder
¼ teaspoon ground ginger
⅛ teaspoon ground red pepper

■ In a 3-quart casserole combine chow mein noodles, shredded wheat biscuits, and toasted nuts. Set aside. In a 1-cup measure combine cooking oil, soy sauce, garlic powder, ginger, and red pepper. Pour over cereal mixture, tossing well to coat evenly.

■ Cook, uncovered, on 100% power (high) for 5½ to 6½ minutes or till hot, stirring twice. Cool (mix will crisp during standing). Makes about 6 cups mix (12 servings).

Holiday Party Mix

For less salt, use unsalted pretzels and nuts. (Pictured on pages 24–25.)

3 cups bite-size
   wheat squares cereal
2 cups round toasted oat
   cereal
2 cups small pretzels
1 cup mixed nuts
¼ cup butter *or* margarine
1 tablespoon Worcestershire
   sauce
¼ teaspoon onion powder
¼ teaspoon celery salt
   Several drops bottled hot
   pepper sauce

■ In a 3-quart casserole combine wheat squares, oat cereal, pretzels, and nuts. Set aside. In a 1-cup measure combine butter or margarine, Worcestershire sauce, onion powder, celery salt, and hot pepper sauce. Cook, uncovered, on 100% power (high) for 1 to 1½ minutes or till butter is melted, stirring once. Drizzle butter mixture over cereal mixture, tossing well to coat evenly.

■ Cook, uncovered, on high for 5½ to 6½ minutes or till hot, stirring twice during cooking. Cool (mix will crisp during standing). Makes about 7½ cups (15 servings).

Honey-Sunflower Mix

Microwave mixes crisp as they cool, not as they cook.

5 cups puffed wheat cereal
1 cup pretzel sticks
1 cup peanuts
½ cup toasted sunflower nuts
¼ cup toasted wheat germ
½ cup honey
¼ cup packed brown sugar
¼ cup butter *or* margarine

■ In a 3-quart casserole combine cereal, pretzels, peanuts, sunflower nuts, and wheat germ. Set aside. In a 2-cup measure combine honey, sugar, and butter. Cook, uncovered, on 100% power (high) for 1½ to 2½ minutes or till butter is melted and sugar is dissolved, stirring once. Pour honey mixture over cereal mixture, tossing to coat evenly. Cook, uncovered, on high for 6 minutes, stirring every 2 minutes. Cool, stirring occasionally (mix will crisp as it stands). Makes 7½ cups (15 servings).

Low-wattage oven: For *mix*, cook on high for 9 minutes.

Dilly Toasted Nuts

Stir the nuts often so they heat evenly.

1 tablespoon butter *or*
   margarine
1 teaspoon dried dillweed
¼ teaspoon celery salt
2 cups walnut halves, pecan
   halves, blanched whole
   almonds, raw peanuts, raw
   cashews, *or* shelled
   pumpkin seeds (10
   ounces)

■ In a 1½-quart casserole combine butter, dillweed, and celery salt. Cook, uncovered, on 100% power (high) for 30 to 40 seconds or till melted. Stir in nuts. Cook, uncovered, for 6 to 7 minutes or till toasted, stirring every 2 minutes the first 4 minutes, then every 30 seconds. Spread nuts out to cool. Makes 2 cups (8 servings).

Peppery Nuts: Prepare Dilly Toasted Nuts as above, *except* omit dillweed and substitute *salt* for celery salt. Add 1 teaspoon *Worcestershire sauce,* ⅛ teaspoon *ground red pepper,* and several drops bottled *hot pepper sauce* to butter before melting.

Nutty Orange Popcorn

Pop the popcorn on your range if you don't have a microwave popper.

10 cups popped popcorn
   (2½ quarts)
1 cup cashews *or* peanuts
¼ cup butter *or* margarine
1 tablespoon finely shredded
   orange peel
¼ teaspoon ground nutmeg
¼ cup honey

■ In a 3-quart casserole combine popcorn and nuts. Set aside. In a 2-cup measure combine butter or margarine, orange peel, and nutmeg. Cook, uncovered, on 100% power (high) for 45 to 60 seconds or till butter is melted. Stir in honey. Pour over popcorn mixture, stirring to coat evenly.

■ Cook, uncovered, on high for 5 minutes, stirring 3 times. Cool (mix will crisp during standing). Break into pieces. Makes 9 cups (9 servings).

Low-wattage oven: For *popcorn mix,* cook on high for 6 minutes.

TIP **Popping Popcorn in the Microwave**

Popcorn is a cinch to micro-cook. For best results, follow these hints and the manufacturer's popping directions.
- Use only 600- to 700-watt ovens, because low-wattage ovens heat unevenly and leave too many unpopped kernels.
- Use packaging or a corn popper specifically designed for a microwave oven. Don't use a casserole or paper bag because the heat may cause the casserole to break or the bag to catch fire.
- Don't exceed the maximum time or the popcorn will scorch.
- Don't try to repop unpopped kernels. Discard them.

Sugar and Spice Bites

This crunchy snack mix tastes like cinnamon toast.

¼ cup butter *or* margarine
⅓ cup sugar
1 teaspoon ground cinnamon
⅛ teaspoon ground nutmeg
   Dash ground cloves
4 cups bite-size shredded
   wheat biscuits *or* corn,
   bran, *or* oat squares cereal
½ cup raisins *or* chopped dried
   apples

■ In a 2-quart casserole cook butter or margarine on 100% power (high) for 45 to 60 seconds or till melted. In a small bowl combine sugar, cinnamon, nutmeg, and cloves.

■ Add cereal to melted butter, tossing to coat. Add sugar mixture, then toss to coat. Cook, uncovered, on high for 3 to 4 minutes more or till cereal is heated through. Stir in raisins or apples. Cool (mix will crisp during standing). Makes 4½ cups (9 servings).

Crispy Squares

To save on cleanup, line the ungreased dish with greased foil.

¼ cup butter *or* margarine
1 6¼-ounce package (4 cups)
   tiny marshmallows
1 teaspoon vanilla
3 cups crisp rice cereal
1 cup cornflakes
1 cup peanuts, raisins, candy-
   coated milk chocolate
   pieces, *or* candy-coated
   peanut butter-flavored
   pieces

■ In a 2-quart casserole cook butter, uncovered, on 100% power (high) for 45 to 60 seconds or till melted. Stir in marshmallows and cook, uncovered, for 1 to 1½ minutes or till marshmallows are puffed. Stir till smooth. (If not smooth, cook 15 seconds more.) Stir in vanilla, then rice cereal, cornflakes, and peanuts. Spread in a greased 12x7½x2-inch baking dish. Chill for 1 hour. Cut into bars. Makes 24 servings.

Crispy Peanut Butter Squares: Prepare Crispy Squares as above, *except* add ¼ cup *peanut butter* to the melted butter. Stir till smooth before adding the marshmallows.

S'More

This kids' favorite is even easier in the microwave.

2 graham cracker squares
½ of a 1- to 1½-ounce bar milk
   chocolate
1 large marshmallow, halved

■ On a plate top *one* cracker square with chocolate, marshmallow, and remaining cracker square. Cook, uncovered, on 100% power (high) for 10 to 15 seconds or till marshmallow puffs. Cool 1 minute. Serves 1.

Something More S'More: Prepare S'More as above, *except* top chocolate with 2 halved *maraschino cherries or* 4 thin *banana slices,* or spread bottom cracker with 2 teaspoons *peanut butter.*

Nutrition Analysis

		Per Serving						Percent U.S. RDA Per Serving						
	Number of servings	Calories	Protein (g)	Carbohydrate (g)	Fat (g)	Sodium (mg)	Potassium (mg)	Protein	Vitamin A	Vitamin C	Thiamine	Riboflavin	Niacin	Calcium	Iron
Barbecue-Style Ham Bites (p. 29)	8	127	13	12	3	849	331	19	6	27	30	8	13	1	6
Beer and Cheese Dip (p. 37)	8	171	7	3	14	475	77	11	12	2	1	8	1	19	2
Chili con Queso Dip (p. 37)	8	181	9	4	15	231	111	14	15	49	2	10	2	25	3
Choose-a-Filling Meatballs (p. 26)	5	129	12	9	5	174	213	18	3	8	4	8	12	3	10
Cider and Ginger Pork Kabobs (p. 29)	9	68	6	4	3	150	201	10	2	44	9	10	10	1	4
Citrus Shrimp (p. 33)	6	63	11	2	1	147	143	17	0	4	1	1	0	4	6
Creamy Vegetable Dip (p. 38)	18	50	1	2	4	51	56	2	7	17	1	3	1	3	1
Crispy Peanut Butter Squares (p. 42)	24	109	3	12	6	92	65	3	5	4	5	5	11	1	3
Crispy Squares (p. 42)	24	94	2	11	5	76	48	3	5	4	5	4	9	1	3
Deviled Meatballs (p. 28)	9	135	12	10	5	322	220	18	5	23	5	7	13	2	10
Dilly Toasted Nuts (p. 41)	8	208	4	5	21	70	139	7	1	1	7	2	1	3	6
Five-Spice Chicken Wingettes (p. 31)	16	38	6	0	1	86	57	9	0	1	1	2	10	0	1
Glazed Sausage Links (p. 30)	12	134	6	9	8	562	131	9	0	4	13	4	7	1	3
Herbed Swiss Dip (p. 37)	8	182	9	3	13	142	59	14	10	2	1	7	0	29	2
Holiday Party Mix (p. 40)	15	149	4	16	8	269	106	6	5	10	12	5	14	2	12
Honey-Sunflower Mix (p. 40)	15	190	5	22	11	125	160	8	2	0	11	3	12	2	6
Hot Cheese Dip (p. 37)	8	176	8	3	15	484	106	12	12	3	1	9	0	21	2
Layered Fiesta Spread (p. 37)	8	325	23	10	21	693	378	35	10	2	6	14	13	24	14
Nutty Orange Popcorn (p. 41)	9	187	4	18	13	84	97	6	4	2	6	3	2	1	5
Oriental Snack Mix (p. 40)	12	201	5	18	13	370	145	8	0	0	5	8	6	3	6
Peppery Nuts (p. 41)	8	209	4	5	21	90	136	7	2	1	7	2	1	3	5
Pizza Nachos (p. 36)	12	203	9	17	11	435	97	14	3	8	5	7	4	15	1
Quick Nachos (p. 36)	12	170	7	17	8	359	69	11	3	10	1	5	2	15	1
Scallops w/ Butter (p. 33)	6	114	9	2	8	224	227	13	7	0	4	2	4	2	6
Scallops w/ Citrus-Ginger Butter (p. 33)	6	115	9	2	8	224	233	13	7	4	4	2	4	2	6
Scallops w/ Garlic or Herb Butter (p. 33)	6	115	9	2	8	222	231	14	7	0	4	2	4	2	6
Scallops w/ Onion-Mustard Butter (p. 33)	6	116	9	2	8	234	232	14	7	1	4	2	4	2	6
Scallops w/ Peppery Butter (p. 33)	6	114	9	2	8	225	227	13	7	0	4	2	4	2	6
Shrimp-Stuffed Mushrooms (p. 34)	10	62	5	2	4	78	189	8	3	3	3	11	9	4	5
S'More (p. 42)	1	153	2	25	6	111	109	4	1	0	1	7	3	4	4
Something More S'More (p. 42)	1	161	2	27	6	111	118	4	1	0	1	7	3	4	4
South-of-the-Border-Style Meatballs (p. 28)	9	128	12	5	6	258	181	19	6	39	4	8	13	4	10
Sugar and Spice Bites (p. 42)	9	154	1	27	6	191	95	2	5	0	12	19	24	3	31
Taco Chicken Nuggets (p. 30)	12	72	12	2	1	47	103	18	0	0	2	3	26	1	2

BEVERAGES

Whether you want a quick warmer in the morning or a relaxing drink after dinner, your microwave fills the order easily, quickly, and conveniently. Microwave drinks can be as simple as heating water and adding a mix. Other beverages might call for additional steps, but usually they require no more than simmering spiced juices for flavor or cooking a fruit base.

Beginning with beverages
If you are just learning about microwave cooking, beverages are a good place to start because they're so simple. Beyond stirring, you won't need to master any special cooking techniques.

As for power levels, you'll usually heat beverages on high. The exceptions are a few spiced drinks that, because of the need to blend flavors, cook longer on a lower power setting.

Heating and reheating
The microwave oven cooks small amounts best, so most of the beverages in this chapter serve one, two, or four people. Cooking larger amounts in the microwave saves little time and is best left to the range-top.

We heated all of our beverages to 180°. Increase or decrease the timings if you prefer drinks hotter or cooler. Or, if you have a temperature probe and you know what temperature you prefer, use it to program the timing.

Easy cleanup
A large glass measuring cup is ideal for microwave beverages because you can measure, mix, cook, and pour all from the same container. Or, use even fewer dishes by making individual servings in microwave-safe mugs.

Cappuccino-Cream Mix
(see recipe, page 50)

Spiced Orange-Tea Mix
(see recipe, page 50)

Hot Currant Punch
(see recipe, page 47)

Spiced Apple Cordial
(see recipe, page 49)

Zippy Tomato Cocktail
(see recipe, page 49)

Banana Nog
(see recipe, page 47)

45

Rich Hot Chocolate

⅓ cup sugar
¼ cup water
 2 squares (2 ounces)
   unsweetened chocolate,
   cut up
2½ cups milk
   Chocolate curls (optional)

■ In a 4-cup measure combine sugar, water, and chocolate. Cook, uncovered, on 100% power (high) for 1 to 2 minutes or till chocolate is melted, stirring once. Stir in milk (see photo 1). Cook, uncovered, on high for 5 to 8 minutes more or till hot, stirring twice. Beat with a rotary beater till frothy, if desired. Serve immediately in 4 mugs. Garnish with chocolate curls, if desired (see large photo). Makes 4 (6-ounce) servings.

Peppermint Hot Chocolate: Prepare Rich Hot Chocolate as above, *except* stir in 1 or 2 drops *peppermint extract* after melting the chocolate. Garnish with a *candy cane,* if desired.

S'More Hot Chocolate: Prepare Rich Hot Chocolate as above, *except* stir in ⅓ cup *marshmallow creme* after melting the chocolate. Garnish with *tiny marshmallows or marshmallow creme,* if desired.

Using a wooden spoon, slowly stir the milk into the hot chocolate mixture, as shown above. The chocolate's heat warms the milk and cuts the cooking time. Finish cooking, then garnish and serve as shown at right.

Banana Nog

Pictured on pages 44–45.

2½ cups milk
½ cup dry instant eggnog
1 medium banana, cut up
⅛ teaspoon ground nutmeg

■ In a blender container or food processor bowl combine ½ *cup* of the milk, dry instant eggnog, and banana pieces. Cover and blend or process till mixture is smooth.

■ In a 4-cup measure combine blended mixture, remaining milk, and nutmeg. Cook, uncovered, on 100% power (high) for 6 to 9 minutes or till hot, stirring twice. Serve in 4 small mugs. Sprinkle each serving with additional nutmeg, if desired. Makes 4 (6-ounce) servings.

Hot Currant Punch

Pictured on pages 44–45.

½ cup red currant jelly
¼ cup water
2 cups cranberry juice cocktail
1 cup unsweetened pineapple juice
¼ cup lemon juice
Lemon peel strip (optional)

■ In a 4-cup measure combine jelly and water. Cook, uncovered, on 100% power (high) for 1½ to 2½ minutes or till jelly is melted.

■ Stir in cranberry juice cocktail, pineapple juice, and lemon juice. Cook, uncovered, on high for 4 to 6 minutes or till hot, stirring once. Serve in 5 heat-proof punch cups. If desired, garnish each serving with a lemon peel strip. Makes 5 (6-ounce) servings.

Low-wattage oven: For *punch,* cook on high for 8 to 10 minutes.

Peanutty Cocoa

Mixing this cocoa in your blender makes it foamy.

2 cups milk
¼ cup creamy peanut butter
3 tablespoons instant chocolate malted milk powder

■ In a blender container combine milk, peanut butter, and malted milk powder. Cover and blend till smooth. Pour into a 4-cup measure. Cook, uncovered, on 100% power (high) for 4½ to 6½ minutes or till mixture is hot, stirring once. Serve in 4 small mugs. Makes 4 (5-ounce) servings.

TIP Reheating Cocoa

To reheat a mug of cocoa, pour ⅔ cup cold cocoa into a microwave-safe mug. Cook on 100% power (high) for the following times:
For 1 mug: 1 to 2 minutes   **For 2 mugs:** 2 to 3 minutes

Lemony Spiced Cider

Cooking on medium power brings out the wonderful spice flavor.

6 whole cloves, cracked
4 inches stick cinnamon, broken
2 2x1-inch strips lemon peel
2 cups apple cider *or* juice
1 tablespoon honey
   Lemon slice halves (optional)

■ Tie cloves, cinnamon, and lemon peel in a 6-inch square of cheesecloth (see photo 1). In a 4-cup measure combine apple cider or juice, honey, and the spice bag. Cook, uncovered, on 100% power (high) for 6 to 9 minutes or till boiling, stirring once. Cook, uncovered, on 50% power (medium) for 10 minutes to blend flavors (see photo 2). Remove spice bag. Pour into 4 mugs. Float a lemon slice half atop each serving, if desired (see photo 3). Makes 4 (6-ounce) servings.

Low-wattage oven: If your microwave oven has no 50% power (medium), use 30% power (defrost).

Lemony Spiced Wine: Prepare Lemony Spiced Cider as above, *except* use only *1½ cups* cider. Add ½ cup *rosé wine* after removing spice bag. Cook, uncovered, on 100% power (high) for 30 to 60 seconds or till heated through.

1

A cheesecloth bag takes the hassle out of removing spices. Place the cloves, stick cinnamon, and lemon peel in the center of a 6-inch square of cheesecloth. Bring the cheesecloth ends up around the spices and lemon peel, and tie with string.

2

Cook the cider and spice bag on 100% power (high) till boiling. Then cook on 50% power (medium) for 10 minutes. Cooking the cider at a lower power level releases and blends the spice and lemon flavors.

3

To serve, remove the spice bag. Pour the cider into mugs. If desired, cut two lemon slices in half and float a slice atop each serving of cider.

Zippy Tomato Cocktail

Pictured on pages 44–45.

1 12-ounce can tomato juice
   or vegetable juice cocktail
½ cup beef broth
1 tablespoon lemon juice
1 teaspoon Worcestershire
   sauce
¼ teaspoon prepared
   horseradish
2 *or* 3 drops bottled hot
   pepper sauce
¼ cup vodka
   Celery sticks (optional)

■ In a 4-cup measure combine tomato juice or vegetable juice cocktail, beef broth, lemon juice, Worcestershire sauce, horseradish, and bottled hot pepper sauce.

■ Cook, uncovered, on 100% power (high) for 7 to 9 minutes or till hot, stirring once. Stir in vodka. Pour into 2 mugs to serve. If desired, serve with celery sticks as stirrers. Makes 2 (8-ounce) servings.

Hot Pineapple-Rum Float

Savor the tropical flavors of rum, ginger, pineapple, and orange.

1 6-ounce can (¾ cup)
   unsweetened pineapple
   juice
⅓ cup orange juice
2 tablespoons rum
⅛ teaspoon ground ginger
½ cup vanilla ice cream

■ In a 2-cup measure combine pineapple juice, orange juice, rum, and ginger. Cook, uncovered, on 100% power (high) for 2 to 4 minutes or till the mixture is heated through.

■ Stir, then pour into 2 small mugs. Top *each* with ¼ *cup* ice cream. Sprinkle with additional ginger, if desired. Makes 2 (5-ounce) servings.

Spiced Apple Cordial

Pictured on pages 44–45.

3 to 4 medium apples, cored
6 inches stick cinnamon,
   broken
2 tablespoons water
2 cups sugar
1 750-milliliter bottle
   (3½ cups) dry white wine
1½ cups brandy

■ Chop apples (you should have 2½ cups). In a 1½-quart casserole combine apples, cinnamon, and water. Cook, covered, on 100% power (high) for 3 to 5 minutes or till apples are tender, stirring once.

■ Add sugar. Stir till dissolved. Cool. Combine apple mixture, wine, and brandy. Pour into a 2-quart ceramic or glass jar. Cover and store in a cool place for 2 to 4 weeks.

■ To serve, strain through several layers of cheesecloth, reserving apples. Serve liqueur in cordial glasses. Serve apples over ice cream. Cover and store liqueur in a cool, dry place. Store apples, covered, in the refrigerator for up to 2 weeks. Makes 5½ cups liqueur or 22 (4-ounce) servings.

Spiced Orange-Tea Mix

Pictured on pages 44–45.

1 cup orange-flavored instant breakfast drink powder
⅔ cup instant tea powder
½ cup sugar
1 teaspoon ground cinnamon
¼ teaspoon ground cloves
   Whole stick cinnamon (optional)

■ Combine drink powder, tea powder, sugar, ground cinnamon, and cloves. Store up to 4 months in an airtight container. Stir before using. Makes 2 cups mix (enough for 12 servings).

■ For *each* serving, in a microwave-safe mug stir *1 rounded tablespoon* mix into ⅔ cup *water*. Cook, uncovered, on 100% power (high) for 1 to 2 minutes or till hot. If desired, serve with a cinnamon stick.

For 2 servings: Cook on high for 2 to 3 minutes.
For 4 servings: Cook on high for 5 to 8 minutes, rearranging once.

Hot Chocolate Mix

Store in an airtight container for up to 4 months.

1½ cups nonfat dry milk powder
½ cup powdered nondairy creamer
½ cup sugar
½ cup unsweetened cocoa powder

■ Combine milk powder, nondairy creamer, sugar, and cocoa powder. Stir before using. Makes about 2⅓ cups mix (enough for 7 servings).

■ For *each* serving, in a microwave-safe mug stir ⅓ *cup* mix into ½ cup *water*. Cook, uncovered, on 100% power (high) 1 to 2 minutes or till hot.

For 2 servings: Cook on high for 2 to 3 minutes.
For 4 servings: Cook on high for 3½ to 5½ minutes, rearranging once.

> **Mocha Mix:** Prepare Hot Chocolate Mix as above, *except* stir 3 to 4 tablespoons *instant coffee crystals* into mix.

Cappuccino-Cream Mix

Pictured on pages 44–45.

1½ cups orange liqueur
½ cup instant Italian-style coffee powder
¼ cup packed brown sugar
   Whipped cream *or* pressurized dessert topping
   Finely shredded orange peel (optional)

■ Combine liqueur, coffee powder, and brown sugar. Stir till mixed. Cover and store up to 2 months in the refrigerator. Makes about 2 cups mix (enough for 10 servings). For *each* serving, in a microwave-safe mug stir *3 tablespoons* mix into ½ cup *water*. Cook, uncovered, on 100% power (high) for 1 to 2 minutes or till hot. Top with whipped cream or dessert topping and orange peel, if desired.

For 2 servings: Cook on high for 2½ to 3½ minutes.
For 4 servings: Cook on high for 3½ to 5½ minutes.

Heating Beverages

Pour the desired amount of cold liquid into the container. Heat, uncovered, on 100% power (high) for time shown in chart or till water is boiling or milk is hot.

Note: Timings are for 600- to 700-watt microwave ovens and will be longer in low-wattage ovens.

Liquid	Amount	Container	Cooking time
Water	½ cup	1-cup measure	1½ to 2½ minutes
	1 cup	2-cup measure	2½ to 4 minutes
	1½ cups	2-cup measure	3 to 5 minutes
	2 cups	4-cup measure	4 to 6 minutes*
	3 cups	4-cup measure	7 to 9 minutes*
Milk	½ cup	1-cup measure	1 to 2 minutes
	1 cup	2-cup measure	2½ to 3½ minutes
	2 cups	4-cup measure	4 to 5 minutes
	3 cups	4-cup measure	6 to 8 minutes

Nutrition Analysis

	Number of servings	Calories	Protein (g)	Carbohydrate (g)	Fat (g)	Sodium (mg)	Potassium (mg)	Protein	Vitamin A	Vitamin C	Thiamine	Riboflavin	Niacin	Calcium	Iron
			Per Serving					**Percent U.S. RDA Per Serving**							
Banana Nog (p. 47)	4	163	5	24	6	91	348	8	5	8	5	16	1	18	1
Cappuccino-Cream Mix (p. 50)	10	205	1	42	4	50	160	1	0	0	0	0	2	5	1
Hot Chocolate Mix (p. 50)	7	187	9	32	4	179	475	14	11	2	7	25	2	28	5
Hot Currant Punch (p. 47)	5	172	0	44	0	10	129	0	0	60	2	2	1	2	4
Hot Pineapple-Rum Float (p. 49)	2	174	2	25	4	30	271	3	3	44	6	6	2	6	2
Lemony Spiced Cider (p. 48)	4	73	0	18	0	4	146	0	0	2	2	1	1	1	3
Lemony Spiced Wine (p. 48)	4	83	0	16	0	4	137	0	0	1	1	1	1	1	2
Mocha Mix (p. 50)	7	190	9	32	4	179	475	14	11	2	7	25	2	28	5
Peanutty Cocoa (p. 47)	4	200	9	15	13	173	332	13	4	3	5	13	14	16	3
Peppermint Hot Chocolate (p. 46)	4	232	7	28	13	75	347	10	4	4	4	16	2	14	6
Rich Hot Chocolate (p. 46)	4	232	7	28	13	75	347	10	4	4	4	16	2	19	6
S'More Hot Chocolate (p. 46)	4	262	7	35	13	81	350	10	4	5	4	16	2	20	6
Spiced Apple Cordial (p. 49)	22	144	0	20	0	0	5	0	0	0	0	0	0	0	0
Spiced Orange-Tea Mix (p. 50)	12	83	1	21	0	1	342	1	13	67	1	3	2	1	2
Zippy Tomato Cocktail (p. 49)	2	115	2	8	0	565	430	3	27	51	5	4	9	2	9

BREADS AND CEREALS

You can sum up the advantages of microwave bread making in one word—speed! Our quick breads cook five times faster than normal, our yeast doughs rise six times faster, and a muffin cooks in a minute. That's fast!

Browning microwave bread
About the only drawback to microwave bread is the crust; it doesn't brown or crisp. As you glance through this chapter, you'll find we compensate for this lack of browning and crisping with a few simple tricks.

Nutty Caramel Rolls
(see recipe, page 56)

Some of our quick bread recipes, for example, ask you to start with whole grains, an easy way to get breads that are naturally darker than those based on white flour. Other recipes want you to grease and coat the pan or dish with crumbs, wheat germ, or nuts for crustlike color. And still others have you sprinkling on a topping before cooking.

Microwave bread basics
Since you can't stir microwave bread for even cooking, you'll need to turn the dish. Turning helps prevent the microwaves from concentrating on one spot.

In general, microwaves cook foods in dish corners before foods in the center. Eliminate this problem by cooking bread in round or ring-shaped dishes. Or, if you can use foil, cut small pieces to shield foods in corners from overcooking.

Most breads cook best on 50 percent or medium power. Check your owner's manual to see what medium power is for your microwave oven. If it's more than 50 percent, your bread will take less time to cook. Muffins, because they're small, cook on high power.

If your microwave has a low setting, you can proof (raise) yeast dough in it. For best results, bake yeast breads conventionally.

Testing for doneness

Deciding when bread is done can be tricky because it won't brown. To test for doneness, scratch the wet surface with a wooden toothpick. If it's done, the bread will be cooked underneath.

Keeping bread fresh tasting

Micro-cooked breads tend to dry out after cooking. To keep them moist, wrap in clear plastic wrap; or top with a glaze immediately after cooling.

Cereal from the microwave

Cooking grains and cereals in your microwave saves more on cleanup than cooking time, but that still means easier breakfasts. Just cook and serve all in the same dish so there's no dirty saucepan to wash.

Nutty Fruit Granola
(see recipe, page 64)

Cranberry-Orange Loaf
(see recipe, page 57)

Whole Wheat Muffins
(see recipe, page 63)

Raising yeast dough

Herbed Whole Wheat Bread

Save even more time by using quick-rising dry yeast. You'll find you can reduce the first rising time to 15 minutes and the second to 5 minutes.

3½ to 4 cups all-purpose flour
2 packages active dry yeast
¼ cup snipped parsley
1 teaspoon dried thyme, crushed
¾ teaspoon celery seed
2 cups water
¼ cup packed brown sugar
¼ cup shortening
1 teaspoon salt
2 cups whole wheat flour

■ Before you begin, test your microwave oven to determine if it can be used for raising bread dough (see tip, page 56, and photo 1).

■ In a large mixer bowl stir together *2½ cups* of the all-purpose flour, yeast, parsley, thyme, and celery seed. In a 4-cup measure combine 2 cups water, brown sugar, shortening, and salt. Cook, uncovered, on 100% power (high) for 1 to 2 minutes or till warm (115° to 120°) and shortening is almost melted (see photo 2). Add to flour mixture. Beat with an electric mixer on low speed for ½ minute, scraping sides of bowl constantly. Beat on high speed 3 minutes. Using a spoon, stir in whole wheat flour and as much of the remaining all-purpose flour as you can.

■ Turn dough out onto a lightly floured surface. Knead in enough of the remaining all-purpose flour to make a moderately stiff dough that is smooth and elastic (6 to 8 minutes total) (see photo 3). Shape into a ball. Place in a lightly greased microwave-safe mixing bowl and turn once to grease the surface.

■ Pour 3 cups *water* into a 4-cup measure. Cook, uncovered, on high for 6½ to 8½ minutes or till boiling. Move measure to the back of the oven.

■ Cover dough with waxed paper. Heat dough and water on 10% power (low) for 13 to 15 minutes or till dough is almost double. Punch dough down (see photo 4). Cover and let rest for 10 minutes.

■ Grease two 8x4x2-inch loaf dishes. Divide dough in half. Shape each half into a loaf and place in prepared loaf dishes. Cover dough with waxed paper. Heat dough and water on low for 6 to 8 minutes or till nearly double (see photo 5).

■ In a *conventional* oven, bake bread at 375° for 30 to 35 minutes or till done. Run a narrow metal spatula around edges to loosen. Remove from pan. Cool thoroughly on a wire rack. Cut into slices (see photo 6). Makes 2 loaves (36 servings).

Low-wattage oven: Not recommended.

1

Remember to test your microwave oven to make sure it is suitable for proofing bread. If 2 tablespoons margarine melts completely in less than 4 minutes on your oven's lowest setting (10% power), the setting has too much power and will kill the yeast before the bread has a chance to rise.

2

After heating the shortening mixture, small lumps will be left in the liquid, as shown. At this stage, the mixture is 115° to 120°—the temperature at which yeast grows. If you have a temperature probe, use it to stop the heating at 115° to 120°. Then add the shortening mixture to the flour mixture.

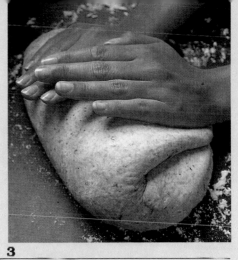

3

Turn the dough out onto a lightly floured surface. Knead by using the heels of your hands to push the dough down and away from you, and your fingertips to fold it back toward you.

4

Proof (raise) the dough in your microwave oven till it's doubled in size. Lightly press two fingertips ½ inch into the dough. If an indentation remains, the dough has doubled. Punch the dough down, then pull the edges to the center, as shown. Turn over. Place the dough on a lightly floured surface to rest before shaping.

5

Cover the loaf dishes with waxed paper for the final proofing stage. Then, with the hot water in the back of the oven, heat the loaves on low till the dough is nearly double, as shown.

6

Bake the loaves in a conventional oven to get a brown, crisp crust, as shown. Remove the loaves from the dishes and place them on a wire rack to cool thoroughly. Then slice and serve.

Fruit-Filled Cinnamon Rolls

The Nutty Caramel Rolls are pictured on pages 52–53.

1¾ to 2¼ cups all-purpose flour
1 package active dry yeast
½ cup milk
2 tablespoons sugar
2 tablespoons butter *or* margarine
1 teaspoon finely shredded orange peel (optional)
½ teaspoon salt
1 egg
3 cups water
1 tablespoon butter *or* margarine
¼ cup sugar
1 teaspoon ground cinnamon
½ cup mixed dried fruit bits *or* raisins

TIP **Raising Yeast Bread Dough**

Before you begin, check your owner's manual to see if proofing (raising) is recommended. Or, use this test to see if you can proof yeast dough in your microwave oven. Place 2 tablespoons cold *stick* margarine in a custard cup in the center of the oven. Cook, uncovered, on 10% power (low) 4 minutes. If the margarine completely melts in less than 4 minutes, you can't proof dough in your oven (see photo 1).

Use only stick margarine, not corn oil spread.

■ Refer to photos, page 55. Before you begin, test your microwave oven to determine if it can be used for raising bread dough (see tip, left).

■ In a mixer bowl combine *1 cup* of the flour and yeast. In a 2-cup measure combine ½ cup milk; 2 tablespoons sugar; 2 tablespoons butter or margarine; orange peel, if desired; and salt. Cook, uncovered, on 100% power (high) for 30 to 60 seconds or till warm (115° to 120°) and butter is almost melted. Stir to dissolve sugar. Add to flour mixture. Add egg. Beat with an electric mixer for ½ minute, scraping sides of bowl constantly. Beat on high speed for 3 minutes. Using a spoon, stir in as much of the remaining flour as you can.

■ Turn dough out onto a lightly floured surface. Knead in enough of the remaining flour to make a moderately soft dough that is smooth and elastic (3 to 5 minutes total). Shape into a ball. Place in a lightly greased microwave-safe mixing bowl and turn once to grease surface.

■ Meanwhile, pour water into a 4-cup measure. Cook, uncovered, on high for 6½ to 8½ minutes or till boiling. Move cup to back of oven. Cover dough with waxed paper. Heat dough and water on 10% power (low) for 10 to 12 minutes or till almost double. Punch dough down. Cover and let rest for 10 minutes.

■ Meanwhile, grease an 8x1½-inch round baking dish. In a 1-cup measure cook 1 tablespoon butter or margarine, uncovered, on 100% power (high) for 30 to 40 seconds. Combine ¼ cup sugar and cinnamon. On a lightly floured surface roll dough into a 12x8-inch rectangle. Brush melted butter over dough. Sprinkle with cinnamon mixture. Sprinkle mixed dried fruit or raisins over dough. Roll up, jelly-roll style, starting at one of the long ends. Slice into twelve 1-inch pinwheels. Arrange, cut side down, in the prepared dish. Return the cup of water to the back of the oven. Heat dough, covered with waxed paper, and water on 10% power (low) for 8 to 10 minutes or till nearly doubled. In a *conventional* oven bake rolls at 375° for 18 to 20 minutes. Cool for 1 minute. Loosen edges. Invert onto a wire rack. Serve warm. Makes 12 rolls.

Low-wattage oven: Not recommended.

Nutty Caramel Rolls: Prepare and shape Fruit-Filled Cinnamon Rolls as directed above, *except* omit fruit. In the 8x1½-inch round baking dish place 3 tablespoons *butter or margarine*. Cook, uncovered, on high for 40 to 50 seconds or till melted. Stir in ½ cup packed *brown sugar* and 1 tablespoon *light corn syrup*. Cook, uncovered, on high for 1½ to 2 minutes or till boiling, stirring once. Sprinkle ⅓ cup *nuts* atop. Place rolls, cut side down, in the baking dish. Continue as directed, *except* invert onto a serving platter.

Cranberry-Orange Loaf

Pictured on pages 52–53.

3 tablespoons toasted wheat
   germ
¾ cup all-purpose flour
½ cup whole wheat flour
⅓ cup sugar
1 teaspoon baking powder
¼ teaspoon baking soda
¼ teaspoon salt
1 beaten egg
½ teaspoon finely shredded
   orange peel
½ cup orange juice
¼ cup cooking oil
½ cup coarsely chopped
   cranberries
⅓ cup chopped pecans

■ Grease an 8x4x2-inch loaf dish. Coat bottom and sides of dish with *2 tablespoons* of the wheat germ. Set aside. Combine flours, sugar, baking powder, soda, and salt. Combine egg, peel, juice, and oil. Add orange mixture to flour mixture. Stir till moistened. Fold in berries and nuts.

■ Spread batter in the prepared dish. Sprinkle with remaining wheat germ. Shield the corners with foil (see photo 1). Cook, uncovered, on 50% power (medium) for 8 minutes, giving the dish a half-turn after 4 minutes. Remove shields (see photo 2). If loaf is not done, give the dish a half-turn and cook on 100% power (high) for 30 seconds to 2 minutes more. (Scratch the slightly wet surface near center with a toothpick. The loaf should be cooked underneath.)

■ Cool 10 minutes on wire rack. Loosen edges. Remove from dish. Invert onto wire rack. Cool thoroughly. Immediately after cooling, cover loaf till serving time or wrap and store overnight. Makes 1 loaf (16 servings).

Low-wattage oven: Cook on high for 7 to 9 minutes.

1
Microwaves hit a baking dish from two sides at the dish's corners, cooking foods in the corners faster. If your owner's manual recommends using foil, prevent overcooking by shielding the corners with it. Use only small pieces of foil in proportion to the food's size, and keep metal from touching metal.

2
Remove the foil pieces and check the loaf for doneness. The bread should start to pull away from the dish, but may still be wet on the surface. Scratch the wet surface near the center with a toothpick. If done, the loaf will be cooked underneath. If not done, cook on high for 30 seconds to 2 minutes more and test again.

Chocolate and Whole Wheat Ring

Wheat germ, walnuts, whole wheat flour, chocolate pieces, and coconut—great ingredients that add up to great flavor!

2 tablespoons toasted wheat germ
2 tablespoons ground walnuts
1 cup all-purpose flour
½ cup whole wheat flour
2 teaspoons baking powder
¼ teaspoon salt
½ cup butter *or* margarine
½ cup sugar
2 eggs
⅔ cup milk
⅓ cup miniature semisweet chocolate pieces
⅓ cup chopped walnuts
¼ cup coconut

■ Grease a microwave-safe 10-cup ring mold. Combine wheat germ and 2 tablespoons walnuts, then coat the ring mold. Set aside.

■ In a small mixing bowl stir together the all-purpose flour, whole wheat flour, baking powder, and salt. In a large mixer bowl beat butter or margarine and sugar with an electric mixer on medium speed till fluffy. Add eggs, one at a time, beating after each addition. Add flour mixture and milk alternately to beaten mixture, beating till smooth.

■ Spoon *half* of the batter into the prepared dish. Combine chocolate pieces, ⅓ cup walnuts, and coconut. Sprinkle over batter. Top with remaining batter (see photo, below).

■ Cook, uncovered, on 50% power (medium) for 12 minutes, giving the dish a quarter-turn every 3 minutes. If not done, cook on 100% power (high) for 30 seconds to 2 minutes more (see photo 2, page 57). Cool in the dish on a wire rack for 10 minutes. To loosen, run a narrow metal spatula around edges. Invert onto a serving platter. Remove dish. Serve warm. Makes 1 ring (16 servings).

Low-wattage oven: Cook on high for 7 to 9 minutes, turning the dish every 2 minutes.

To create the layers, spoon half of the batter into the prepared ring mold. Sprinkle the mixture of chocolate pieces, nuts, and coconut over the batter. Spoon the remaining batter over the top, as shown. The ring mold will not be as full as for conventional baking because the batter rises so much during microwave cooking.

Chocolate and
Whole Wheat Ring

Technique:
Making muffins

Ready-to-Cook Fruit 'n' Bran Muffins

Refrigerate this honey-sweetened batter. Then cook as many muffins as you need. The batter keeps up to 2 weeks.

½ cup water
1½ cups whole bran cereal
¼ cup shortening
1 cup buttermilk *or* sour milk
2 beaten eggs
¼ cup packed brown sugar
¼ cup honey
1¼ cups all-purpose flour
2½ teaspoons baking powder
1 teaspoon ground cinnamon
½ teaspoon baking soda
¼ teaspoon salt
¾ cup mixed dried fruit
   bits *or* raisins
   Desired topping (optional)
   (see tip)

■ Cook water on 100% power (high) for 1½ to 2 minutes or till boiling. In a mixing bowl combine water, bran, and shortening. Add buttermilk, eggs, brown sugar, and honey. Mix well. Combine flour, baking powder, cinnamon, soda, and salt. Add to bran mixture. Stir till moistened (see photo 1). Fold in fruit. Refrigerate in an airtight container up to 2 weeks.

■ Line 6-ounce custard cups or a microwave-safe muffin pan with paper bake cups. For each muffin, spoon *2 slightly rounded tablespoons* of batter into a paper cup (see photo 2). For custard cups, arrange in a ring on a plate. Sprinkle topping over batter, if desired (see photo 3). Cook, uncovered, on 100% power (high) for specified time or till done, giving the plate or pan a half-turn every minute (see photo, page 62). (Scratch the slightly wet surface with a wooden toothpick. The muffin should be cooked underneath.) If using custard cups, remove muffins from the oven as they are done. Remove muffins from the cups or pan. Let stand on a wire rack for 5 minutes (see photo 4). Serve warm. Makes 24.

For 1 muffin: Cook on high for 30 to 60 seconds.
For 2 muffins: Cook on high for 1 to 2 minutes.
For 4 muffins: Cook on high for 1½ to 2½ minutes.
For 6 muffins: Cook on high for 2 to 3½ minutes.

TIP Top o' the Muffins

Choose a topping to sprinkle on the muffins in this chapter.
Sugar 'n' Spice Topping: Combine 2 teaspoons *sugar* and ¼ teaspoon ground *cinnamon or* ground *nutmeg.* Sprinkle ¼ *teaspoon* on each muffin. Tops 8 or 9 muffins.
Nutty Graham Topping: Combine 2 *graham cracker squares,* coarsely crushed (2 tablespoons), and 1 tablespoon finely chopped *nuts.* Sprinkle *1 teaspoon* on each muffin. Tops 10 muffins.
Streusel Topping: Stir together 3 tablespoons all-purpose *flour,* 1 tablespoon *brown sugar,* and ¼ teaspoon ground *cinnamon.* Stir in 1 tablespoon melted *butter or margarine.* Sprinkle *1 teaspoon* on each muffin. Tops 12 muffins.

1

Overmixing causes tunnels and peaks to form in muffins as they cook. To prevent overmixing, add the flour mixture to the bran cereal mixture and stir gently just till moistened, as shown.

2

Line 6-ounce custard cups or a microwave muffin pan with paper bake cups. Spoon 2 tablespoons of the muffin batter into the cups, as shown. You'll notice that, after chilling, the batter has risen slightly and is stiffer than before.

3

For even cooking, arrange the custard cups on a plate, leaving the center open. If you like, sprinkle a topping over the batter in the cups. Clockwise, from front center, are: Streusel Topping, Sugar 'n' Spice Topping, Nutty Graham Topping, and a muffin without any topping.

4

Even if they are done, fresh-from-the-microwave muffins will have wet tops like the one in front above. After standing 5 minutes, the top will dry as it did on the muffin in the back. Check for doneness by scratching the wet surface with a toothpick. You should find a cooked texture underneath the surface.

Basic Muffins

¾ cup all-purpose flour
2 tablespoons sugar
1 teaspoon baking powder
⅛ teaspoon salt
1 beaten egg yolk
⅓ cup milk
3 tablespoons cooking oil
Desired topping (see tip, page 60)

■ In a mixing bowl combine flour, sugar, baking powder, and salt. Make a well in the center of the flour mixture. Combine egg yolk, milk, and cooking oil. Add all at once to flour mixture. Stir just till moistened (see photo 1, page 61). Line a microwave-safe muffin pan or six 6-ounce custard cups with paper bake cups. For each muffin, spoon *2 slightly rounded tablespoons* of batter into each paper cup (see photo 2, page 61). Prepare topping. Sprinkle atop each.

■ For custard cups, arrange on a plate, leaving the center open (see photo 3, page 61). Cook batter in cups or microwave-safe muffin pan, uncovered, on 100% power (high) for 1½ to 3 minutes or till done, giving the plate or pan a half-turn every minute (see photo below, and photo 4, page 61). (Scratch the slightly wet surface with a wooden toothpick. The muffin should be cooked underneath.)

■ If using custard cups, remove muffins from oven as they are done. Remove muffins from the pan or custard cups. Let stand for 5 minutes on a wire rack. Serve warm. Makes 6 muffins.

Place the filled muffin pan in your microwave oven. Cook according to the recipe directions, giving the muffin pan a half-turn every minute, as shown. These Basic Muffins are topped with the Streusel Topping.

Surprise-Filled Muffins: Prepare Basic Muffins as above, *except* spoon *1 rounded tablespoon* muffin batter into *each* muffin cup or custard cup. Add 1 teaspoon *jam, jelly, cream cheese, peanut butter, or semisweet chocolate pieces* to each cup. Top each with 2 tablespoons more batter.

Cheese and Nut Muffins: Prepare Basic Muffins as above, *except* stir ¼ cup (1 ounce) finely shredded *cheddar cheese*, 2 tablespoons finely chopped *nuts*, and 1 teaspoon dried *parsley flakes* into the dry ingredients.

Blueberry Muffins: Prepare Basic Muffins as above, *except* add ½ teaspoon finely shredded *lemon peel* and dash ground *cloves* to dry ingredients. Then carefully fold in ⅓ cup fresh *or* thawed frozen *blueberries* into batter.

Whole Wheat Muffin Mix

See the Whole Wheat Muffins topped with our Nutty Fruit Granola on pages 52–53.

  5 cups all-purpose flour
2½ cups whole wheat flour
  1 cup packed brown sugar
  3 tablespoons baking powder
  1 tablespoon ground cinnamon
1½ teaspoons salt
  2 cups shortening that does
      not require refrigeration
  1 beaten egg
⅓ cup milk
      Nutty Fruit Granola (see
      recipe, page 64), granola,
      or other desired topping
      (see tip, page 60)

■ Refer to photos, pages 61 and 62. Combine all-purpose flour, whole wheat flour, brown sugar, baking powder, cinnamon, and salt. With a pastry blender, cut in shortening till mix resembles coarse crumbs. Store in an airtight container up to 6 weeks at room temperature or 6 months in freezer. (Bring to room temperature before use.) Makes 12 cups.

■ To bake muffins, in a mixing bowl place *1¼ cups* mix. Combine egg and milk. Add to dry ingredients. Stir just till moistened. Line a microwave-safe muffin pan or six 6-ounce custard cups with paper bake cups. For each muffin, spoon *2 slightly rounded tablespoons* batter into a paper bake cup. Top with *1 teaspoon* crushed granola or other topping.

■ For custard cups, arrange on a plate, leaving center open. Cook, uncovered, on 100% power (high) for 2 to 3 minutes or till done, giving the dish a half-turn every minute. (Scratch the slightly wet surface with a wooden toothpick. The muffin should be cooked underneath.) If using custard cups, remove muffins from oven as they are done. Remove muffins from the pan or cups. Let stand on a wire rack for 5 minutes. Serve warm. Makes 6 muffins.

> **Apple-and-Nut Whole Wheat Muffins:** Prepare muffins as directed above, *except* decrease milk to ¼ cup and add ½ teaspoon *vanilla.* Fold ¼ cup chopped, peeled *apple* and ¼ cup chopped *walnuts* into the batter. Continue as directed above.

Quick Caramel-Pecan Rolls

A golden caramel topping crowns these pale biscuits.

  3 tablespoons butter *or*
      margarine
¼ cup packed brown sugar
  1 tablespoon light corn syrup
½ teaspoon ground cinnamon
¼ cup chopped pecans,
      peanuts, *or* walnuts
  1 package (6) refrigerated
      biscuits

■ In a 1-cup measure cook butter or margarine, uncovered, on 100% power (high) for 40 to 50 seconds or till melted. Stir in brown sugar, corn syrup, and cinnamon. Cook, uncovered, on high for 30 to 40 seconds or till sugar is dissolved. Spoon mixture into a microwave-safe muffin pan or six 6-ounce custard cups lined with paper bake cups. Sprinkle chopped nuts atop. Place 1 biscuit over nuts in each cup.

■ For custard cups, arrange on plate, leaving center open. Cook, uncovered, on high 1 to 1½ minutes or till done, giving a half-turn after 30 seconds. Let stand 1 minute. Invert onto plate. Serve warm. Makes 6.

Low-wattage oven: Not recommended.

Crisping a cereal mix

Nutty Fruit Granola

Pictured on pages 52–53.

2½ cups regular rolled oats
½ cup coconut
½ cup coarsely chopped
    walnuts, almonds, *or*
    pecans
⅓ cup sesame seed
⅓ cup toasted wheat germ
½ cup honey
¼ cup cooking oil
¾ cup mixed dried fruit bits
½ cup chopped pitted dates

■ Line a 15x10x1-inch baking pan with foil. Set aside. In a large microwave-safe mixing bowl combine rolled oats, coconut, chopped nuts, sesame seed, and toasted wheat germ. Combine honey and cooking oil. Stir into the oat mixture till evenly coated (see photo 1).

■ Cook, uncovered, on 100% power (high) for 8 to 10 minutes or till mixture is toasted, stirring every 2 minutes for the first 4 minutes, then every minute (see photo 2).

■ Stir in the mixed dried fruit bits and dates (see photo 3). Spread the granola mixture in the foil-lined pan (see photo 4). Cool (mix will crisp during standing). When cool, break into clumps. Store in an airtight container for up to 2 weeks. Makes about 7 cups granola (14 servings).

TIP Toasting Nuts

Just as you can toast granola in the microwave, you can also toast nuts for cooking or snacking. In a 2-cup measure cook whole or chopped nuts on 100% power (high) for specified time or till toasted, stirring every minute the first 3 minutes, then every 30 seconds. Open whole nuts to see if they're toasted inside. Spread out to cool. Let stand 15 minutes (nuts will continue to toast on standing).

Nuts	Amount	Cooking time
Raw peanuts	1 cup	4 to 5 minutes
	½ cup	3 to 4 minutes
Walnuts	1 cup	4 to 5 minutes
	½ cup	3 to 4 minutes
Pecans	1 cup	3 to 4 minutes
	½ cup	2 to 3 minutes
Almonds	1 cup	2 to 3 minutes
	½ cup	2 to 3 minutes

1

Mix and cook in the same container. In a microwave-safe mixing bowl combine oats, coconut, nuts, sesame seed, and wheat germ. Stir together honey and cooking oil and drizzle over the oat mixture, as shown. For even cooking, stir the mixture till the dry ingredients are coated.

2

During cooking, stir the coated oat mixture every 2 minutes for the first 4 minutes, then every minute. This ensures even toasting. The mixture should turn golden.

3

When the rolled oat mixture is toasted, stir in the mixed dried fruit bits and dates. The fruit doesn't need to cook.

4

Spread the cooked granola in the foil-lined pan, as shown. You will notice that the granola crisps as it cools. When cool, break the granola into clumps. Store in an airtight container at room temperature.

TIP Great Granola Fix-Ups

Here are seven ways to use crispy homemade Nutty Fruit Granola:

- Stir ¼ cup granola into an 8-ounce carton of your favorite flavored yogurt.
- Sprinkle ¼ cup granola over a serving of ice cream.
- Top muffin or quick bread batter with granola before microwave cooking.
- Pour milk over a ½-cup serving of granola and fruit for breakfast.
- Pack granola in a plastic bag for a brown-bag treat.
- Layer pudding and granola for a quick parfait. Dollop with whipped topping, then sprinkle with more granola.
- Sprinkle about 1 teaspoon granola onto a pancake just after the batter is poured onto the griddle.

Herbed Rice Pilaf

Basil fans take note: Your favorite herb is great in place of the sage.

1 tablespoon butter
¼ cup finely chopped onion
¼ cup thinly sliced celery
½ teaspoon dried sage, crushed
1 teaspoon instant chicken
   bouillon granules
1 cup quick-cooking rice
¼ cup snipped parsley
2 tablepoons toasted slivered
   almonds

■ In a 1-quart casserole cook butter on 100% power (high) for 30 to 40 seconds or till melted. Stir in onion, celery, and sage. Cook, covered, on high for 3 to 4 minutes or till vegetables are nearly tender. Stir in bouillon granules and 1 cup *water*.

■ Cook, uncovered, on high for 2 to 3½ minutes or till water is boiling. Stir in uncooked rice. Let stand, covered, for 5 minutes. Stir in parsley and almonds. Makes 4 servings.

Cocoa Cereal Mix

Cook and serve in the same bowl.

1 cup quick-cooking farina
1 cup nonfat dry milk powder
⅓ cup unsweetened cocoa
   powder
¼ cup sugar
⅛ teaspoon salt

■ Mix farina, milk powder, cocoa, sugar, and salt. Store in an airtight container up to 2 months. Stir before using. Makes 2¼ cups (6 servings).

■ For *each* serving, in microwave-safe cereal bowl combine ¾ cup *water* and ⅓ cup mix. Cook 1 serving, uncovered, on 70% power (medium-high) 3 to 5 minutes or till bubbly, stirring once. Let stand 1 minute.

For 2 servings: Cook 6 to 8 minutes, stirring every 2 minutes.

Low-wattage oven: Cook on 100% power (high) instead of medium-high.

Raisin-and-Spice Oatmeal Mix

Remove the bowls from the oven when the cereal bubbles.

2 cups quick-cooking rolled
   oats
½ cup nonfat dry milk powder
½ cup raisins
⅓ cup chopped pecans
⅓ cup packed brown sugar
1 teaspoon ground cinnamon
½ teaspoon finely shredded
   orange peel
¼ teaspoon ground nutmeg

■ Combine all ingredients and ¼ teaspoon *salt*. Store in an airtight container up to 2 months. Stir before using. Makes 3 cups (6 servings).

■ For *each* serving, in a microwave-safe cereal bowl combine ¾ cup *water* and ½ cup mix. Cook 1 serving, uncovered, on 70% power (medium-high) for 2 to 3 minutes or till bubbly. Let stand 1 minute. Stir.

For 2 servings: Cook 4 to 6½ minutes, stirring once.

Low-wattage oven: Cook on 100% power (high) instead of medium-high.

Cooking Cereals

For 1 or 2 servings, cook cereal in individual microwave-safe bowls. For 4 servings, use a 1-quart bowl.

Combine water, cereal, and a dash *salt*. Cook, uncovered, on 100% power (high) for time shown

or till mixture thickens and boils, stirring twice. Let stand 1 minute. Stir before serving.

	Servings	Water	Cereal	Cooking time
Quick-cooking oatmeal	1	¾ cup	⅓ cup	2 to 3 minutes
	2	¾ cup each	⅓ cup each	3 to 5 minutes
Quick-cooking farina	1	¾ cup	2½ tablespoons	2 to 3 minutes
	2	¾ cup each	2½ tablespoons each	4 to 6 minutes
	4	2¾ cups	⅔ cup	8 to 10 minutes

Nutrition Analysis

	Number of servings	Per Serving						Percent U.S. RDA Per Serving							
		Calories	Protein (g)	Carbohydrate (g)	Fat (g)	Sodium (mg)	Potassium (mg)	Protein	Vitamin A	Vitamin C	Thiamine	Riboflavin	Niacin	Calcium	Iron
Apple-and-Nut Whole Wheat Muffins (p. 63)	6	200	4	19	12	121	111	7	1	1	9	6	5	6	7
Basic Muffins (p. 62)	6	153	3	17	8	103	39	4	1	0	7	5	4	5	5
Blueberry Muffins (p. 62)	6	157	3	18	8	103	46	4	2	2	8	6	4	6	5
Cheese and Nut Muffins (p. 62)	6	188	4	17	12	132	59	6	4	2	8	7	4	9	6
Chocolate and Whole Wheat Ring (p. 58)	16	183	3	19	11	144	85	5	5	0	7	5	3	5	5
Cocoa Cereal Mix (p. 66)	6	217	10	43	1	175	355	16	8	2	17	25	7	22	9
Cranberry-Orange Loaf (p. 57)	16	120	2	14	7	74	73	3	1	6	8	3	3	2	4
Fruit-Filled Cinnamon Rolls (p. 56)	12	150	3	26	4	130	98	5	3	1	10	8	6	2	7
Herbed Rice Pilaf (p. 66)	4	144	3	22	5	135	101	5	9	14	8	3	5	3	7
Herbed Whole Wheat Bread (p. 54)	36	86	2	16	2	60	54	4	1	1	8	5	5	1	5
Nutty Caramel Rolls (p. 56)	12	193	3	32	6	135	104	5	3	1	11	8	6	3	9
Nutty Fruit Granola (p. 64)	14	230	5	32	11	4	216	7	2	0	13	3	3	2	8
Quick Caramel-Pecan Rolls (p. 63)	6	162	2	22	8	275	78	3	3	0	8	4	4	2	6
Raisin-and-Spice Oatmeal Mix (p. 66)	6	245	8	41	6	411	386	12	33	2	40	26	27	29	38
Ready-To-Cook Fruit 'n' Bran Muffins (p. 60)	24	92	2	16	3	134	119	3	5	3	6	6	5	4	6
Surprise-Filled Muffins (p. 62)	6	170	3	21	8	104	44	4	1	1	7	6	4	6	5
Whole Wheat Muffin Mix (p. 63)	6	167	4	18	9	122	87	6	1	0	8	6	4	6	6

CAKES AND COOKIES

Microwave cakes and cookies fit today's hectic life-styles, because you can cook them up fast and still have great flavor and quality. Whether you want a fast batch of bar cookies, cupcakes, or a quick cake ring, you'll find what you need in this chapter.

Layer cakes on the double
Microwave cakes cook in one-third to one-fourth the time of conventionally cooked cakes. But because two cake layers won't fit into a microwave oven at once, you'll have to make one-layer cakes. You can still serve a layered cake, though. Just split the one layer in half (either crosswise or horizontally) and stack with the frosting or filling.

Choosing the right power
We cooked our cakes on 50% power (medium) to assure a delicate texture. (If medium power in your microwave oven is greater than 50 percent, cook on medium, but follow the low-wattage timings.) The cakes finish with 1 to 2 minutes on high to dry the surfaces. Cupcakes, because they're small, cook on high.

Turn cakes and cookies during cooking so no spots overcook.

Browning microwave cakes
Like breads, microwave cakes and cookies lack a brown and crispy crust. To add eye appeal, we chose recipes for this chapter that include whole grains, cocoa, or spices. For those cakes and cookies that do have light-colored crusts, we call for a frosting, sauce, or glaze.

When it comes to foods with firm crusts such as angel cakes, sponge cakes, pound cakes, and nonbar cookies, stick with your conventional oven for best results.

Apricot Fruitcake
(see recipe, page 76)

Pineapple-Carrot Cupcakes
(see recipe, page 75)

Testing for doneness
If you can't look for a browned crust, how can you tell when the cake or cookies are done? Test by scraping the surface with a toothpick. If done, you'll find a cooked texture underneath.

Keep cakes and cookies moist
After they've cooked, microwave-baked products tend to dry out faster than conventionally cooked ones. To hold in the moisture, wrap or frost the cake or cookies immediately after cooling.

Chocolate Cake
(see recipe, page 72)

Cooking a one-layer cake

Yellow Cake

The refreshing orange frosting adds color to the cake.

1 cup all-purpose flour
1 teaspoon baking powder
⅛ teaspoon salt
⅓ cup butter *or* margarine
⅔ cup sugar
½ teaspoon vanilla
1 egg
⅔ cup milk
   Orange-Butter Frosting

■ Grease the bottom of an 8x1½-inch round baking dish and line with waxed paper (see photo 1). Set aside. Combine flour, baking powder, and salt. In a mixer bowl beat butter or margarine with an electric mixer for ½ minute. Add sugar and vanilla. Beat till fluffy. Add egg. Beat till combined. Add flour mixture and milk alternately to beaten mixture, beating well. Spread evenly in the prepared dish (see photo 2).

■ Cook cake layer, uncovered, on 50% power (medium) for 10 minutes (see photo 3), giving dish a quarter-turn every 3 minutes. If not done, cook on 100% power (high) for 30 seconds to 2 minutes or till the surface is nearly dry (see photo 4).

■ Cool cake on a wire rack 5 minutes. To loosen, run a narrow metal spatula around dish edges and slightly under waxed paper. Invert onto rack. Remove waxed paper (see photo 5). Cool. Frost with Orange-Butter Frosting immediately after cooling (see photo 6). Makes 8 servings.

Low-wattage oven: Cook on high for 6 to 8 minutes.

Orange-Butter Frosting: In a bowl combine 3 tablespoons *butter or margarine*, ½ teaspoon finely shredded *orange peel*, 1 tablespoon *orange juice*, and ½ teaspoon *vanilla*. Gradually add 1 to 1½ cups sifted *powdered sugar*, beating to a smooth, spreading consistency.

TIP Fast-Cooking Cupcakes

Just about any of our cake batters make good microwave cupcakes. Line a microwave-safe muffin pan or 6-ounce custard cups with paper bake cups. Spoon 2 tablespoons batter into each bake cup. Arrange custard cups in a circle on a plate. Cook, uncovered, on 100% power (high) till done, giving the dish a half-turn every minute. Allow 1 to 2 minutes for 4 cupcakes and 2 to 3 minutes for 6 cupcakes. Cool for 5 minutes on a wire rack. Remove from pan or custard cups and cool for 10 minutes. Cover or frost immediately.

1

Lining the dish with waxed paper helps eliminate the rubbery layer that forms on the bottom of the cake. When you remove the waxed paper, the rubbery layer will come with it. To fit the waxed paper, trace the bottom of the dish on waxed paper with scissors, as shown. Cut out the shape. Grease the dish. Line with the circle.

2

Spread the cake batter evenly in the prepared baking dish to ensure even cooking. Unlike in a conventional oven, cake batter in a microwave does not spread into an even layer as it cooks.

3

Cakes tend to cook from the edges to the center, as shown. To prevent some spots from cooking faster than others, turn the dish as directed in the recipe. Because the oven cycles on and off on medium power, you'll notice the cake breathing—rising when the power is on and falling when it is off. This is normal.

4

To test if the cake is done, scratch the slightly wet surface near the center of the cake with a wooden toothpick. If done, you'll find a cooked texture underneath.

5

After loosening the cake from the dish and inverting it onto a wire rack, remove the waxed paper. The rubbery layer that formed on the bottom of the cake will come off as you peel off the waxed paper, as shown.

6

Frosting is one way to dress up the pale appearance of your microwave cake. It also keeps the cake from drying out. The top of the cake will be moist and difficult to frost, so we recommend frosting the bottom (the waxed-paper side). If you can't frost the cake right after cooling, wrap it in clear plastic wrap to keep moist.

Chocolate Cake

To layer, cut in half crosswise and stack. (Pictured on pages 68–69.)

1 cup all-purpose flour
2 tablespoons unsweetened
    cocoa powder
1 teaspoon baking powder
½ teaspoon baking soda
⅛ teaspoon salt
⅓ cup butter *or* margarine
⅔ cup sugar
1 egg
⅔ cup water
    Mocha-Butter Frosting

■ Refer to photos, page 71. Grease the bottom of an 8x1½-inch round baking dish. Line with waxed paper. Combine flour, cocoa, baking powder, soda, and salt. In a mixer bowl beat butter ½ minute. Add sugar. Beat till fluffy. Add egg. Beat well. Add flour mixture and water alternately to mixture. Beat just till combined. Spread evenly in dish.

■ Cook, uncovered, on 50% power (medium) for 10 minutes, giving dish a quarter-turn every 3 minutes. If not done, cook on 100% power (high) for 30 seconds to 2 minutes or till surface is nearly dry. Cool in dish on a wire rack for 5 minutes. Remove and invert on rack. Remove waxed paper. Cool. Frost immediately with Mocha-Butter Frosting. Serves 8.

Low-wattage oven: Cook on high for 6 to 8 minutes.

Mocha-Butter Frosting: Stir together 2 tablespoons *water* and 1 teaspoon *instant coffee crystals*. Set aside. In a small mixer bowl beat 3 tablespoons *butter* till light and fluffy. Gradually add 1½ cups sifted *powdered sugar* and 2 tablespoons *unsweetened cocoa powder,* beating well. Beat in coffee liquid and 1 teaspoon *vanilla*. Add ¾ to 1 cup sifted *powdered sugar,* beating till spreadable.

Pumpkin-Raisin Cake

The nutty topping saves you the work of frosting this moist cake.

3 tablespoons toasted wheat
    germ
1 cup all-purpose flour
¾ teaspoon ground cinnamon
½ teaspoon baking soda
½ teaspoon finely shredded
    orange peel
⅛ teaspoon ground ginger
⅓ cup butter *or* margarine
⅔ cup packed brown sugar
2 eggs
⅓ cup canned pumpkin
¼ cup buttermilk *or* sour milk
⅓ cup raisins
¼ cup chopped nuts
2 tablespoons brown sugar
1 tablespoon butter *or*
    margarine, softened

■ Refer to photos, page 71. Grease an 8x1½-inch round baking dish. Coat with wheat germ. Set aside. Combine flour, ¼ *teaspoon* of the cinnamon, baking soda, orange peel, and ginger. In a small mixer bowl beat ⅓ cup butter or margarine for ½ minute. Add ⅔ cup brown sugar. Beat till fluffy. Add eggs, one at a time, beating after each addition. Combine pumpkin and buttermilk. Add dry ingredients and buttermilk mixture alternately to beaten mixture, beating just till combined. Fold in raisins. Spread evenly in prepared dish. For topping, combine nuts, 2 tablespoons brown sugar, 1 tablespoon butter or margarine, and remaining ½ teaspoon cinnamon. Sprinkle over batter.

■ Cook, uncovered, on 50% power (medium) for 16 minutes, giving the dish a quarter-turn every 4 minutes. If not done, cook on 100% power (high) for 30 seconds to 2 minutes. Cool in the dish on a wire rack. Serve warm or cool. Makes 8 servings.

Low-wattage oven: Cook on high for 12 minutes.

Applesauce Cake

This cake makes a great after-school treat.

1 cup all-purpose flour
½ teaspoon baking powder
½ teaspoon ground cinnamon
¼ teaspoon baking soda
¼ teaspoon salt
¼ teaspoon ground nutmeg
⅛ teaspoon ground cloves
⅓ cup butter *or* margarine
⅔ cup packed brown sugar
1 egg
¾ cup applesauce
½ cup finely chopped walnuts
¼ cup packed brown sugar
1½ teaspoons cornstarch
3 tablespoons milk
1 tablespoon butter *or* margarine
¼ cup crushed granola

■ Refer to photos, page 71. Grease the bottom of an 8x1½-inch round baking dish and line with waxed paper. Mix flour, baking powder, cinnamon, soda, salt, nutmeg, and cloves. In a mixer bowl beat ⅓ cup butter or margarine for ½ minute. Add ⅔ cup sugar. Beat till fluffy. Add egg. Beat well. Add flour mixture and applesauce alternately to beaten mixture. Beat till combined. Stir in nuts. Spread evenly in the dish.

■ Cook, uncovered, on 50% power (medium) for 10 minutes, giving the dish a quarter-turn every 3 minutes. If not done, cook on 100% power (high) for 30 seconds to 2 minutes or till the surface is nearly dry. Cool on a wire rack for 5 minutes. Loosen, then invert onto the wire rack. Remove the waxed paper. Cool thoroughly.

■ For topping, in a 2-cup measure combine ¼ cup sugar and cornstarch. Stir in milk. Add 1 tablespoon butter or margarine. Cook, uncovered, on high for 1½ to 2½ minutes or till bubbly. Stir after 1 minute, then every 30 seconds. Place cake on a plate, top side up. Spread topping over cake. Sprinkle with granola. Makes 8 servings.

Low-wattage oven: For *cake*, cook on high for 7 to 9 minutes.

Pineapple-Raisin Upside-Down Cake

A cake that makes its own topping! Just cook the cake and invert it. (Pictured on pages 6–7.)

1 8-ounce can pineapple slices (juice pack)
2 tablespoons butter *or* margarine
⅓ cup packed brown sugar
2 tablespoons raisins
1 cup all-purpose flour
1¼ teaspoons baking powder
¼ teaspoon salt
⅓ cup shortening
⅔ cup sugar
½ teaspoon vanilla
2 eggs

■ Refer to photos, page 71. Drain pineapple, reserving liquid. Halve pineapple slices. In an 8x1½-inch round baking dish cook butter or margarine, uncovered, on 100% power (high) for 40 to 50 seconds or till melted. Stir in brown sugar and *1 tablespoon* of the reserved pineapple liquid. Add water to remaining liquid, if necessary, to equal ⅓ cup total. Set aside. Arrange pineapple in the dish. Sprinkle with raisins.

■ Combine flour, baking powder, and salt. In a mixer bowl beat shortening for ½ minute. Add sugar and vanilla. Beat till fluffy. Add eggs. Beat till combined. Add flour mixture and juice mixture alternately to beaten mixture. Beat till combined. Spread over mixture in dish.

■ Cook, uncovered, on 50% power (medium) for 16 minutes, giving the dish a quarter-turn every 4 minutes. If not done, cook on 100% power (high) for 30 seconds to 2 minutes more. Let stand in the dish on a wire rack for 5 minutes. Loosen edge. Invert cake onto a serving platter. Remove the dish. Serve warm. Makes 8 servings.

Low-wattage oven: For *cake*, cook on high for 10 to 12 minutes.

Peach-Walnut Torte

Peach-Walnut Torte

Make this four-layer torte from one cake layer. (Pictured on the cover.)

¾ cup all-purpose flour
¼ teaspoon baking soda
¼ teaspoon salt
3 tablespoons butter *or* margarine
½ cup packed brown sugar
1 egg
½ cup milk
½ cup finely crushed vanilla wafers (11 wafers)
¼ cup ground walnuts (about 1 ounce)
1 cup fresh peach *or* nectarine slices, *or* 1 cup frozen unsweetened peach slices, thawed, *or* one 8¾-ounce can peach slices (juice pack)
   Lemon juice
1 cup whipping cream

■ Refer to photos, page 71. Grease the bottom of an 8x1½-inch round baking dish. Line with waxed paper. Combine flour, soda, and salt. In a mixer bowl beat butter or margarine for ½ minute. Add sugar. Beat till blended. Add egg. Beat well. Add flour mixture and milk alternately to beaten mixture, beating till combined. Combine vanilla wafers and ground nuts. Stir into batter. Spread in the prepared dish.

■ Cook, uncovered, on 50% power (medium) for 10 minutes, giving dish a quarter-turn every 3 minutes. If not done, cook on 100% power (high) 30 seconds to 2 minutes or till surface is nearly dry. Cool on wire rack 5 minutes. Loosen edges. Invert onto rack. Remove waxed paper. Cool.

■ Split cake in half horizontally. Halve each layer crosswise, making 4 thin half circles. Brush fresh peaches with lemon juice. (Or, drain thawed or canned fruit.) To assemble, beat whipping cream till soft peaks form. Place *one* half circle of cake on a plate. Spread with *one-fourth* of the whipped cream. Top with second cake layer. Spread with another *one-fourth* of the whipped cream. Arrange *half* of the fruit atop. Repeat with remaining cake layers and whipped cream. Chill up to 2 hours. Before serving, top with remaining peach slices. Makes 6 servings.

Low-wattage oven: Not recommended.

Pineapple-Carrot Cake

The cupcake version is pictured on pages 68–69. (See tip, page 70.)

1 cup all-purpose flour
1 cup sugar
1 teaspoon baking powder
½ teaspoon ground cinnamon
¼ teaspoon baking soda
¼ teaspoon ground nutmeg
⅛ teaspoon salt
1 cup finely shredded carrot
1 8¼-ounce can crushed pineapple
1 beaten egg
⅓ cup cooking oil
¼ cup finely chopped pecans *or* walnuts
   Cream Cheese Frosting
   Thin carrot strips

■ Refer to photos, page 71. Grease the bottom of an 8x1½-inch round baking dish. Line with waxed paper. Combine flour, sugar, baking powder, cinnamon, soda, nutmeg, and salt. Add shredded carrot, *undrained* pineapple, egg, and cooking oil. Stir just till combined. Stir in nuts. Spread evenly in prepared dish. Cook, uncovered, on 50% power (medium) 20 minutes, giving dish a quarter-turn every 5 minutes. If not done, cook on 100% power (high) 30 seconds to 2 minutes. Cool on wire rack 5 minutes. Loosen edges. Invert. Remove waxed paper. Cool. Frost with Cream Cheese Frosting. Top with carrot strips. Makes 8 servings.

Low-wattage oven: For *cake*, cook on high for 12 to 14 minutes.

Cream Cheese Frosting: In a small mixer bowl combine ½ of a 3-ounce package *cream cheese*, 2 tablespoons *butter or margarine*, and ½ teaspoon *vanilla*. Beat till fluffy. Gradually add 1 cup sifted *powdered sugar*, beating till spreadable.

Making a ring-shaped cake

Apricot Fruitcake

Pictured on pages 68–69.

1½ cups water
2 cups raisins
1 cup snipped dried apricots
2 tablespoons finely crushed graham crackers (1 *or* 2 squares)
1½ cups all-purpose flour
1 teaspoon baking powder
1 teaspoon ground cinnamon
½ teaspoon ground nutmeg
¼ teaspoon salt
¼ teaspoon ground allspice
¼ teaspoon ground cloves
1 8-ounce package pitted whole dates, snipped (1⅓ cups)
1 cup coarsely chopped red *or* green candied cherries
¾ cup broken pecans
½ cup toasted slivered almonds
½ cup butter *or* margarine
2 eggs
1 cup packed brown sugar
¼ cup brandy *or* orange juice
¼ cup orange juice
    Orange Icing (optional)

■ In a 4-cup measure heat water, uncovered, on 100% power (high) for 3 to 5 minutes or till boiling. Add raisins and snipped apricots. Let stand for 5 minutes. Drain well (see photo 1).

■ Meanwhile, grease a 10-inch microwave-safe fluted tube dish. Coat with crushed graham crackers (see photo 2). Set aside.

■ In a large mixing bowl stir together flour, baking powder, cinnamon, nutmeg, salt, allspice, and cloves. Add drained fruit, dates, candied cherries, pecans, and almonds. Stir till fruit and nuts are well coated with the flour mixture.

■ In a 2-cup measure cook butter or margarine, uncovered, on high for 1 to 2 minutes or till melted. In a medium mixing bowl beat eggs till foamy. Add melted butter or margarine, brown sugar, brandy, and orange juice. Stir till combined. Stir egg mixture into fruit mixture. Spoon fruitcake batter into the prepared dish. Spread the batter evenly.

■ Cook, uncovered, on 50% power (medium) for 25 to 30 minutes or till done, giving the dish a quarter-turn every 5 minutes (see photo 3). If not done, cook on high for 30 seconds to 2 minutes or till the surface is nearly dry. (Scratch the slightly wet surface near the center with a wooden toothpick. The cake should be cooked underneath.)

■ Cool in the baking dish on a wire rack for 5 minutes. Invert onto the wire rack and remove the dish. Cool thoroughly.

■ Wrap the fruitcake in a brandy- or fruit-juice-moistened cheesecloth (see photo 4). Overwrap the fruitcake with foil. For a blended and mellow flavor, store the moistened and wrapped fruitcake in the refrigerator for 3 to 4 weeks before serving. Remoisten the cheesecloth as needed after 1 week. Serve drizzled with Orange Icing, if desired. Makes 24 servings.

Low-wattage oven: Cook on high for 20 to 25 minutes.

Orange Icing: In a small mixing bowl beat together 1 cup sifted *powdered sugar,* ½ teaspoon finely shredded *orange peel,* and 1½ teaspoons *orange juice.*

1

Add the raisins and apricots to the boiling water. Let stand for 5 minutes. Drain well, as shown. The plumped fruit helps keep the microwave-cooked fruitcake moist.

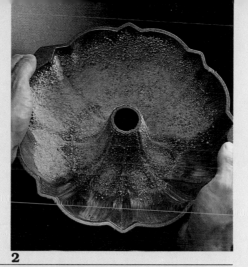

2

Coating the greased fluted tube dish with crumbs helps prevent the fruitcake from sticking to the dish and gives the fruitcake a mock crust. Be sure to tilt the dish to make sure the sides and center stem are well covered, as shown.

3

For more even cooking, turn the dish as directed in the recipe. The ring shape prevents microwaves from overcooking the edges before the center is done.

4

Wrap the cooled fruitcake in a brandy- or fruit-juice-soaked cheesecloth, then overwrap with foil to keep the cake moist as it mellows in the refrigerator.

Syrup-Glazed Citrus Cake Ring

Graham cracker crumbs give this cake a golden finish.

2 tablespoons finely crushed graham crackers (1 *or* 2 squares)
1½ cups all-purpose flour
1½ teaspoons baking powder
1 teaspoon finely shredded lemon peel
⅛ teaspoon salt
½ cup butter *or* margarine
¾ cup sugar
2 eggs
⅔ cup orange juice
⅔ cup orange juice
⅓ cup sugar
½ teaspoon finely shredded lemon peel
1 tablespoon lemon juice

Orange-Liqueur-Glazed Citrus Cake Ring: Prepare syrup-Glazed Citrus Cake Ring as above, *except* decrease orange juice in syrup to ½ cup, then stir in 2 tablespoons *orange liqueur* after cooking.

■ Grease a 9-inch microwave-safe ring mold. Coat with crushed graham crackers (see photo 2, page 77). Set aside. In a small mixing bowl stir together flour, baking powder, 1 teaspoon lemon peel, and salt. In a small mixer bowl beat butter or margarine with an electric mixer on medium speed ½ minute. Gradually add ¾ cup sugar, beating till fluffy.

■ Add eggs, one at a time, beating after each addition. Scrape bowl frequently. Gradually add flour mixture and ⅔ cup orange juice alternately to egg mixture, beating just till combined. Spread batter evenly in prepared dish (see photo 2, page 71).

■ Cook, uncovered, on 50% power (medium) for 10 minutes, giving the dish a quarter-turn every 3 minutes (see photo 3, page 77). If not done, cook on 100% power (high) for 30 seconds to 2 minutes or till surface is nearly dry (see photo 4, page 71). Cool in the dish on a wire rack for 5 minutes. Invert onto a serving plate and remove the dish.

■ Meanwhile, for syrup, in a 4-cup measure combine ⅔ cup orange juice, ⅓ cup sugar, ½ teaspoon lemon peel, and lemon juice. Cook, uncovered, on 100% power (high) for 2 to 3 minutes or till bubbly, stirring after 1½ minutes.

■ With a long-tined fork, poke holes all over top of warm cake. Slowly spoon the syrup glaze over cake (see photo, below). Cool the cake thoroughly. Makes 12 servings.

Low-wattage oven: For *cake,* cook on high for 7 to 9 minutes.

Use a long-tined fork to poke holes all over the top of the warm cake so the syrup can soak in. Slowly spoon the syrup over the cake, as shown. Let cool. Because the syrup adds moistness, gloss, and flavor to the cake, there's no need to add frosting.

Spicy Cake Ring

Top off each serving of this pound cake-like ring right—with ice cream!

2 tablespoons finely crushed graham crackers (1 *or* 2 squares)
1½ cups all-purpose flour
1 teaspoon baking powder
1 teaspoon ground cinnamon
⅛ teaspoon salt
⅛ teaspoon ground nutmeg
⅛ teaspoon ground cloves
½ cup butter *or* margarine
⅔ cup sugar
2 eggs
¾ cup milk
Powdered sugar

■ Grease a 9-inch microwave-safe ring mold. Coat with crushed graham crackers (see photo 2, page 77). Set aside. In a small mixing bowl combine flour, baking powder, cinnamon, salt, nutmeg, and cloves.

■ In a small bowl beat butter or margarine with an electric mixer on medium speed for ½ minute. Add sugar and beat till fluffy. Add eggs, one at a time, beating well. Add flour mixture and milk alternately to beaten mixture, beating after each addition just till combined. Spread batter evenly in the prepared dish (see photo 2, page 71).

■ Cook, uncovered, on 50% power (medium) for 8 minutes, giving the dish a quarter-turn every 3 minutes (see photo 3, page 77). If not done, cook on 100% power (high) for 30 seconds to 2 minutes or till surface is nearly dry (see photo 4, page 71).

■ Cool in the dish on a wire rack for 5 minutes. Invert onto a wire rack and remove dish. Cool thoroughly. Cover cake immediately after cooling. To serve, sprinkle with powdered sugar. Makes 12 servings.

Low-wattage oven: Not recommended.

Black Forest Cake Ring

Indulge in the classic ingredient combination of Black Forest cake: chocolate and cherries.

¼ cup toasted wheat germ
2 cups all-purpose flour
¾ cup sugar
1 teaspoon baking soda
½ teaspoon ground cinnamon
⅛ teaspoon salt
2 beaten eggs
½ cup cooking oil
2 teaspoons vanilla
1 21-ounce can cherry pie filling
1 6-ounce package (1 cup) semisweet chocolate pieces
1 cup chopped walnuts

■ Generously grease a 10-inch microwave-safe fluted tube dish. Coat with wheat germ (see photo 2, page 77). Set aside. In a large mixing bowl stir together flour, sugar, baking soda, cinnamon, and salt. Set aside.

■ In a small mixing bowl combine eggs, cooking oil, and vanilla. Add egg mixture and pie filling to flour mixture. Mix well. Stir in chocolate pieces and nuts. Spread batter evenly in prepared dish (see photo 2, page 71).

■ Cook, uncovered, on 50% power (medium) for 18 minutes, giving the dish a quarter-turn every 5 minutes (see photo 3, page 77). If not done, cook on 100% power (high) for 30 seconds to 3 minutes or till surface is nearly dry (see photo 4, page 71).

■ Cool in the dish on a wire rack for 15 minutes. Invert onto wire rack and remove dish. Cool thoroughly. Cover immediately after cooling. Makes 12 to 14 servings.

Low-wattage oven: Cook on high for 17 to 20 minutes.

Layering bar cookies

Triple-Layer Brownies

Bite into three great layers: oatmeal, chocolate, and frosting.

1 square (1 ounce) unsweetened chocolate
3 tablespoons butter *or* margarine
¾ cup quick-cooking rolled oats
⅓ cup all-purpose flour
⅓ cup packed brown sugar
¼ teaspoon baking soda
¼ cup butter *or* margarine
½ cup all-purpose flour
¼ teaspoon baking powder
⅓ cup sugar
2 tablespoons water
1 slightly beaten egg
½ teaspoon vanilla
⅓ cup chopped nuts
Chocolate Frosting

■ In a medium microwave-safe mixing bowl cook chocolate and 3 tablespoons butter or margarine, uncovered, on 100% power (high) for 1½ to 3 minutes or till melted. Set aside.

■ In a small mixing bowl stir together oats, ⅓ cup flour, brown sugar, and baking soda. In a 1-cup measure cook ¼ cup butter or margarine, uncovered, on high for 45 to 60 seconds or till melted. Stir into oat mixture. Pat oat mixture into an ungreased 8x8x2-inch baking dish (see photo 1). Cook, uncovered, on 50% power (medium) for 3 to 4 minutes or till surface appears dry, giving the dish a quarter-turn after 2 minutes. Cool on a wire rack for 10 minutes.

■ Meanwhile, in a small mixing bowl stir together ½ cup flour and baking powder. Set aside. Stir sugar and water into melted chocolate mixture. Add egg and vanilla. Stir gently just till combined. Add flour mixture to chocolate mixture. Stir till combined. Stir in nuts. Spread evenly over cooked oat layer (see photo 2).

■ Cook, uncovered, on 50% power (medium) for 5 to 7 minutes or till done, shielding corners if necessary and giving the dish a quarter-turn every 3 minutes (see photo 3). (Scratch the slightly wet surface near the center with a wooden toothpick [see photo 4]. The brownies should be cooked underneath.) Cool on a wire rack. Frost with Chocolate Frosting. Cut into bars. Store in a covered container. Makes 24 bars.

Low-wattage oven: For *oatmeal layer,* cook on high for 3 to 4 minutes. For *chocolate layer,* cook on high for 3 to 5 minutes.

Chocolate Frosting: In a small microwave-safe mixing bowl combine 1 square (1 ounce) *unsweetened chocolate* and 1 tablespoon *butter or margarine*. Cook, uncovered, on 100% power (high) for 1½ to 2½ minutes or till melted. Stir in 1 cup sifted *powdered sugar* and ½ teaspoon *vanilla*. Stir in enough *hot water* (about 1½ tablespoons) to make a spreadable frosting.

1

For the first layer of the bar cookies, pat the oat mixture evenly into the bottom of an ungreased 8x8x2-inch baking dish.

2

Spread the chocolate mixture over the warm oatmeal layer. The heat from the just-cooked oatmeal layer will help the chocolate layer cook more evenly.

3

As you are cooking the bar cookies, turn the dish as directed in the recipe so the bars will cook more evenly. If your owner's manual recommends using foil, and the corners of the cookies are done before the rest, shield the corners with small pieces of foil.

4

To test if the bar cookies are done, scratch the slightly wet surface near the center with a wooden toothpick. If done, a cooked texture will have formed underneath. Cool and frost, then cut into 24 bars.

Chocolate Chip Bars

A must for a microwave cookbook: chocolate chip cookies in a bar.

2 tablespoons toasted wheat germ
⅓ cup sugar
¼ cup all-purpose flour
¼ cup whole wheat flour
¼ teaspoon baking powder
3 tablespoons butter *or* margarine
1 beaten egg yolk
¼ cup milk
½ teaspoon vanilla
⅓ cup miniature semisweet chocolate pieces
¼ cup finely chopped walnuts *or* pecans

■ Grease a 9x5x3-inch loaf dish. Line the bottom with waxed paper (see photo 1, page 71). Sprinkle with wheat germ. Set aside.

■ In a mixing bowl combine sugar, all-purpose flour, whole wheat flour, and baking powder. Cut in butter or margarine till mixture resembles coarse crumbs. Combine egg yolk, milk, and vanilla. Add to dry ingredients. Stir mixture just till blended. Stir in chocolate pieces. Spread batter evenly in prepared dish. Sprinkle with nuts.

■ If your owner's manual recommends using foil, shield corners with foil (see photo 1, page 57). Cook on 50% power (medium) for 5 to 7 minutes or till done, giving dish a half-turn every 3 minutes (see photo 3, page 81). Remove foil shields after 5 minutes (see photo 2, page 57). (When done, the surface may still be wet, but a wooden toothpick inserted near the center should come out clean.)

■ Cool on a wire rack for 10 minutes. Invert onto the wire rack and peel off waxed paper (see photo 5, page 71). Invert again. Cool thoroughly on the rack. Cut into bars. Store in a covered container. Makes 8 servings.

Low-wattage oven: Cook on 100% power (high) for 4 to 5 minutes, turning once.

Six-Layer Bars

¼ cup butter *or* margarine
1 cup finely crushed graham crackers (about 14 squares)
½ of a 6-ounce package (½ cup) semisweet chocolate pieces
½ cup almond brickle pieces
½ cup coconut
½ cup chopped nuts
½ of a 14-ounce can (about ⅔ cup) *sweetened condensed* milk

■ In an 8x8x2-inch baking dish cook butter or margarine, uncovered, on 100% power (high) for 45 to 60 seconds or till melted. Stir in crushed graham crackers. Pat into an even layer in the bottom of the dish. Cook, uncovered, on high about 1 minute or till set. Layer chocolate pieces, almond brickle pieces, coconut, and nuts atop graham cracker layer. Pour sweetened condensed milk over all.

■ Cook, uncovered, on 50% power (medium) for 6 to 7 minutes or till set, giving the dish a half-turn after 4 minutes. Cool on a wire rack. Cut into bars. Makes 24 bars.

Low-wattage oven: For *layers,* cook on high for 6 to 7 minutes.

Cocoa-Raspberry Torte

Whip up this easy pound-cake torte any time you need a special dessert.

1 frozen loaf pound cake
1 10-ounce package frozen red raspberries *or* strawberries
2 tablespoons cornstarch
1 teaspoon finely shredded orange peel
2 tablespoons orange juice
¾ cup sifted powdered sugar
2 tablespoons unsweetened cocoa powder
1 tablespoon butter *or* margarine, melted
1 to 2 tablespoons milk

■ Cut frozen pound cake horizontally into 3 layers. Set aside. For filling, in a medium microwave-safe mixing bowl cook berries, uncovered, on 100% power (high) for 2 to 3 minutes or till slushy. Stir together cornstarch, orange peel, and orange juice, then stir into berries. Cook, uncovered, on high for 3 to 4 minutes or till bubbly, stirring every minute. Cook, uncovered, for 30 seconds more. Use a fork to slightly mash berries. Cover and chill filling about 1½ hours.

■ Place *one* layer of cake on a serving platter. Spread *half* of the berry filling on top. Top with second cake layer, then remaining berry filling. Top with last cake layer. Cover and chill for several hours or overnight.

■ About 1 hour before serving, make glaze. In a mixing bowl stir together powdered sugar and cocoa powder. Stir in melted butter or margarine. Stir in enough of the milk to make of glazing consistency. Spoon over cake, drizzling down sides. Cover and chill till serving time. Makes 12 servings.

Nutrition Analysis

	Number of servings	Calories	Protein (g)	Carbohydrate (g)	Fat (g)	Sodium (mg)	Potassium (mg)	Protein	Vitamin A	Vitamin C	Thiamine	Riboflavin	Niacin	Calcium	Iron
			Per Serving							Percent U.S. RDA Per Serving					
Applesauce Cake (p. 73)	8	331	4	45	16	239	188	7	8	1	10	7	5	6	12
Apricot Fruitcake (p. 76)	24	249	3	42	9	88	333	5	12	4	8	6	5	4	9
Black Forest Cake Ring (p. 79)	12	448	6	61	22	127	173	9	4	4	14	9	7	3	12
Chocolate Cake (p. 72)	8	352	3	58	13	292	51	5	10	0	7	6	5	4	7
Chocolate Chip Bars (p. 82)	8	175	3	20	11	59	85	4	4	0	6	4	3	3	5
Cocoa-Raspberry Torte (p. 83)	12	182	2	30	6	112	63	3	5	6	4	4	2	2	5
Orange-Liqueur-Glazed Citrus Cake Ring (p. 78)	12	230	3	35	9	156	80	5	7	17	8	6	5	4	5
Peach-Walnut Torte (p. 75)	6	415	5	41	26	254	233	8	21	4	11	12	7	8	10
Pineapple-Carrot Cake (p. 75)	8	385	4	56	17	166	138	5	35	7	11	6	5	5	7
Pineapple-Raisin Upside-Down Cake (p. 73)	8	298	3	44	13	164	116	5	4	5	9	6	5	5	8
Pumpkin-Raisin Cake (p. 72)	8	295	5	41	13	8	55	75	2	2	0	1	4	1	3
Six-Layer Bars (p. 82)	24	121	2	13	8	55	75	2	2	0	1	4	1	3	2
Spicy Cake Ring (p. 79)	12	197	3	25	9	151	57	5	7	0	7	7	4	5	6
Syrup-Glazed Citrus Cake Ring (p. 78)	12	224	3	34	9	156	87	5	7	15	8	6	5	4	5
Triple-Layer Brownies (p. 80)	24	123	2	16	6	58	50	2	3	0	3	2	2	1	1
Yellow Cake (p. 70)	8	299	3	42	14	212	63	5	10	2	8	7	4	6	5

CANDY

How sweet it is! Candy making in the microwave oven can be as simple as stirring nuts into melted chocolate or as involved as cooking sugar syrups.

Melt-and-stir candies
Once you've tried them, you'll think your microwave was invented for melt-and-stir candies. You simply melt chocolate or caramels and stir in the remaining ingredients. In this chapter, you'll find not only melt-and-stir treats, but also a melting-time chart (in case you want to concoct your own recipes).

Classic-candy making
You can micro-cook nut brittles, fudge, and divinity, but these classic candies take a little practice. Still, once you get the knack of accurately timing the sugar syrup and working quickly, you'll be able to turn out great candy every time.

Testing for doneness
For best results with the classics, it's a good idea to test for doneness after the minimum cooking time. If the mixture hasn't reached the right stage, continue cooking and test every 30 seconds.

You can tell if the candy has cooked long enough by using a thermometer or a water test. We have included instructions for both methods in our recipes.

Candy thermometers
Two kinds of thermometers are available for microwave candy making. One, a microwave candy thermometer, contains no metal parts and can be used while the microwave is on. The other is a quick-recovery thermometer, which cannot be used in the oven, but gives an immediate reading once the candy mixture is out of the oven. You can't use your oven's temperature probe because it cannot register the high temperatures that are necessary for candy making.

Shortcut Fudge
(see recipe, page 90)

Chocolate Truffles
(see recipe, page 91)

Peanut Butter and Chocolate Squares
(see recipe, page 91)

Of the two kinds of candy thermometers, our Test Kitchen had best results with the quick-recovery thermometer.

If you use a thermometer, check its accuracy in boiling water each time you make candy. The thermometer should read 212°. If it registers higher or lower, increase or decrease the final cooking temperature of your candy accordingly.

The water test
Another accurate gauge of candy temperature is the water test. As sugar syrups get hotter, they react differently in cold water. At lower temperatures, mixtures form soft balls. Then, as their temperatures rise, mixtures form harder balls and eventually brittle threads.

To use the water test, drop some of the candy syrup into a bowl of cold, but not icy, water. Using your fingers, form the syrup into a ball. The way the syrup reacts will tell you if it's cooked long enough.

Candy cookware
When making the classic candies, use heavy-duty glass containers that are free from cracks and chips and have not been stressed by falls. Stressed glass may shatter from the heat of the syrup. You also can use a special plastic casserole like the one on page 87.

Storing candy
Generally, you can keep candy for two to three weeks if it is stored in tightly covered containers. Most kinds should be stored at room temperature. However, soft chocolate candies need to be stored in the refrigerator.

Avoid storing different types of candies in the same container, because hard candies will become soft and sticky and soft candies will dry out. Layer hard candies between sheets of waxed paper and put soft candies in bonbon cups to keep their shapes.

Nut Brittle
(see recipe, page 86)

Cherry Divinity
(see recipe, page 88)

Making nut brittle

Nut Brittle

Pictured on pages 84–85.

¾ teaspoon baking soda
1 cup sugar
½ cup light corn syrup
1¼ cups raw peanuts *or* coarsely chopped raw cashews, almonds, pecans, *or* walnuts
1 tablespoon butter *or* margarine

■ Lightly butter two large baking sheets or 15x10x1-inch baking pans, then set aside. Sift baking soda, then set aside.

■ In a 1-quart heavy-duty glass or Tupperware Ultra 21 casserole combine sugar and corn syrup. (Mixture will be stiff.) Cook, uncovered, on 100% power (high) for 2½ to 3½ minutes or till sugar is dissolved and mixture comes to boiling, stirring twice to help dissolve sugar. Avoid splashing mixture onto sides of casserole. Stir in nuts.

■ Without stirring, cook, uncovered, on high for 4 minutes more. Stir in butter or margarine (see photo 1). Cook, uncovered, for 2 to 3 minutes more or till candy reaches hard-crack stage (295° to 305°) and syrup is a clear, golden color. After 2 minutes, check candy every 30 seconds. To test for hard-crack stage, drop syrup into *very cold* water. The syrup should separate into hard, brittle threads that snap easily (see photo 2).

■ Quickly sprinkle baking soda over mixture, stirring constantly (see photo 3). Immediately pour onto prepared pans, dividing mixture in half. If desired, stretch candy thin by cooling for 1 minute, then using two forks to lift and pull it (see photo 4). Cool; break into pieces. Store tightly covered at room temperature. Makes 1 pound (16 servings).

Low-wattage oven: For *sugar and corn syrup mixture,* cook on high for 4 to 5 minutes. For *nut mixture,* cook on high for 4 minutes. For *nut mixture after adding butter,* cook on high for 5 to 6 minutes, checking every 30 seconds after 5 minutes.

Nutmeg Brittle: Prepare Nut Brittle as above, *except* add ¼ teaspoon ground *nutmeg* with the butter or margarine.

1

Add the butter when the nut mixture is thick and syrupy and has the golden brown color of caramelized sugar. Continue cooking till the syrup reaches the hard-crack stage.

2

You can tell when the syrup reaches the hard-crack stage by adding a few drops from a spoon to a bowl of *very cold,* but not icy, water. The syrup should separate into hard, brittle threads that snap easily. If threads don't form, cook the syrup for 30 seconds more. Test again with fresh water and a clean spoon.

3

Once the candy has reached the hard-crack stage, quickly stir in the sifted baking soda. The soda reacts with the candy mixture and causes it to foam. This makes the brittle light and tender. Sifting the baking soda first prevents lumps of soda in the brittle.

4

Quickly pour the mixture onto the greased baking sheets. You'll find the candy easier to handle if you divide it in half. Let it cool for 1 minute, then use 2 forks to lift and pull the candy, stretching it thin. The thinner you stretch it, the more brittle it will be.

Making divinity

Divinity

Make divinity on a dry day. (Cherry Divinity is shown on pages 84–85.)

2 egg whites
2½ cups sugar
½ cup light corn syrup
⅓ cup water
1 teaspoon vanilla

■ Line two large baking sheets with waxed paper, then set aside. Place egg whites in a large mixer bowl. Set aside till ready to beat.

■ In a 4-cup glass measure stir together sugar, corn syrup, and water. Cook, uncovered, on 100% power (high) for 4½ to 5½ minutes or till mixture comes to a full boil over the entire surface, stirring every minute. Avoid splashing mixture onto sides of measure.

■ Without stirring, cook, uncovered, on high for 4 to 6 minutes more or till candy reaches hard-ball stage (250° to 266°). The syrup should remain bubbly over the entire surface (see photo 1). After 4 minutes, check candy every 30 seconds. To test for hard-ball stage, drop syrup into *very cold* water. The syrup should form a hard but pliable ball (see photo 2). Set hot syrup aside.

■ Immediately beat egg whites with a sturdy, freestanding electric mixer on high speed till stiff peaks form (tips stand straight). *Gradually* pour hot mixture in a thin stream over egg whites, beating on high speed and scraping sides of the bowl occasionally (see photo 3). This should take about 3 minutes. Add vanilla. Continue beating on high speed, scraping bowl occasionally, for 3 to 6 minutes or just till candy starts to lose its gloss (see photo 4). Quickly drop candy from a teaspoon onto the prepared baking sheets (see photo 5). Makes about 40 pieces.

Low-wattage oven: Not recommended.

Peppermint Divinity: Prepare Divinity as above, *except* stir in ¼ cup coarsely crushed *hard peppermint candies* immediately after the candy starts to lose its gloss.

Cherry Divinity: Prepare Divinity as above, *except* stir in ½ cup chopped *red or green candied cherries* immediately after the candy starts to lose its gloss.

Nut Divinity: Prepare Divinity as above, *except* stir in ½ cup chopped *pecans, walnuts, or hazelnuts (filberts)* immediately after the candy starts to lose its gloss.

Chocolate Swirled Divinity: Prepare Divinity as above, *except* stir in ½ cup *miniature semisweet chocolate pieces* immediately after the candy starts to lose its gloss. Stir just till swirled.

1

Cook the syrup on high till it comes to a full boil, stirring every minute. Then continue cooking, without stirring, until the syrup reaches the hard-ball stage. Throughout the cooking time, the syrup should boil over its entire surface, as shown.

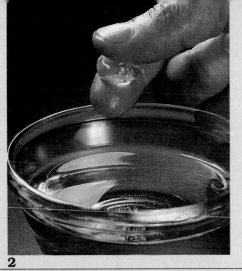

2

To test for the hard-ball stage, add a few drops of the hot syrup from a spoon to *very cold,* but not icy, water. With your fingers, shape the syrup into a ball in the water. When you remove the ball from the water, you should be able to change its shape, as shown, but not flatten it.

3

Beat the egg whites with a sturdy, freestanding mixer set on high speed. You'll need the power from a sturdy mixer because the mixture is so dense. Gradually pour the syrup in a thin stream (slightly less than ⅛-inch diameter) over the egg whites; scrape bowl occasionally. This should take about 3 minutes.

4

Continue to beat the candy on high speed until it just begins to lose its gloss, as shown. This should take 3 to 6 minutes. When you lift the beaters, the mixture should fall in a ribbon that mounds on itself and does not disappear into the remaining candy mixture.

5

Once the candy is beaten to the right stage, work fast so you can shape all the candy before it begins to set. With 2 teaspoons, quickly drop the divinity onto the baking sheets lined with waxed paper, using the second teaspoon to push the candy off the first spoon, as shown.

TIP Saving Divinity

Sometimes it's hard to tell if you've beaten divinity to the right stage. Test the mixture by dropping a spoonful onto waxed paper. If it flattens, beat ½ to 1 minute more and test again.

If the mixture is too stiff and has a rough surface, beat in *hot water,* a few drops at a time, till the mixture is a softer consistency.

If it mounds just right and has a smooth surface, quickly stir in any remaining ingredients and drop the candy into bite-size pieces.

Shortcut Fudge

This recipe makes three different flavors. (Pictured on pages 84–85.)

½ cup butter *or* margarine
2 cups sugar
1 5-ounce can (⅔ cup)
    evaporated milk
2 cups tiny marshmallows
1 6-ounce package (1 cup)
    semisweet chocolate
    pieces *or* butterscotch-
    flavored pieces *or* peanut
    butter-flavored pieces
½ teaspoon vanilla
½ cup chopped walnuts *or*
    peanuts, *or* toasted
    coconut (optional)

■ Line an 8x8x2-inch baking pan with foil, extending foil over the edges of the pan. Butter the foil, then set the pan aside.

■ In a 3-quart casserole place butter or margarine. Cook, uncovered, on 100% power (high) for 1 to 2 minutes or till melted. Stir in sugar and evaporated milk. Cook, uncovered, on high for 7 to 10 minutes or till candy reaches soft-ball stage (234° to 240°), stirring every 3 minutes. After 7 minutes, check every 30 seconds. To test for soft-ball stage, drop syrup into *very cold* water. The syrup should form a ball that *immediately* flattens and runs between your fingers (see photo, below).

■ Add marshmallows; chocolate, butterscotch-flavored, or peanut butter-flavored pieces; and vanilla. Stir till marshmallows and pieces are melted and blended into mixture. Add nuts, if desired. Quickly turn fudge into the prepared pan. While fudge is warm, score into 1-inch squares.

■ Cool to room temperature, then cover and chill in the refrigerator for several hours or till firm. When fudge is firm, grasp the foil edges and lift the foil and fudge out of the pan. Remove foil. Cut fudge into squares. Store tightly covered in the refrigerator. Makes 2 pounds (64 pieces).

Low-wattage oven: For *soft-ball stage,* cook on high 11 to 13 minutes.

To tell if the syrup for the candy has reached the soft-ball stage, add a few drops of syrup from a spoon to *very cold,* but not icy, water. With your fingers, shape the drops into a ball in the cold water. When you remove the ball from the water, it should *immediately* flatten and run between your fingers, as shown.

Chocolate Truffles

These tiny morsels pack a lot of flavor. (Pictured on pages 84–85.)

1 6-ounce package (1 cup) semisweet chocolate pieces
⅓ cup butter *or* margarine
3 tablespoons milk
1 beaten egg yolk
3 tablespoons orange juice or desired liquor or liqueur*
Unsweetened cocoa powder, powdered sugar, chocolate-flavored sprinkles, coconut, *or* chopped *or* ground nuts

■ In a 4-cup measure combine chocolate, butter or margarine, and milk. Cook the mixture, uncovered, on 100% power (high), for 1½ to 2½ minutes or till soft enough to stir smooth, stirring once during cooking (see photo 2, page 92).

■ Gradually stir about *half* of the hot mixture into beaten egg yolk. Return all of the mixture to the 4-cup measure. Cook, uncovered, about 1 minute or till bubbly, stirring every 30 seconds.

■ Stir in orange juice, liquor, or liqueur. Cover and chill about 1 hour or till mixture is cool, evenly thickened, and smooth, stirring occasionally.

■ Beat the cooled chocolate mixture with an electric mixer on medium speed about 2 minutes or till slightly fluffy. Cover and chill about 15 minutes or till mixture holds its shape.

■ Drop from a level teaspoon onto a baking sheet lined with waxed paper. Cover and chill about 30 minutes or till firm. Roll into balls, then roll in cocoa powder, powdered sugar, chocolate sprinkles, coconut, or nuts. Store covered in the refrigerator. Makes ¾ pound (about 48 pieces).

Liquor options: Use rum, Irish whiskey, brandy, kirsch, amaretto, hazelnut liqueur, coffee liqueur, praline liqueur, *or* orange liqueur.

Peanut Butter and Chocolate Squares

These layered candies will be easier to cut if you let them stand at room temperature for a half hour after chilling. (Pictured on pages 84–85.)

⅔ cup sifted powdered sugar
½ cup peanut butter
1 tablespoon honey
2 teaspoons milk
¼ cup chopped peanuts
1 6-ounce package (1 cup) semisweet chocolate pieces
2 tablespoons peanut butter
2 tablespoons chopped peanuts

■ Line an 8x4x2-inch loaf pan with foil, extending foil over edges of pan. Butter the foil, then set the pan aside.

■ In a 1-quart casserole combine powdered sugar, ½ cup peanut butter, honey, and milk. Cook, uncovered, on 100% power (high) for 1 to 2 minutes or till sugar is dissolved, stirring once. Stir in ¼ cup peanuts. Pour peanut butter mixture into the prepared pan. Spread evenly.

■ Wash casserole. In the same casserole, combine chocolate and 2 tablespoons peanut butter. Cook, uncovered, on high, for 1½ to 2½ minutes or till soft enough to stir smooth, stirring once during cooking (see photo 2, page 92). Spread chocolate mixture over peanut butter mixture. Sprinkle with 2 tablespoons peanuts. Press lightly. Cool to room temperature. Cover and chill several hours or till firm. When firm, lift the foil and candy from pan. Remove foil. Cut into squares. Store tightly covered in the refrigerator. Makes 1 pound (24 pieces).

Nutty Caramel Clusters

Peanuts, pecans, and almonds: you'll find them all here!

25 vanilla caramels
 1 tablespoon butter *or* margarine
 1 tablespoon milk
 1 cup sliced almonds
 ½ cup cocktail peanuts
 ½ cup pecan halves
 ½ cup semisweet chocolate pieces
 2 teaspoons shortening

■ Grease a baking sheet or line one with waxed paper, then set aside. In a 1-quart casserole combine caramels, butter or margarine, and milk. Cook, uncovered, on 100% power (high) for 1 to 2 minutes or till soft enough to stir smooth, stirring once during cooking (see photo 1). Stir in almonds, peanuts, and pecans. Drop from a teaspoon onto the prepared baking sheet.

■ In a 1-cup measure combine chocolate pieces and shortening. Cook, uncovered, on high, for 1 to 2 minutes or till soft enough to stir smooth, stirring once during cooking (see photo 2).

■ Drizzle chocolate over each cluster. Cool to room temperature, then cover and chill till firm. Store tightly covered in the refrigerator. Makes about 1¼ pounds (25 pieces).

1 Cook the caramel mixture on 100% power (high), stirring once, till soft enough to stir smooth. Some of the caramels will retain their shape and won't look melted, but you'll still be able to stir them until they are smooth.

2 Just like caramels, chocolate pieces retain their shape even when melted. Cook on high, stirring once, till the pieces are soft enough to stir smooth. Remember, some of the chocolate pieces won't look melted.

TIP Easy Candies

Use the timings in the charts for toasting nuts (see page 64) and melting caramels and chocolate (see opposite).

Chocolate-Caramel Snappers: Arrange 1½ cups toasted *pecan halves* in clusters of 3 on a greased, foil-lined baking sheet. Melt ½ of a 14-ounce package *vanilla caramels* with 1 tablespoon *each milk* and *butter or margarine.* Spoon some over each cluster. Let stand 20 minutes. Melt ½ cup *semisweet chocolate pieces* and 2 teaspoons *shortening,* then spoon over caramel. Cover; chill till firm.

Chocolate Clusters: Melt 1 cup *semisweet chocolate pieces* and 1 tablespoon *shortening.* Stir in 1½ cups *nuts, chow mein noodles,* or *tiny marshmallows* (or a combination of these). Drop from a spoon onto a baking sheet lined with waxed paper. Cover; chill till firm.

Melting Caramels and Chocolate

Place the unwrapped caramels or chocolate squares or pieces in the specified container. Cook them, uncovered, on 100% power (high), stirring every minute, for the time shown in chart or till the caramels or chocolate are soft enough to stir together till smooth. Some pieces won't look melted.

Ingredient	Amount	Container	Cooking time
Caramels	14	1-cup measure	30 to 60 seconds
	½ of 14-ounce package	2-cup measure	1 to 2 minutes
	14-ounce package	4-cup measure	2½ to 3½ minutes
Chocolate squares	1 ounce (1 square)	1-cup measure	1 to 2 minutes
	2 ounces (2 squares)	1-cup measure	1½ to 2½ minutes
Chocolate pieces	½ cup	1-cup measure	1½ to 2 minutes
	6-ounce package (1 cup)	2-cup measure	2 to 2½ minutes
	12-ounce package (2 cups)	4-cup measure	2½ to 3 minutes

Nutrition Analysis

	Per Serving							Percent U.S. RDA Per Serving							
	Number of servings	Calories	Protein (g)	Carbohydrate (g)	Fat (g)	Sodium (mg)	Potassium (mg)	Protein	Vitamin A	Vitamin C	Thiamine	Riboflavin	Niacin	Calcium	Iron
Cherry Divinity (p. 88)	40	67	0	17	0	5	6	0	0	0	0	0	0	0	1
Chocolate Swirled Divinity (p. 88)	40	72	0	17	1	5	10	0	0	0	0	0	0	0	1
Chocolate Truffles (p. 91)	48	32	0	2	3	15	17	0	1	1	0	0	0	0	1
Divinity (p. 88)	40	61	0	16	0	5	3	0	0	0	0	0	0	0	1
Nut Brittle (p. 86)	16	148	3	22	6	67	77	5	1	0	7	1	9	1	4
Nut Divinity (p. 88)	40	71	0	16	1	5	12	0	0	0	1	0	0	0	1
Nutmeg Brittle (p. 86)	16	148	3	22	6	67	77	5	1	0	7	1	9	1	4
Nutty Caramel Clusters (p. 92)	25	118	2	11	8	26	94	3	0	0	3	4	3	3	3
Peanut Butter and Chocolate Squares (p. 91)	24	102	3	9	7	41	84	4	0	0	1	1	7	1	2
Peppermint Divinity (p. 88)	40	65	0	16	0	8	3	0	0	0	0	0	0	0	1
Shortcut Fudge (p. 90)	64	58	0	9	3	18	17	1	1	0	0	1	0	1	1

EGGS AND CHEESE

Eggs are quick to make, so why cook them in your microwave? That's easy: You don't have to heat up the kitchen, you can cook and serve in the same dish, and you can turn out the fluffiest scrambled eggs every time.

Extras on eggs
You can scramble, poach, or fry eggs in your microwave, but you'll need to follow some special cooking techniques.

For instance, if you're scrambling eggs, mix the yolks and whites well so the yolks won't cook before the whites. Also, before you fry or poach eggs, prick the membranes covering the yolks and whites two or three times so they won't explode. To fry eggs in your microwave, you'll need a special browning dish.

With a little practice, you'll learn which of your favorite egg recipes work best in the microwave. But take a tip from our Test Kitchen: Leave soufflés and quiches for the conventional oven and hard-cooked eggs for the range-top.

We tested our recipes with large eggs, so if you use a different size, adjust the time accordingly.

Cheese tricks
Cheese is another good yet delicate microwave subject. The microwave oven is great for softening or melting cheese quickly, but take care not to overcook cheese or it will become stringy and tough.

Here are some tips that we discovered give the best cheesy results.

When our recipes call for a large amount of cheese, you'll notice we ask you to cook it on medium,

Mexicali Scrambled Eggs
(see recipe, page 98)

instead of high, to avoid over-cooking. Because cheese is so delicate, we suggest that you sprinkle small amounts over hot food after cooking. The cheese will melt while the food stands.

In testing recipes, we found sauces made with natural, rather than process, cheese are more likely to separate and curdle. So when you can, choose process Swiss or American cheese.

Cider-Cheese Fondue
(see recipe, page 102)

Technique:
Poaching eggs

Huevos Rancheros

Have your eggs Mexican-style—poached in a fiery tomato sauce.

Tortilla Cups *or* tortilla
  chips
¼ cup chopped onion
1 tablespoon water
1 clove garlic, minced
½ teaspoon chili powder
2 10-ounce cans tomatoes and
    green chili peppers
4 eggs
½ cup shredded Monterey Jack
    cheese (2 ounces)
Bottled hot pepper sauce

■ Prepare Tortilla Cups, if desired (see photo 1). Set aside. In a 1½-quart casserole combine onion, water, garlic, and chili powder. Cook, covered, on 100% power (high) for 1 to 2 minutes or till onion is tender. Add *undrained* tomatoes and peppers. Cook, covered, for 6 to 8 minutes or till boiling over entire surface, stirring twice.

■ Carefully break eggs, one at a time, into a custard cup, then slide onto hot tomato sauce. Prick each yolk and white 3 times with a wooden toothpick (see photo 2). Cook, covered, on high for 2 to 3 minutes or till eggs are nearly done (see photo 3), giving the dish a half-turn once. Let stand, covered, for 2 minutes.

■ To serve, carefully spoon eggs and sauce into Tortilla Cups or serve over tortilla chips. Sprinkle with shredded cheese (see photo 4). Pass hot pepper sauce. Makes 4 servings.

> **Tortilla Cups:** Place four 6- to 7-inch *flour tortillas* between layers of paper towels. Heat on 100% power (high) for 45 to 60 seconds or till pliable. Line four 10-ounce custard cups with tortillas. Lightly brush tortillas with *cooking oil* (see photo 1). Cook, uncovered, on high for 2 to 4 minutes or till tortilla surfaces are dry, rearranging cups once. Remove tortillas from custard cups. Cool on a wire rack.

1

Fit the softened tortillas into the custard cups and lightly brush with oil. The oil helps the tortillas crisp as they cook.

2

Carefully break the eggs, one at a time, into a custard cup, then slide onto the hot sauce. Prick each yolk and each white 3 times with a wooden toothpick, as shown. This lets steam escape so it does not build up and burst the egg yolk or white.

3

Remove the eggs from the oven when they are almost done, as shown. Then let them stand in the covered casserole about 2 minutes or until they are done just the way you like them. You'll find the eggs continue cooking in the sauce for a few minutes after you remove them from the oven.

4

Once the eggs are done, carefully spoon one egg and some of the tomato sauce into each Tortilla Cup or over tortilla chips. Sprinkle with the Monterey Jack cheese and pass the hot pepper sauce at the table. Serve with fresh grapes, cantaloupe, or other fruit.

Eggs Creole

The spicy blend of tomatoes and seasonings earns this dish its name.

1   7½-ounce can tomatoes,
    cut up
⅓ cup finely chopped celery
2   tablespoons finely chopped
    onion
2   tablespoons finely chopped
    green pepper
¼ teaspoon sugar
⅛ teaspoon salt
⅛ teaspoon ground red pepper
    Dash ground cloves
1   bay leaf
1   tablespoon cold water
1   teaspoon cornstarch
4   eggs
½ cup shredded cheddar
    cheese (2 ounces)

■ In a 1½-quart casserole combine *undrained* tomatoes, celery, onion, green pepper, sugar, salt, red pepper, cloves, and bay leaf. Cook, covered, on 100% power (high) for 4 to 6 minutes or till vegetables are tender, stirring once.

■ Combine water and cornstarch, then stir into tomato mixture. Cook, uncovered, on high for 1½ to 3½ minutes or till thickened and bubbly, stirring every 30 seconds. Remove bay leaf. Cover to keep warm.

■ Pour 1 cup *water* into a 1-quart casserole. Cook, uncovered, on high for 2½ to 4½ minutes or till boiling over entire surface. Carefully break eggs, one at a time, into a custard cup, then slide into water. Prick each yolk and white 3 times with a wooden toothpick (see photo 2, page 97). Cook, covered, on high for 1½ to 2½ minutes or till nearly done (see photo 3, page 97). Let stand, covered, for 2 minutes.

■ To serve, remove eggs from water with a slotted spoon and place on top of tomato mixture in the casserole. Sprinkle with shredded cheese (see photo 4, page 97). Let stand for 1 minute to melt cheese. Serve from the casserole. Makes 4 servings.

Mexicali Scrambled Eggs

Serve with avocado slices and corn muffins for a light supper. (Pictured on pages 94–95.)

4   eggs
¼ cup milk
⅛ teaspoon pepper
    Several dashes bottled hot
    pepper sauce
    Dash salt
¼ cup diced fully cooked ham,
    chicken, beef, *or* pork
1   2-ounce can mushroom
    stems and pieces, drained
2   tablespoons chopped canned
    green chili peppers,
    drained
¼ cup shredded cheddar
    cheese (1 ounce)
    Dairy sour cream *or* chili
    sauce

■ In a 1-quart casserole combine eggs, milk, pepper, hot pepper sauce, and salt. Beat with a fork till yolks and whites are well mixed. Stir in meat, mushrooms, and chili peppers.

■ Cook, uncovered, on 100% power (high) for 3 to 5 minutes or till eggs are almost set, pushing cooked portions to the center after 1½ minutes, then every 30 seconds (see photo 2, opposite). Season to taste. Sprinkle with shredded cheese. Let stand till cheese starts to melt. Serve with sour cream or chili sauce. Makes 2 or 3 servings.

Anything-Goes Scrambled Eggs

Mix and match the different ingredients and you'll find that almost anything goes in these fluffy eggs.

4 ounces bulk pork sausage *or* ground beef
¼ cup chopped onion
1 cup chopped broccoli *or* whole kernel corn, cooked and drained, *or* frozen pea pods, thawed and halved crosswise
6 eggs
⅓ cup milk
¼ teaspoon dried oregano, basil, *or* thyme, crushed
¼ teaspoon salt
⅛ teaspoon pepper
1 medium tomato, sliced

■ In a 9-inch pie plate crumble sausage or beef, then add onion. Cover with waxed paper. Cook on 100% power (high) for 2 to 4 minutes or till no pink remains in meat, stirring once. Drain off fat. Stir in vegetable. Cook, covered, for 1 to 2 minutes or till vegetable is hot.

■ In a medium mixing bowl combine eggs, milk, herb, salt, and pepper. Beat with a fork till yolks and whites are well mixed. Pour egg mixture over meat mixture in dish (see photo 1). Cook, uncovered, on high for 1½ minutes. Push cooked portions to the center of the dish (see photo 2). Continue cooking for 2½ to 3½ minutes more or till eggs are almost set, pushing cooked portions to the center every 30 seconds. Let stand for 5 minutes. Serve over tomato slices. Makes 4 servings.

Low-wattage oven: For *eggs,* cook on high for 7 minutes, pushing cooked portions to the center every 45 to 60 seconds.

TIP Scrambling Eggs

In a bowl, for each egg, add 1 tablespoon *milk,* a dash *salt,* and a dash *pepper.* Using a fork, beat egg mixture till yolks and whites are well mixed. For each egg, add 1 teaspoon *butter or margarine* to mixture. In a 10-ounce custard cup (or a 1-quart casserole for 4 to 6 eggs) cook, uncovered, on 100% power (high) for the time given below or till almost set, pushing cooked portions to the center after 1½ and 3 minutes, then every 30 seconds. Let stand till eggs are set. Stir before serving.

For 1 egg: 1 to 1½ minutes
For 2 eggs: 1½ to 2½ minutes
For 4 eggs: 3 to 5 minutes
For 6 eggs: 4 to 6 minutes

1

Before adding the egg mixture, be sure the yolks and whites are well mixed. If they aren't, the yolks will cook before the whites because of their higher fat content. Pour the egg mixture over the hot meat mixture, as shown. The heat from the meat will speed the cooking of the eggs.

2

Cook the mixture for 1½ minutes. Then, because the eggs at the edges cook first, push the cooked portions to the center, letting the uncooked portions flow to the edges, as shown. Cook 2½ to 3½ minutes more or till almost set, pushing the cooked portions to the center every 30 seconds. Eggs will finish cooking as they stand.

French Omelet

Just remember these three easy omelet steps: fill it, fold it, and flip it!

3 eggs
2 tablespoons water
2 teaspoons snipped parsley
    (optional)
    Dash salt
    Dash pepper
1 teaspoon butter *or*
    margarine
    Desired filling *or* topping
    (optional)

■ In a small mixing bowl combine eggs, water, snipped parsley (if desired), salt, and pepper. Beat with a fork till yolks and whites are well mixed. Set aside.

■ In a 9-inch pie plate cook butter or margarine on 100% power (high) for 30 to 40 seconds or till melted. Spread butter with spatula to coat the pie plate evenly. Add egg mixture to pie plate and cook, uncovered, on high for 2½ to 3½ minutes or till eggs are set but still shiny, pushing cooked edges toward center every 30 seconds.

■ To serve, place filling, if desired, on one half of the omelet. Fold omelet in half. Slide omelet to edge of pie plate. Tilt pie plate, then invert to roll omelet onto a warm plate. Add topping, if desired. Makes 1 or 2 servings.

Cooked Vegetable Filling: In a 10-ounce covered casserole cook ½ cup chopped *zucchini, carrot, green pepper, mushrooms, onion, or celery* in 1 tablespoon *butter or margarine* on 100% power (high) for 2 to 3 minutes or till tender.

Fresh Vegetable Filling: Choose from ½ cup *alfalfa sprouts*, chopped *tomato, or* sliced *avocado.*

Cheese Filling: Shred ½ cup of your favorite *cheese.*

Meat or Seafood Filling: In a 10-ounce covered casserole heat ⅓ cup chilled, chopped, cooked *beef, pork, lamb, ham, chicken, shrimp, crab, tuna, or salmon* on 100% power (high) for 30 to 60 seconds or till heated through.

Topping: Top omelet with shredded or grated *cheese,* chopped *tomato,* crumbled cooked *bacon, or* chopped *nuts.*

Dessert Fruit Filling and Topping: Choose from ½ cup *berries, sliced peaches, pineapple chunks, mandarin orange sections, or banana slices.* Dollop fruit with *dairy sour cream.* Sprinkle omelet with *brown sugar or powdered sugar.*

**French Omelet with Fresh
Vegetable Filling**

Cider-Cheese Fondue

Cook, serve, and reheat all in the same dish. (Pictured on pages 94–95.)

2 cups shredded Muenster,
    cheddar, *or* Swiss cheese
    (8 ounces)
1 tablespoon all-purpose flour
¼ teaspoon ground nutmeg *or*
    dried dillweed
⅓ cup apple juice, apple
    cider, *or* dry white wine
    Bread cubes *or* vegetable *or*
    fruit dippers

■ In a medium mixing bowl combine cheese, flour, and nutmeg or dillweed, then toss to coat. Set aside.

■ In a 1-quart casserole cook juice or wine, uncovered, on 100% power (high) about 1 minute or till hot. Add cheese mixture to hot liquid.

■ Cook, uncovered, on 50% power (medium) for 3 to 5 minutes or till cheese is melted and mixture is hot, stirring every 2 minutes.

■ Reheat in the casserole, as necessary, on 50% power (medium) for 1 to 2 minutes. (Or, keep warm in a fondue pot over fondue burner.) Serve with bread cubes or vegetable or fruit dippers. Makes 4 servings.

Low-wattage oven: For *cheese,* cook on high for 3 to 4 minutes.

Calico Macaroni And Cheese

In testing, we found process cheese gives a satiny-smooth sauce.

1 cup elbow macaroni
1 cup loose-pack frozen
    mixed vegetables
⅓ cup chopped green pepper
2 tablespoons water
1 cup milk
1 tablespoon all-purpose flour
⅛ teaspoon pepper
1 cup shredded process Swiss
    cheese *or* American cheese
    (4 ounces)
    Grated Parmesan cheese
    (optional)
    Paprika (optional)
    Chopped tomato (optional)
    Chopped green pepper
    (optional)

■ On the range-top cook macaroni according to package directions. Drain well.

■ Meanwhile, in a 1-quart casserole combine mixed vegetables, ⅓ cup green pepper, and water. Cook, covered, on 100% power (high) for 2 to 3 minutes or till crisp-tender. Drain. Combine milk, flour, and pepper. Stir into vegetable mixture. Cook, uncovered, on high for 4 to 7 minutes or till slightly thickened and bubbly, stirring every minute.

■ Add Swiss or American cheese and stir till melted. Stir in cooked macaroni. If desired, sprinkle with Parmesan cheese and paprika. Cook, uncovered, on high for 2½ to 3½ minutes or till heated through. If desired, garnish with tomato and green pepper. Makes 4 servings.

Poaching and Frying Eggs

To **poach eggs,** pour 1 cup *hot water* into a 1 quart casserole. Cook, uncovered, on 100% power (high) 2 to 3 minutes or till boiling over entire surface. Carefully break eggs, one at a time, into custard cup; add to water. Prick each yolk and white 3 times with a toothpick. Cook, covered, on high for time shown till nearly done. Let stand.

Eggs	Cooking time	Standing time
1 egg	30 to 60 seconds	2 minutes
2 eggs	1 to 1½ minutes	2 minutes
4 eggs	1½ to 2½ minutes	2 minutes

If you have a browning dish, you can **fry eggs** in your microwave oven. Preheat the browning dish on 100% power (high) for 2 minutes (3½ minutes in a low-wattage oven). Add 1 tablespoon *cooking oil* and carefully break the eggs into the preheated dish. Prick each yolk and white 3 times with a wooden toothpick. Cook, covered, on high for the time shown or till cooked to desired doneness.

Eggs	Cooking time
1 egg	30 to 60 seconds
2 eggs	1 to 2 minutes
4 eggs	2 to 3 minutes

Nutrition Analysis

	Number of servings	Calories	Protein (g)	Carbohydrate (g)	Fat (g)	Sodium (mg)	Potassium (mg)	Protein	Vitamin A	Vitamin C	Thiamine	Riboflavin	Niacin	Calcium	Iron
		Per Serving						**Percent U.S. RDA Per Serving**							
Anything-Goes Scrambled Eggs (p. 99)	4	201	14	6	13	427	337	22	27	59	14	20	5	10	12
Calico Macaroni and Cheese (p. 102)	4	305	16	36	11	130	304	24	53	20	26	22	13	37	10
Cider-Cheese Fondue (p. 102)	4	225	13	5	17	355	102	21	13	0	1	11	1	41	2
Eggs Creole (p. 98)	4	156	10	5	10	307	249	16	19	20	5	13	2	14	8
French Omelet (p. 100)	1	193	12	1	15	311	133	19	13	0	5	18	0	6	12
w/ Cheese Filling (p. 100)	1	420	26	2	34	661	189	40	25	0	6	30	1	47	14
w/ Cooked Vegetable Filling (p. 100)	1	305	13	4	27	427	268	20	26	21	7	21	4	8	13
w/ Dessert Fruit Filling and Topping (p. 100)	1	265	13	12	18	321	294	20	16	71	6	21	1	9	14
w/ Fresh Vegetable Filling (p. 100)	1	197	13	2	15	312	146	20	14	2	6	19	1	6	13
w/ Meat or Seafood Filling (p. 100)	1	281	27	1	18	347	296	41	13	0	7	24	14	7	21
Huevos Rancheros (p. 96)	4	236	13	23	11	298	350	20	35	100	11	16	8	21	16
Mexicali Scrambled Eggs (p. 98)	2	269	21	5	18	647	242	32	16	43	16	30	7	20	15

FISH AND SEAFOOD

Fish take to the microwave oven as they take to water. From cod to shrimp, the microwave's combination of quick cooking and steam is hard to beat.

Fast, fast, fast
As you might expect, fish and seafood cook quicker in your microwave oven than they do conventionally. That's because micro-cooking allows you to poach, boil, or steam food without waiting for a pot of water to heat.

For the speediest cooking, cover your fish or seafood with a lid or vented plastic wrap to hold the steam. Then cook on high unless we tell you otherwise in the recipe.

The quick thaw
You can also thaw fish and seafood in the microwave, with help from our chart on page 123. One tip to remember: make sure each frozen piece is completely defrosted before beginning a recipe. Otherwise, the thawed portions will cook faster than the still-frozen parts.

The tough assignment
Developing a microwave recipe for crispy coated fish was our biggest challenge in this chapter.

Because crumb coatings underneath fish tend to get soggy, we've left the bottoms of our fish uncoated. But, if you own a browning dish, you can cook fish that's coated on all sides. Just put a little cooking oil in the dish for fish with fried-on-the-range-top look and flavor.

Cooked right all over
Keep an eye out when cooking high-fat fish such as salmon. Fatty portions of the fish may cook faster than nonfatty areas. We recommend shielding the fatty parts with foil. (First, check your owner's manual to see if you can use foil in your oven.)

Oriental-Style Scallops
(see recipe, page 120)

Thinner portions of a fish fillet also cook faster. To prevent overcooking, trim off, fold under, or overlap these parts to get an even thickness. Or, shield thinner portions with foil.

You'll know it's done
Whether cooked in a microwave or a conventional oven, fish and seafood look the same when done. Fish is cooked if it flakes when you test it with a fork. Shrimp turn pink, scallops become opaque, and clam and oyster shells open.

Throw away any shrimp with uncurled tails and any unopened clams or oysters. And do not micro-cook live lobsters, crabs, or crawfish.

**Salmon Steaks
with Horseradish Sauce**
(see recipe, page 109)

Halibut Kabobs
(see recipe, page 109)

Shrimp Creole
(see recipe, page 120)

Stuffing a whole fish

Snapper with Mushroom Stuffing

1   1½- to 2-pound fresh *or* frozen whole dressed red snapper *or* other fish with head and tail removed
1   5-ounce package regular long grain and wild rice mix
1   cup sliced fresh mushrooms
¼   cup chopped onion
2   tablespoons butter *or* margarine
2   tablespoons chopped pimiento
½   cup frozen peas
1   tablespoon butter *or* margarine
1   teaspoon lemon juice

■ Thaw fish, if frozen (see chart, page 123). For stuffing, prepare rice mix according to package directions. In a 1½-quart casserole combine mushrooms, onion, and 2 tablespoons butter or margarine. Cook, covered, on 100% power (high) for 2 to 3 minutes. Add pimiento.

■ Gently stir in frozen peas and cooked rice (see photo 1). Set aside. In a custard cup cook 1 tablespoon butter or margarine, uncovered, on high for 30 to 40 seconds or till melted. Stir in lemon juice.

■ Rinse fish and pat dry. Enlarge fish cavity by cutting toward tail (see photo 2). Place in a 12x7½x2-inch baking dish. Brush inside and outside of fish with lemon mixture. Spoon about ¾ *cup* of the stuffing into cavity (see photo 3). Place remaining stuffing in a casserole and set aside.

■ Cover the stuffed fish with vented clear plastic wrap (see photo 4). Cook on high for 10 to 12 minutes or till fish flakes easily with a fork, giving the dish a half-turn after 6 minutes (see photo 5). If necessary, use small pieces of foil to shield the tail end.

■ Let fish stand, covered, while cooking remaining stuffing. Cook stuffing, covered, on high for 2 to 3 minutes or till heated through, stirring once. Serve fish with additional stuffing. Makes 6 to 8 servings.

Low-wattage oven: Make sure the dish will fit into your microwave oven before trying this recipe.

TIP   Cooking Whole Fish

When it comes to micro-cooking, a fish is not a fish is not a fish; they vary in weight and in size. Before you begin one of our recipes, remove the head and tail and weigh the fish. If it's heavier or lighter than our suggested weight, increase or decrease the cooking time accordingly. We recommend removing the fish's head and tail because steam may cause the eyes to pop and the tail to overcook. What's more, with no head and tail, the fish will fit more easily into your microwave oven.

1

For the stuffing, when the onion and mushrooms are tender, add the frozen peas. They'll cook as the stuffing heats.

2

Once the fish has been thawed and rinsed, enlarge the cavity by cutting from the head end toward the tail end. Pull back the skin as you cut to make cutting easier. Enlarging the cavity gives more room to spoon the stuffing into the fish.

3

Place the rinsed fish in a 12x7½x2-inch baking dish and brush with the butter mixture. Then loosely spoon the stuffing into the fish cavity to generously fill, as shown.

4

Before cooking, cover the stuffed fish with clear plastic wrap. Turn back the corner of the wrap to create a vent for steam to escape, as shown. A lid would also work as a cover.

5

Perfectly cooked fish should flake when tested with a fork, as shown. If the thinner tail end is done before the rest of the fish, shield it with a small piece of foil, as shown. (First, check your owner's manual to see if you can use foil in your oven.)

Bulgur-Stuffed Fish

Look for bulgur in your grocer's cereal section or alongside the grains.

1 1- to 1½-pound fresh *or*
   frozen whole dressed fish
   with head and tail removed
½ cup bulgur
⅓ cup finely chopped, seeded
   cucumber
¼ cup finely shredded carrot
2 tablespoons snipped parsley
2 tablespoons thinly sliced
   green onion
2 teaspoons lemon juice
⅛ teaspoon dried basil,
   crushed
   Dash pepper

■ Refer to photos, page 107. Thaw fish, if frozen (see chart, page 123). For stuffing, prepare bulgur according to package directions.

■ Meanwhile, in a medium mixing bowl combine cucumber, carrot, parsley, green onion, lemon juice, basil, and pepper. Add cooked bulgur and toss gently to combine. Set aside.

■ Rinse fish and pat dry. Enlarge fish cavity by cutting toward tail. Place fish in a 10x6x2-inch baking dish. Spoon about *½ cup* of stuffing into fish cavity. Place remaining stuffing in a small casserole and set aside.

■ Cover fish with vented clear plastic wrap. Cook on 100% power (high) for 8 to 10 minutes or till fish flakes easily with a fork, giving the dish a half-turn after 5 minutes. If necessary, use small pieces of foil to shield the tail end. Let stand, covered, while cooking remaining stuffing. Cook stuffing, covered, on high for 1 to 2 minutes or till heated through, stirring once. Serve the stuffing with the fish. Makes 4 or 5 servings.

Herbed Corn-Bread-Stuffed Trout

2 6- to 8-ounce whole dressed
   trout with heads removed
¼ cup chopped celery
¼ cup chopped green pepper
3 tablespoons butter *or*
   margarine
1 cup corn bread stuffing mix
⅛ teaspoon ground sage
⅛ teaspoon pepper
3 to 4 tablespoons chicken
   broth *or* water
1 tablespoon butter *or*
   margarine

■ Refer to photos, page 107. Thaw fish, if frozen (see chart, page 123). For stuffing, in a 1-quart casserole combine celery, green pepper, and 3 tablespoons butter or margarine. Cook, covered, on 100% power (high) for 1½ to 2½ minutes or till tender. Stir in corn bread stuffing mix, sage, and pepper. Add enough chicken broth or water to just moisten stuffing mix and toss gently to combine. Set aside.

■ In a custard cup cook 1 tablespoon butter or margarine, uncovered, on high for 30 to 40 seconds or till melted. Set aside. Rinse fish and pat dry. Enlarge the fish cavities by cutting toward tails. Place fish in a 10x6x2-inch baking dish. Brush inside and outside of *each* fish with melted butter. Spoon about *½ cup* of the stuffing into the cavity of *each* fish. Place remaining stuffing in a small casserole and set aside.

■ Cover the fish with vented clear plastic wrap. Cook on high for 4 to 6 minutes or till fish flakes easily with a fork, giving the dish a half-turn after 3 minutes. If necessary, use small pieces of foil to shield tails.

■ Let fish stand, covered, while cooking remaining stuffing. Cook stuffing, covered, on high for 1 to 2 minutes or till heated through, stirring once. Serve the warm stuffing with the fish. Makes 2 servings.

Salmon Steaks with Horseradish Sauce

Serve these pleasantly pungent steaks with steamed vegetables and warm rolls. (Pictured on pages 104–105.)

2   6- to 8-ounce fresh *or* frozen
    salmon *or* halibut steaks,
    cut ¾ to 1 inch thick
1   tablespoon butter *or*
    margarine
1   tablespoon snipped chives
2   teaspoons cornstarch
⅛   teaspoon salt
    Dash white pepper
⅔   cup milk
2   teaspoons prepared
    horseradish
½   teaspoon lemon juice
    Fresh chives (optional)

■ Thaw fish steaks, if frozen (see chart, page 123). Place steaks in an 8x8x2-inch baking dish. Cover with vented clear plastic wrap (see photo 4, page 107). Cook on 100% power (high) for 4 to 8 minutes or till fish flakes easily with a fork, turning fish over after 1 minute (see photo 5, page 107). Let stand, covered, while preparing sauce.

■ For sauce, in a 2-cup measure cook butter or margarine, uncovered, on high for 30 to 40 seconds or till melted. Add 1 tablespoon chives, cornstarch, salt, and white pepper, then stir till smooth. Stir in milk. Cook, uncovered, on high for 1½ to 3 minutes or till thickened and bubbly, stirring every 30 seconds. Stir in horseradish and lemon juice. To serve, spoon sauce over salmon steaks. If desired, garnish with fresh chives. Makes 4 servings.

Halibut Kabobs

Pictured on pages 104–105.

1   pound fresh *or* frozen
    halibut steaks, cut 1 inch
    thick
3   tablespoons cooking oil
3   tablespoons dry white wine
3   tablespoons lemon juice
½   teaspoon salt
½   teaspoon dried oregano,
    crushed
1   medium zucchini, cut
    into ¼-inch slices
1   tablespoon water
8   cherry tomatoes

■ Thaw halibut steaks, if frozen (see chart, page 123). Trim off skin. Cut halibut steaks into 1-inch cubes.

■ For marinade, in a mixing bowl combine cooking oil, wine, lemon juice, salt, and oregano. Add fish cubes and stir gently to coat. Cover and marinate in the refrigerator for 1 hour, stirring gently once or twice.

■ Meanwhile, in a 1-quart casserole place zucchini and water. Cook, covered, on 100% power (high) for 2 minutes. Drain and let zucchini stand till cool enough to handle.

■ Drain fish, reserving marinade. On four 9-inch-long wooden skewers alternately thread fish cubes, zucchini, and cherry tomatoes. Place in a 12x7½x2-inch baking dish. Pour reserved marinade over kabobs. Cover with vented clear plastic wrap (see photo 4, page 107). Cook on high for 3 to 6 minutes or till fish flakes easily with a fork, giving the dish a half-turn after 2 minutes (see photo 5, page 107). Makes 4 servings.

Low-wattage oven: Not recommended.

Cooking thin fillets

Gazpacho Fillets

The sauce tastes like gazpacho, a fresh-tasting Spanish summer soup.

1 pound fresh *or* frozen fish
  fillets
1 cup water
1 large tomato
¼ cup chopped, seeded
  cucumber
¼ cup chopped green pepper
¼ cup chopped celery
2 tablespoons chopped onion
1 tablespoon lemon juice
½ teaspoon sugar
½ teaspoon instant chicken
  bouillon granules
⅛ teaspoon pepper
  Few dashes bottled hot
  pepper sauce
2 tablespoons tomato paste
  Celery leaves (optional)

■ Thaw fish, if frozen (see photo 1, opposite, and chart, page 123). In a 2-cup measure cook water, uncovered, on 100% power (high) for 2½ to 3½ minutes or till boiling. Spear tomato with a fork. Carefully dip tomato into the hot water for 12 seconds (see photo 2). Hold tomato under cold water till cool enough to handle. Remove peel and seeds, then chop tomato. (You should have ¾ to 1 cup.)

■ In an 8x8x2-inch baking dish stir together chopped tomato, cucumber, green pepper, celery, onion, lemon juice, sugar, bouillon granules, pepper, and hot pepper sauce. Arrange fish fillets on top of vegetables with thicker portions toward the edges of the dish. Turn under any thin portions of fillets to obtain an even thickness of about ½ inch (see photo 3). Sprinkle fillets with salt and pepper.

■ Cover with a lid or vented clear plastic wrap (see photo 4). Cook on high for 6 to 9 minutes or till fish flakes easily with a fork, giving the dish a half-turn after 4 minutes (see photo 5, page 107).

■ Carefully transfer fish to a serving platter. Cover to keep warm. For sauce, stir tomato paste into tomato mixture in baking dish. Cook, uncovered, on high about 1 minute or till heated through. If desired, garnish platter with celery leaves. Serve sauce over cooked fish fillets (see large photo). Makes 4 servings.

TIP The Thick and Thin of Fish Fillets

When you face the freezer case, you'll discover all shapes and sizes of fish. In microwave cookery, the thickness of the fish is especially important, because it affects the timing and evenness of cooking. We based our fillet recipes on a ½-inch thickness, unless we indicate otherwise. If you want to buy fillets that are about ½ inch thick, try perch, turbot, walleyed pike, and orange roughy. You can expect flounder, sole, and whiting fillets to be thinner, and haddock, red snapper, and cod to be thicker. Don't worry if your fillets are not exactly ½ inch thick all over; you can compensate. Just halve thicker fillets, or fold, stack, or trim thinner pieces.

1

One of the handiest microwave tricks is thawing frozen fish. Defrost on 30% power (medium-low) according to the directions on page 123. During thawing, separate and turn the fish fillets once so they'll thaw more evenly, as shown. After thawing, the fish should be pliable on the outside, but slightly icy in the center.

2

For fast and easy peeling, loosen the skin of a tomato. First, use a fork to dip the tomato into boiling water for 12 seconds, as shown. Then hold the tomato under cold water until cool enough to peel.

3

Fish fillets vary in thickness and shape, so they need help to cook evenly in the microwave. First, place any thick areas toward the outer edges of the dish where they'll cook faster. Then turn under any thin portions to obtain an even thickness of about ½ inch, as shown.

4

To cook, cover the fillets and vegetables with a lid or vented clear plastic wrap, as shown above. After cooking, carefully transfer the fish fillets to a serving platter and cover to keep warm while you make the sauce. To serve, spoon the sauce over fillets, as shown at right.

Broccoli-Stuffed Fish Rolls

For the radish-accordion garnish, make several crosswise slits in a radish, cutting to, but not through, the other side. Chill in ice water.

4 thin fish fillets (about 1 pound total)
1 10-ounce package frozen broccoli spears
4 green onions, halved lengthwise
1 tablespoon water
1 tablespoon butter *or* margarine
⅓ cup dry white wine
½ teaspoon dried basil, crushed
¼ teaspoon salt
1 cup thinly sliced celery
1 tablespoon cold water
2 teaspoons cornstarch
   Celery leaves (optional)
   Radish accordions (optional)

■ Thaw fish, if frozen (see photo 1, page 111, and chart, page 123). Place frozen broccoli spears, green onions, and 1 tablespoon water in an 8x8x2-inch baking dish. Cover with vented clear plastic wrap (see photo 4, page 107). Cook on 100% power (high) for 5 to 7 minutes or till crisp-tender, giving the dish a half-turn and separating broccoli spears once. Remove broccoli and green onions from the baking dish and discard liquid. Drain vegetables on paper towels.

■ In a custard cup cook butter or margarine on high for 30 to 40 seconds or till melted. Brush fish fillets with melted butter or margarine. Place *one-fourth* of the broccoli and green onions across the center of *each* fillet, cutting onions as necessary. Roll up fish loosely (see photo, below). Fasten securely with wooden toothpicks, if necessary. Arrange fish rolls, seam side down, in the same 8x8x2-inch baking dish.

■ Combine wine, basil, and salt. Pour over fish. Cook, covered, on high for 4 to 6 minutes or till fish flakes easily with a fork, giving the dish a half-turn once (see photo 5, page 107). Transfer fish to a serving platter, reserving cooking liquid. Cover fish to keep warm.

■ For sauce, measure reserved cooking liquid in a 2-cup measure. If necessary, add enough water to equal ⅔ cup total. Add celery. Cook, covered, on high for 4 to 6 minutes or till celery is just tender. Combine 1 tablespoon cold water and cornstarch. Add to celery mixture. Cook, uncovered, for 1½ to 2½ minutes or till thickened and bubbly, stirring every minute. If desired, garnish the platter with celery leaves and radish accordions. Serve the sauce with the fish. Makes 4 servings.

Arrange the broccoli and green onions across the center of each fish fillet. Trim the onions, if necessary. Roll up each fillet loosely, as shown. Secure with wooden toothpicks, if necessary.

Broccoli-Stuffed Fish Rolls

Coating thick fillets

Breaded Fish Fillets

1 pound fresh *or* frozen fish
  fillets, cut ½ inch thick
2 tablespoons butter *or*
  margarine
¼ cup fine dry bread crumbs
½ teaspoon curry powder
⅛ teaspoon salt
  Dash garlic powder
  Tomato rose (optional)
  Fresh parsley (optional)

■ Thaw fish, if frozen (see photo 1, page 111, and chart, page 123). In a custard cup cook butter or margarine, uncovered, on 100% power (high) for 40 to 50 seconds or till melted, then set aside. For crumb coating, in a small mixing bowl combine bread crumbs, curry powder, salt, and garlic powder. Set aside.

■ Separate fish into fillets. Arrange on waxed paper. Brush with melted butter or margarine (see photo 1). Coat the tops and sides of fillets with crumb coating (see photo 2). Arrange fillets, coated side up, in an 8x8x2-inch baking dish, with thicker portions toward the edges of the dish. Turn under any thin portions of fillets to obtain an even thickness of about ½ inch (see photo 3, page 111).

■ Cook, uncovered, on high for 4 to 7 minutes or till fish flakes easily with a fork, giving the dish a half-turn after 4 minutes (see photo 5, page 107). Gently brush off any dry-looking crumb coating (see photo 3). Use a wide spatula to transfer fish to a serving platter (see photo 4). If desired, garnish with a tomato rose and parsley sprigs. Makes 4 servings.

TIP **Crumbs for Coating Fish**

Crushed crackers coat fish just as well as dry bread crumbs and offer a slightly different flavor. Just look in your cupboard. Instead of bread crumbs, try finely crushed zwieback, finely crushed wheat crackers, or finely crushed shredded wheat wafers. Coat and cook fish, following our directions for Breaded Fish Fillets.

1

Arrange the fish fillets on waxed paper. Use a pastry brush to brush on melted butter or margarine. The butter helps the crumbs cling to the fish.

2

Pat the crumb mixture onto the fillets. Coating only the tops and sides of the fillets, not the bottoms, assures that the crumbs will stay crispy.

3

After cooking the fish, brush off any dry-looking crumbs. Then all you'll taste will be a buttery crumb coating.

4

Use a wide spatula to carefully transfer the fish to a serving platter. For color, garnish with a tomato rose and some parsley. To shape a tomato rose, first make a thin base from the stem end of the tomato, cutting to, but not through, the other side (leave a ½-inch-wide piece of skin attached). Starting at the piece of attached skin, cut a continuous narrow strip of peel from the tomato in a spiral fashion. Taper the end to sever. Finish the rose by curling the strip onto its base.

Cornmeal Fish Fillets

The browning dish cooks the cornmeal coating till it's crunchy.

½ pound fresh *or* frozen fish
    fillets
3 tablespoons all-purpose
    flour
2 tablespoons yellow cornmeal
½ teaspoon paprika
¼ teaspoon seasoned salt
2 tablespoons milk
1 tablespoon cooking oil

■ Thaw fish, if frozen (see photo 1, page 111, and chart, page 123). For coating, in a 9-inch pie plate combine flour, cornmeal, paprika, and seasoned salt. Separate fish into fillets. Dip fillets into milk. Coat on all sides with the cornmeal coating. Set aside.

■ Preheat a 10-inch microwave browning dish on 100% power (high) for 5 minutes. Add cooking oil to dish. Swirl to coat (see photo 1, page 153). Add coated fish fillets. Cook, uncovered, on high for 1 to 1½ minutes or till fillet bottoms are golden brown.

■ Use a wide spatula to carefully turn fish fillets over. Cook, uncovered, for 1 to 2 minutes more or till fish flakes easily with a fork (see photo 5, page 107). Makes 2 servings.

Low-wattage oven: Preheat the browning dish on high for 7 minutes.

Chip 'n' Cheese Fillets

1 pound fresh *or* frozen
    fish fillets
2 to 3 tablespoons creamy
    Italian *or* ranch-style salad
    dressing
½ cup crushed potato chips
¼ cup shredded American *or*
    Swiss cheese (1 ounce)

■ Thaw fish, if frozen (see photo 1, page 111, and chart, page 123). In an 8x8x2-inch baking dish arrange fish fillets with thicker portions toward the edges of the dish. Turn under any thin portions to obtain an even thickness (see photo 3, page 111).

■ Spoon salad dressing over fish. Pat on crushed potato chips (see photo 2, page 115). Cook, uncovered, on 100% power (high) for 4 to 7 minutes or till fish flakes easily with a fork, giving the dish a half-turn once (see photo 5, page 107).

■ Sprinkle with shredded cheese. Cook on high for 30 to 60 seconds more or till cheese just begins to melt. Use a wide spatula to transfer fish to a serving platter (see photo 4, page 115). Makes 4 servings.

Low-wattage oven: For *fish before adding cheese,* cook on high for 7 to 9 minutes, giving the dish a half-turn once.

Fish and Vegetables En Papillote

En papillote (poppy-YOTE) means "cooked and served in paper."

½ pound fresh *or* frozen fish
   fillets
½ cup celery bias-sliced ½ inch
   thick
½ cup carrot bias-sliced ⅛ inch
   thick
¼ cup green onions sliced into
   1-inch pieces
2 tablespoons butter *or*
   margarine
4 teaspoons all-purpose flour
½ teaspoon Dijon-style
   mustard
⅔ cup light cream *or* milk
2 tablespoons coarsely
   chopped cashews

■ Thaw fish, if frozen (see photo 1, page 111, and chart, page 123). In a 1½-quart casserole cook fish, covered, on 100% power (high) for 2 to 4 minutes or till fish flakes easily with a fork (see photo 5, page 107). Drain and break into large pieces. Set aside.

■ In same casserole combine celery, carrot, green onions, and butter or margarine. Cook, covered, on high 3 to 5 minutes or till crisp-tender. Stir in flour and mustard. Stir in cream. Cook, uncovered, 2½ to 4 minutes or till thickened and bubbly, stirring every 30 seconds. Fold in fish.

■ Cut 2 pieces of parchment paper or brown paper into heart shapes about 13x10 inches each. Place *half* of the fish mixture on one side of *each* heart. Top with cashews (see photo 1, below). Fold the other half of the heart over fish mixture. To close packet, begin at the top of the heart and turn edges up 2 or 3 times to seal (see photo 2, below). Work toward the bottom, twisting the tip of the heart several times to secure.

■ Place sealed packets in microwave oven. Cook on high for 3 to 4 minutes or till heated through, turning and rearranging packets after 2 minutes. To serve, place packets on plates. With scissors, cut a large X in tops (see photo 3, below). Fold back each segment. Makes 2 servings.

1
Cut two heart shapes from parchment or brown paper, then spoon half of the fish mixture onto one side of each heart and top with cashews, as shown.

2
To close the packet, begin at the top of the heart and turn the edges of the parchment up two or three times, as shown. Twist at the tip of the heart to secure it.

3
For a dramatic presentation, place the packets on dinner plates. Cut a large X in the top of each. Fold the parchment paper back to show off the filling.

Making seafood dishes

Coquilles St. Jacques

Coquilles St. Jacques (kah-KEYS sang-JZOCK) are traditionally served in coquille shells, as shown opposite.

1	pound fresh *or* frozen shrimp in shells
½	pound fresh *or* frozen scallops
1	tablespoon butter *or* margarine
¼	cup fine dry bread crumbs
¾	cup water
2	tablespoons lemon juice
1	cup sliced fresh mushrooms
¼	cup sliced green onions
3	tablespoons butter *or* margarine, cut up
¼	cup all-purpose flour
¼	teaspoon salt
¼	teaspoon ground nutmeg
1¼	cups light cream *or* milk
2	tablespoons dry white wine *or* dry sherry

■ Thaw shrimp and scallops, if frozen (see chart, page 123). For topping, in a custard cup cook 1 tablespoon butter or margarine, uncovered, on 100% power (high) for 30 to 40 seconds or till melted. Stir in fine dry bread crumbs. Set topping aside.

■ Peel and devein shrimp (see photo 1). Cut any large shrimp or scallops in half (see photo 2). In a 2-quart casserole combine shrimp, scallops, water, and lemon juice. Cook, covered, on high for 5 to 7 minutes or till shrimp are pink and scallops are opaque, stirring twice. Drain seafood well and set aside.

■ In the same casserole combine mushrooms, green onions, and 3 tablespoons butter or margarine. Cook, covered, on high for 2 to 3 minutes or till tender, stirring once.

■ Stir in flour, salt, and nutmeg. Stir in light cream or milk. Cook, uncovered, on high for 3 to 5 minutes or till thickened and bubbly, stirring every minute till slightly thickened, then every 30 seconds. Stir in wine or sherry and cooked shrimp and scallops (see photo 3).

■ Spoon the seafood mixture into 5 or 6 coquille shells, au gratin dishes, 6-ounce custard cups, or a 1-quart casserole (see photo 4). Sprinkle bread-crumb topping over seafood mixture. Cook, uncovered, on high for 1½ to 2½ minutes or till heated through, giving the dish or dishes a half-turn once (see photo 5). Makes 5 or 6 servings.

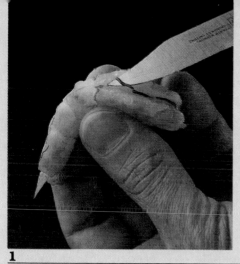

1

After shelling a shrimp, use a sharp knife to make a shallow slit along its back. Then scrape out the black vein with the tip of the knife, as shown.

2

Cut any large shrimp or scallops in half, making them about the same size as the smaller pieces. The more even the size, the more even the cooking.

3

Make a white sauce by cooking the vegetables with flour and milk until the mixture is thickened and bubbly. Stir in the white wine or sherry and the hot cooked seafood, as shown.

4

Spoon the seafood mixture into five or six coquille shells, as shown. You can also use au gratin dishes, 6-ounce custard cups, or a casserole. Sprinkle the mixture with the crumb topping.

5

Arrange the coquille shells in the microwave oven. Cook until the mixture is heated through, giving shells a half-turn once, as shown.

Oriental-Style Scallops

Both bay and sea scallops will work. (Pictured on pages 104–105.)

1 pound fresh *or* frozen
   scallops
½ cup water
1 cup thinly bias-sliced carrots
   (2 medium)
2 tablespoons sliced green
   onion
1 clove garlic, minced
1 tablespoon cooking oil
1 tablespoon cornstarch
½ teaspoon sugar
¼ teaspoon ground ginger
½ cup chicken broth
2 tablespoons soy sauce
2 tablespoons dry sherry
1 6-ounce package frozen
   pea pods

■ Thaw scallops, if frozen (see chart, page 123). Cut any large scallops in half crosswise (see photo 2, page 119). In a 2-quart casserole heat water, uncovered, on 100% power (high) for 1½ to 2½ minutes or till boiling. Add scallops. Cook, covered, for 2 to 4 minutes or till scallops are opaque, stirring twice. Drain scallops and set aside.

■ In the same casserole combine carrots, green onion, garlic, and cooking oil. Cook, covered, on high for 3 to 4 minutes or till crisp-tender. Stir in cornstarch, sugar, and ginger. Stir in chicken broth, soy sauce, and sherry. Cook, uncovered, for 2 to 3 minutes or till thickened and bubbly, stirring every minute. Add frozen pea pods. Cook, uncovered, for 1 to 2 minutes more or till pea pods are crisp-tender, stirring once. Stir in scallops (see photo 3, page 119). Cook, uncovered, for 30 to 60 seconds or till heated through. Makes 4 to 6 servings.

Shrimp Creole

Pictured on pages 104–105.

1 pound fresh *or* frozen
   shrimp in shells
1 medium onion, chopped
½ cup chopped celery
2 cloves garlic, minced
2 tablespoons butter *or*
   margarine
2 tablespoons all-purpose
   flour
1 12-ounce can (1½ cups)
   vegetable juice cocktail
1 bay leaf
2 teaspoons Worcestershire
   sauce
½ teaspoon sugar
½ teaspoon dried thyme,
   crushed
⅛ to ¼ teaspoon ground red
   pepper
   Several dashes bottled hot
    pepper sauce
   Hot cooked rice
   Snipped parsley (optional)

■ Thaw shrimp, if frozen (see chart, page 123). Peel and devein shrimp (see photo 1, page 119). Set aside.

■ In a 2-quart casserole combine onion, celery, garlic, and butter or margarine. Cook, covered, on 100% power (high) for 2 to 4 minutes or till tender. Add flour. Stir till smooth.

■ Stir in vegetable juice cocktail, bay leaf, Worcestershire sauce, sugar, thyme, red pepper, and hot pepper sauce. Cook, uncovered, on high for 4 to 7 minutes or till bubbly, stirring every minute till slightly thickened, then every 30 seconds.

■ Add shrimp. Cook, covered, on high for 3 to 5 minutes or till shrimp turn pink, stirring once. Remove bay leaf. Serve over rice. Garnish with parsley, if desired. Makes 4 servings.

Salmon à la King

A tasty takeoff on chicken à la king.

1 15½-ounce can salmon
1 medium onion, chopped
   (½ cup)
¼ cup chopped green pepper
¼ cup butter *or* margarine
¼ cup all-purpose flour
½ teaspoon instant chicken
   bouillon granules
1 cup light cream *or* milk
½ cup water
1 4-ounce can mushroom
   stems and pieces, drained
2 tablespoons chopped
   pimiento
   Toast points, toasted English
   muffin halves, *or* rusks

■ Drain salmon and remove skin and bones. Break salmon into bite-size pieces. Set aside. In a 1½-quart casserole combine onion, green pepper, and butter or margarine. Cook, covered, on 100% power (high) for 1½ to 2 minutes or till vegetables are crisp-tender.

■ Stir flour and bouillon granules into butter mixture. Stir in light cream or milk and water. Cook, uncovered, on high for 5 to 6 minutes or till thickened and bubbly, stirring every minute till slightly thickened, then every 30 seconds.

■ Fold in salmon, mushrooms, and pimiento. Cook, uncovered, on high for 1 to 2 minutes or till heated through, stirring gently once. Serve over toast points, muffin halves, or rusks. Makes 4 servings.

Dilled Salmon Patties

1 15½-ounce can salmon
½ cup finely chopped onion
½ cup finely chopped celery
1 tablespoon water
¼ cup fine dry bread crumbs
1 beaten egg
1 teaspoon dried dillweed
⅛ teaspoon salt
¼ cup fine dry bread crumbs
6 slices American cheese
6 hamburger buns, split
   and toasted
¼ cup mayonnaise *or* salad
   dressing
6 lettuce leaves, shredded, *or*
   alfalfa sprouts

■ Drain salmon. Remove skin and bones. Flake salmon. In a 1-quart casserole combine onion, celery, and water. Cook, covered, on 100% power (high) for 2½ to 3½ minutes or till tender. Drain. Stir in ¼ cup fine dry bread crumbs, egg, dillweed, and salt. Add salmon. Mix well.

■ Cover and chill in the refrigerator about 30 minutes or till firm enough to shape. Shape salmon mixture into six ¾-inch-thick patties. Coat on all sides with ¼ cup bread crumbs. Arrange patties in a 12x7½x2-inch baking dish. Cook, uncovered, on high for 4 to 6 minutes or till heated through, giving the dish a half-turn after 3 minutes.

■ Place 1 slice of cheese atop each patty. Cook, uncovered, for 30 to 60 seconds or till cheese just begins to melt. Spread the cut surfaces of toasted buns with mayonnaise or salad dressing. Add a salmon patty and shredded lettuce leaves or alfalfa sprouts to each bun. Makes 6 servings.

Low-wattage oven: For *patties,* if the baking dish won't fit, use an 8x8x2-inch baking dish. Cook half at a time on high for 4 to 6 minutes.

Curried Tuna on Rice

Start with ⅔ cup uncooked rice to get 2 cups hot cooked rice.

1 medium apple, cored and
　　coarsely chopped (1 cup)
¼ cup chopped onion
2 tablespoons butter *or*
　　margarine
2 to 3 teaspoons curry powder
2 tablespoons all-purpose
　　flour
¼ teaspoon salt
1⅓ cups milk
1 6½-ounce can tuna
½ cup coarsely chopped
　　peanuts *or* cashews
　　Hot cooked rice
　　Coconut (optional)
　　Raisins (optional)

■ In a 1½-quart casserole combine apple, onion, butter or margarine, and curry powder. Cook, covered, on 100% power (high) for 1½ to 2½ minutes or till just tender, stirring after 1 minute.

■ Stir in flour and salt. Stir in milk. Cook, uncovered, on high for 5 to 8 minutes or till thickened and bubbly, stirring every minute till slightly thickened, then every 30 seconds.

■ Drain and flake tuna. Fold tuna and peanuts or cashews into thickened mixture. Cook, uncovered, on high for 30 to 60 seconds more or till heated through.

■ To serve, spoon mixture over rice. If desired, sprinkle with coconut and raisins. Makes 4 servings.

Saucy Tuna-Mac Casserole

1 cup corkscrew *or* shell
　　macaroni (4 ounces)
1 10¾-ounce can condensed
　　cream of celery soup
¾ cup shredded American
　　cheese (3 ounces)
½ cup milk
2 teaspoons dried minced
　　onion
1 6½-ounce can tuna,
　　drained and flaked
2 hard-cooked eggs, chopped
⅓ cup coarsely crushed
　　shredded wheat biscuits,
　　shredded wheat wafers,
　　or crackers

■ Cook macaroni according to package directions. Drain and set aside.

■ In a 1½-quart casserole combine condensed soup, cheese, milk, and dried onion. Fold in tuna, hard-cooked eggs, and drained macaroni. Cook, uncovered, on 100% power (high) for 7 to 10 minutes or till hot, stirring once after 4 minutes. When done, stir again and sprinkle with shredded wheat biscuits, wafers, or crackers. Makes 4 or 5 servings.

Saucy Salmon-Mac Casserole: Prepare as above, *except* substitute one 7¾-ounce can *salmon,* drained, skin and bones removed, and flaked, for the tuna.

Defrosting Fish and Seafood

Unwrap **whole fish** and remove head and tail (except for trout). Place in a 12x7½x2-inch baking dish. Cover with vented clear plastic wrap. Cook on 30% power (medium-low) as directed, turning the fish over after half of the defrosting time. For fish weighing more than 1 pound, shield tail end with foil after 5 minutes (be sure foil is allowed in your oven). Let stand as directed. Rinse; pat dry.

Frozen food	Amount	Defrosting time	Standing time
Whole dressed fish (head, tail removed)	One 1- to 1½-pound fish	8 to 10 minutes	15 minutes
	One 1½- to 2-pound fish	10 to 12 minutes	15 minutes
Whole dressed trout (head, tail attached)	Two 8- to 10-ounce fish	6 to 8 minutes	10 minutes

Unwrap **fish fillets, steaks,** or **portions**. Place in an 8x8x2- or 12x7½x2-inch baking dish. Cover with vented clear plastic wrap. Cook on 30% power (medium-low) as directed, turning and separating the fish after half of the defrosting time. Let stand as directed. The fish should be pliable and cold on the outside, but still slightly icy in the center of thick areas. Rinse and pat dry.

Frozen food	Amount	Defrosting time	Standing time
Fish fillets	½ pound	3½ to 4½ minutes	10 minutes
	1 pound	6 to 8 minutes	10 minutes
Fish steaks	1 pound	6 to 8 minutes	15 minutes
Unbreaded fish portions	One 12-ounce package	4 to 6 minutes	10 minutes

Unwrap **seafood** and place in a casserole. Cover with the lid. Cook on 30% power (medium-low) as directed, stirring or turning over the seafood once or twice to break it up. Rinse and pat dry.

Frozen food	Amount	Defrosting time
Shrimp in shells	½ pound	3 to 4 minutes
	1 pound	6 to 8 minutes
	1½ pounds	8 to 10 minutes*
Peeled, deveined shrimp	½ pound	4 to 6 minutes
	1 pound	7 to 9 minutes*
	1½ pounds	9 to 11 minutes*
Scallops	½ pound	4 to 6 minutes
	1 pound	8 to 10 minutes*
	1½ pounds	10 to 12 minutes*
Crabmeat	6 ounces	2½ to 3½ minutes

*Note: Timings are for 600- to 700-watt ovens and will be longer in low-wattage ovens.

Cooking Fish and Seafood

For **whole fish,** remove head and tail (except for trout). Place in a shallow baking dish. Cover with vented clear plastic wrap. Cook on 100% power (high) as directed or till fish flakes easily with a fork, giving the dish a half-turn once. Let stand, covered, for 5 minutes.

Food	Amount	Cooking time
Whole dressed fish (head, tail removed)	One 1- to 1½-pound fish	8 to 10 minutes
	One 1½- to 2-pound fish	10 to 12 minutes
Whole dressed trout (head, tail attached)	Two 8- to 10-ounce fish	5 to 7 minutes

For **fillets** or **steaks,** place fish in a shallow baking dish. Arrange with thicker portions toward the outer edges of dish for more even cooking. If fillets vary in thickness, turn under any thin portions to obtain even thickness. Cover with vented clear plastic wrap. Cook on 100% power (high) as directed or till fish flakes easily with a fork.

Food	Amount	Cooking time
Fish fillets (¼ inch thick)	½ pound	2 to 4 minutes
Fish fillets (½ inch thick)	½ pound	3 to 4 minutes
	1 pound	4 to 7 minutes
Fish steaks (¾ to 1 inch thick)	1 pound	4 to 8 minutes

For **seafood,** halve large scallops and devein shrimp. In a casserole place ¼ cup water for each ½ pound of seafood. Heat water, uncovered, on 100% power (high) for 1 to 4 minutes or till boiling. Add seafood. Cook, covered, on high as directed or till shrimp are pink and scallops are opaque, stirring once or twice. Drain well.

Food	Amount	Cooking time
Shrimp in shells	½ pound	2 to 4 minutes
	1 pound	3 to 5 minutes
	1½ pounds	5 to 7 minutes
Peeled, deveined shrimp	½ pound	1½ to 2½ minutes
	1 pound	3 to 5 minutes
	1½ pounds	4 to 6 minutes
Scallops	½ pound	2 to 3 minutes
	1 pound	2 to 5 minutes

Nutrition Analysis

	Number of servings	Per Serving						Percent U.S. RDA Per Serving							
		Calories	Protein (g)	Carbohydrate (g)	Fat (g)	Sodium (mg)	Potassium (mg)	Protein	Vitamin A	Vitamin C	Thiamine	Riboflavin	Niacin	Calcium	Iron
Breaded Fish Fillets (p. 114)	4	167	21	5	7	250	447	32	5	0	3	4	13	2	3
Broccoli-Stuffed Fish Rolls (p. 112)	4	162	22	7	4	275	649	34	33	49	4	6	13	6	5
Bulgur-Stuffed Fish (p. 108)	4	223	23	29	1	83	582	35	41	7	9	5	19	3	12
Chip 'n' Cheese Fillets (p. 116)	4	200	22	6	9	289	581	34	2	8	3	4	14	6	2
Coquilles St. Jacques (p. 118)	5	330	20	14	22	427	431	30	22	18	9	14	16	12	13
Cornmeal Fish Fillets (p. 116)	2	232	22	16	9	283	496	34	8	1	8	7	16	3	4
Curried Tuna on Rice (p. 122)	4	416	23	41	18	707	479	36	8	7	18	13	51	14	14
Dilled Salmon Patties (p. 121)	6	419	22	30	23	994	374	35	10	4	16	19	31	34	15
Fish and Vegetables en Papillote (p. 117)	2	488	26	17	36	304	850	40	205	18	10	15	16	13	11
Gazpacho Fillets (p. 110)	4	114	21	5	1	200	640	32	13	40	4	5	14	2	5
Halibut Kabobs (p. 109)	4	152	23	2	5	136	607	36	6	12	11	5	53	5	2
Herbed Corn-Bread-Stuffed Trout (p. 108)	2	678	41	54	33	1384	1001	63	20	39	15	13	17	13	17
Oriental-Style Scallops (p. 120)	4	183	20	14	4	912	677	31	179	31	14	8	14	6	17
Salmon à la King (p. 121)	4	487	24	25	32	891	481	36	25	33	15	23	42	32	15
Salmon Steaks with Horseradish Sauce (p. 109)	4	192	19	3	11	154	359	29	7	2	9	10	0	6	5
Saucy Salmon-Mac Casserole (p. 122)	4	404	23	34	19	1199	414	35	14	2	24	24	27	33	14
Saucy Tuna-Mac Casserole (p. 122)	4	387	27	34	16	1372	391	41	13	2	24	23	42	22	16
Shrimp Creole (p. 120)	4	262	15	36	7	503	407	23	27	58	13	4	19	8	16
Snapper with Mushroom Stuffing (p. 106)	6	213	24	8	9	178	483	37	6	6	13	7	14	3	7

FRUIT

Fruits and the microwave oven are a natural combination. Need convincing? Take a look at the recipes in this chapter.

In minutes you can micro-cook luscious fruit dishes just the way you like them—juicy, sweet, and nutritious.

Microwave cooking keeps fruit juicy because it's so steamy; apples and pears don't dry out the way they do during conventional-oven baking.

A nutritious bonus

Micro-cooked fruit also packs a nutrition punch. Since the cooking is so much faster, there's less time for the heat to destroy valuable vitamins and minerals.

Cooking fresh fruit

Micro-cooking fresh fruit is sheer simplicity. Start by piercing the skin of whole fruit so it won't pop, or by cutting the fruit into even-size pieces. Arrange the fruit in a dish and add a splash of water.

We found fruit cooks fastest and best on high power, covered with a lid or vented clear plastic wrap. We also suggest stirring or turning pieces during cooking for even heating.

Choose-a-Fruit Crumble
(see recipe, page 136)

Spicy Poached Fruit
(see recipe, page 130)

Thawing, warming, and plumping
Besides cooking fresh-from-the-tree fruit, your microwave is great for defrosting frozen fruit, warming canned fruit, or rehydrating dried fruit. Refer to our charts at the end of this chapter for specific directions.

Jams, jellies, and preserves
Even though cooking fruit is one of its fortes, the microwave oven is not suited for cooking jams, jellies, or preserves. The large quantities and high temperatures required in jam and jelly making are easier and safer on the range-top.

Cream-Cheese-Stuffed Peaches
(see recipe, page 130)

Steaming stuffed fruit

Raisin-Stuffed Apples

You'll find these apples stay juicier than conventionally baked apples.

¼ cup raisins, currants, *or* snipped pitted dates
2 tablespoons chopped walnuts, pecans, peanuts, *or* sunflower nuts
1 tablespoon sugar
⅛ teaspoon ground cinnamon
4 medium baking apples (6 to 7 ounces each)
 Lemon juice
2 tablespoons water

■ For filling, in a small mixing bowl combine raisins, currants, or dates; nuts; sugar; and cinnamon. Set aside.

■ Core apples and peel off a strip around top of each (see photo 1). Brush peeled fruit with lemon juice. Place apples and the water in a 1½-quart casserole. Spoon filling into apples (see photo 2).

■ Cook, covered, on 100% power (high) for 4 to 8 minutes or till tender, rearranging and spooning cooking liquid over apples after 3 minutes (see photo 3). Before serving, spoon liquid over apples again. Serve warm or chilled with liquid. Makes 4 servings.

Chocolate-Raisin-Stuffed Apples: Prepare Raisin-Stuffed Apples as above, *except* decrease raisins, currants, or snipped pitted dates to 3 tablespoons and add 1 tablespoon *miniature semisweet chocolate pieces* to the filling.

TIP Choosing Apples for Micro-Cooking

Do you have trouble telling the good apples from the bad apples—for micro-cooking, that is? If you're looking for apples that will retain their shape and texture, try cooking varieties such as Rome Beauty, Granny Smith, or Rhode Island Greening. When shopping for apples, select those that are firm with smooth skins and relatively free of bruises. If you're not going to use the apples right away, store them in a vented plastic bag in the refrigerator to keep them fresh and crisp.

1

Using a vegetable peeler, trim off a strip at the top of each apple. This prevents the skin from bursting during cooking. Brush the peeled apple with a little lemon juice to keep it from turning brown.

2

After placing the apples and water in the casserole, spoon the raisin-nut filling into the cored centers, as shown.

3

During cooking, remove the cover and rearrange the apples so the steam will cook them evenly. At the same time, spoon some of the cooking liquid over the fruit to moisten it, as shown. Before serving, spoon the liquid over the apples again.

Spicy Poached Fruit

Pictured on pages 126–127.

½ cup water
½ cup apple *or* grape juice *or* cranberry juice cocktail
2 tablespoons honey
3 inches stick cinnamon, broken up
2 whole cloves
1 ⅛-inch-thick gingerroot slice
4 ¼-inch-thick orange slices
4 medium pears *or* apples
Thin orange peel strips (optional)

■ In a 2-quart casserole combine water, juice, honey, cinnamon, cloves, and gingerroot. Add orange slices. Cook, covered, on 100% power (high) for 4 to 6 minutes or till boiling.

■ Meanwhile, core fruit, leaving stems intact on pears, if desired. Peel pears completely (except for a decorative strip around each stem, if desired) or peel a ½-inch-wide strip from top of each apple (see photo 1, page 129). Add fruit to hot mixture. Cook, covered, on high for 4 to 6 minutes or till tender, rearranging and spooning cooking liquid over fruit once (see photo 3, page 129).

■ Before serving, remove spices and orange slices. Serve warm or chilled with cooking liquid. If desired, garnish with thin orange peel strips. Makes 4 servings.

Low-wattage oven: For *fruit,* cook on high for 6 to 8 minutes.

> **Spicy Wine-Poached Fruit:** Prepare Spicy Poached Fruit as above, *except* substitute ¼ cup *sweet white or red wine* (muscat, champagne, Concord, port, *or* Madeira) for the ½ cup juice and increase honey to ¼ cup.

Cream-Cheese-Stuffed Peaches

Pictured on pages 126–127.

2 large peaches *or* nectarines
2 tablespoons water
⅓ cup soft-style cream cheese with pineapple
2 tablespoons raisins
2 tablespoons sugar
Dash ground allspice
1 tablespoon chopped pecans

■ Peel peaches. Cut nectarines or peaches in half lengthwise. Remove and discard the pits. Cut a thin slice from the bottom of each half so the fruit sits level. Arrange halves in an 8x8x2-inch baking dish. Add water to dish. Cover with vented clear plastic wrap. Cook on 100% power (high) for 1½ to 3 minutes or till tender, giving dish a half-turn after 1 minute.

■ For filling, in a small mixing bowl combine cream cheese, raisins, sugar, and allspice. Spoon some of the mixture atop each nectarine or peach half. Cook, uncovered, on high for 30 seconds or till filling is hot. Sprinkle with chopped pecans. Serve warm. Makes 4 servings.

Pineapple-Berry Compote

If you're watching calories, substitute plain yogurt for the sour cream. It contains one-third as many calories.

1 8¼-ounce can pineapple
   chunks
1 to 2 tablespoons brown
   sugar
   Several dashes ground
   nutmeg
1 tablespoon butter *or*
   margarine
½ cup fresh *or* frozen
   blueberries
   Dairy sour cream

■ Drain pineapple, reserving 2 tablespoons liquid. In a 20-ounce casserole stir together reserved pineapple liquid, brown sugar, and nutmeg. Add pineapple. Dot with butter or margarine. Cook, uncovered, on 100% power (high) for 2 to 3 minutes or till boiling. Stir in blueberries. Serve warm topped with sour cream. Makes 2 servings.

Apple-Raisin Compote

Cooking on medium power mellows the flavors.

1½ cups apple juice
¼ teaspoon ground cardamom
   or 3 inches stick
   cinnamon, broken up
½ of an 8-ounce package
   (1 cup) dried apples *or*
   mixed dried fruit
¼ cup raisins

■ In a 1-quart casserole combine apple juice and cardamom or cinnamon. Cook, covered, on 100% power (high) for 3 to 5 minutes or till boiling. Cook, covered, on 50% power (medium) for 5 minutes.

■ Meanwhile, cut large pieces of fruit in half. Add fruit and raisins to the hot mixture. Cook, covered, on high for 3 to 5 minutes or till fruit is softened, stirring once (see photo, below). Serve warm or chilled. Before serving, remove cinnamon. Makes 4 servings.

Low-wattage oven: For *spice mixture,* cook on high for 5 to 7 minutes or till boiling, then cook on high for 5 minutes more before adding fruit.

Cook the dried fruit in the hot juice until it is soft and plump, stirring once, as shown. The fruit absorbs the liquid as it heats.

Glazed Peaches

Walnut Bananas Foster

Walnut Bananas Foster

All the flavor without the flames.

3 medium bananas
   Lime *or* lemon juice
2 tablespoons butter *or*
   margarine
¼ cup packed brown sugar
2 tablespoons orange *or* apple
   juice
¼ cup walnut halves
2 tablespoons light rum *or*
   brandy
   Vanilla ice cream

■ Peel bananas. Slice in half crosswise, then in half lengthwise. Brush with lime or lemon juice and set aside. For sauce, in a 9-inch pie plate cook butter or margarine, uncovered, on 100% power (high) for 40 to 50 seconds or till melted. Stir in brown sugar and orange or apple juice.

■ Add bananas and walnuts. Spoon sauce over to coat. Cook, uncovered, on high for 2 to 3 minutes or till bananas are tender. Stir in rum or brandy. Serve warm with ice cream. Makes 4 servings.

Glazed Peaches

Choose the all-season canned-peach version when fresh fruit is not available locally.

4 medium peaches *or*
   nectarines (1 pound)
1 tablespoon butter *or*
   margarine
¼ cup orange marmalade *or*
   apricot *or* peach preserves
1 tablespoon orange liqueur,
   apricot brandy, *or* orange
   juice
   Vanilla yogurt *or* ice cream
   (optional)
   Sliced *or* slivered almonds,
   toasted (optional)

■ Peel peaches. Cut peaches or nectarines in half lengthwise. Remove and discard pits. Set aside. For glaze, in a 1½-quart casserole cook butter or margarine, uncovered, on 100% power (high) for 30 to 40 seconds or till melted. Stir in marmalade or preserves and liqueur, brandy, or juice.

■ Add fruit. Spoon the glaze over to coat. Cook, covered, on high for 3 to 5 minutes or till fruit is tender, stirring once or twice. Serve warm with vanilla yogurt or ice cream and almonds, if desired. Makes 4 servings.

> **Anytime Glazed Peaches:** Prepare Glazed Peaches as above, *except* substitute one 29-ounce can *peach halves or* one 30-ounce can *unpeeled apricot halves* for the fresh fruit. Drain fruit before adding to glaze. Cook, covered, on high for 3 to 5 minutes or till fruit is heated through, stirring once.

Preparing fruit cobbler

Choose-a-Fruit Cobbler

Whole wheat flour tans the cobbler topping.

4 cups desired fresh *or*
   frozen fruit*
½ cup sugar
4 teaspoons cornstarch
¼ teaspoon ground nutmeg,
   ginger, *or* allspice
⅓ cup water
½ cup all-purpose flour
¼ cup whole wheat flour
2 tablespoons sugar
1 teaspoon baking powder
3 tablespoons butter *or*
   margarine
1 slightly beaten egg yolk
¼ cup milk
   Ice cream *or* light cream
   (optional)

■ For filling, thaw fruit, if frozen (see photo 1). *Do not drain.* In a 1½-quart casserole or an 8x1½-inch round baking dish combine ½ cup sugar, cornstarch, and nutmeg, ginger, or allspice. Stir in water. Add fruit. Cook, uncovered, on 100% power (high) for 6 to 8 minutes or till liquid is thickened and bubbly and fruit is tender, stirring every 2 minutes till slightly thickened, then every minute (see photo 2).

■ Meanwhile, for biscuit topping, in a medium mixing bowl combine all-purpose flour, whole wheat flour, 2 tablespoons sugar, and baking powder. Cut in butter or margarine till mixture resembles coarse crumbs. Combine beaten egg yolk and milk, then add all at once to dry ingredients. Stir just to moisten dry ingredients.

■ Spoon topping onto hot filling, making 6 mounds around the edges of the casserole and leaving the center open (see photo 3). Cook, uncovered, on 50% power (medium) for 6 to 8 minutes or till done, giving the dish a half-turn once. (To check doneness, scratch the slightly wet surface of topping with a wooden toothpick. If done, a cooked texture will have formed underneath, as in photo 4, page 71.) Serve warm with ice cream or light cream, if desired (see photo 4). Makes 6 servings.

Low-wattage oven: For *fruit mixture,* cook on high for 9 to 11 minutes. For *biscuit topping,* cook on high for 3 to 5 minutes.

---

*Fruit options: Unsweetened pitted tart red cherries; sliced, peeled peaches; sliced, peeled fresh apples *or* pears; *or* sliced fresh nectarines.

1

If you're using frozen cherries or peaches, save yourself some time by thawing them in your microwave. In a baking dish cook the fruit, covered, on high for 4 to 6 minutes or until no ice remains, stirring once to break up fruit. Do not drain.

2

Cook the fruit mixture on high until thickened and bubbly, stirring every 2 minutes until the mixture is slightly thickened, then stirring every minute.

3

Before adding the topping, be sure the filling is hot and bubbly; otherwise the topping will not cook completely. Spoon the topping into six mounds, forming a ring around the edges of the casserole, as shown. Don't put a mound in the center because it would take longer to cook than the mounds on the edges.

4

The cobbler is done when the biscuit topping is slightly wet on the surface, but looks cooked underneath. Add a scoop of vanilla ice cream to each serving, spooning some of the sauce over top, if desired.

Choose-a-Fruit Crumble

The plum version with Coconut Topping is pictured on pages 126–127.

4 cups sliced, peeled apples *or* pears, *or* sliced nectarines *or* plums
2 to 3 tablespoons honey
2 tablespoons water
  Oat Topping, Granola Topping, Coconut Topping, *or* Chocolate Topping
  Vanilla ice cream, light cream, *or* milk

■ Place fruit in an 8x1½-inch round baking dish. Combine honey and water (if using pears, omit water). Pour over fruit. Cover with vented clear plastic wrap. Cook on 100% power (high) for 3 to 5 minutes or till fruit is almost tender, stirring once.

■ Meanwhile, prepare desired topping. Sprinkle topping over hot fruit. Cook, uncovered, on high for 2 to 3 minutes or till fruit is tender and topping is heated through, giving the dish a half-turn once. Serve warm with ice cream, light cream, or milk. Makes 4 servings.

Oat Topping: In a small mixing bowl combine ⅓ cup *quick-cooking rolled oats,* 3 tablespoons *all-purpose flour,* 2 tablespoons *brown sugar,* and ½ teaspoon ground *allspice.* Cut in 2 tablespoons *butter or margarine* till crumbly. Stir in ¼ cup chopped *nuts.*

Granola Topping: Crush ¾ cup *granola.* Add 1 tablespoon melted *butter or margarine* and toss to coat.

Coconut Topping: In a small mixing bowl mix together ⅓ cup *crushed graham crackers,* ¼ cup toasted *coconut,* and ⅛ teaspoon ground *ginger.* Add 1 tablespoon melted *butter or margarine* and toss to coat.

Chocolate Topping: In a small bowl combine 2 tablespoons *honey,* 1 tablespoon melted *butter or margarine,* and 2 teaspoons *unsweetened cocoa powder.* In a small mixing bowl pour honey mixture over ¾ cup *crisp rice cereal* and toss to coat.

Caramel-Apple Streusel

Canned apple slices make quick work of this dessert.

2 20-ounce cans sliced apples
16 vanilla caramels
1 tablespoon lemon juice
⅓ cup all-purpose flour
¼ cup sugar
¼ teaspoon ground cinnamon
2 tablespoons butter *or* margarine
  Frozen whipped dessert topping, thawed (optional)

■ Drain apples, reserving ¼ cup of the liquid. Cut up large pieces of apple. Set aside. In a 1½-quart casserole combine reserved apple liquid and caramels. Cook, uncovered, on 100% power (high) for 2 to 3 minutes or till caramels are soft enough to stir smooth, stirring twice during cooking. Add apples and lemon juice. Toss to coat.

■ For topping, in a small mixing bowl combine flour, sugar, and cinnamon. Cut in butter or margarine till mixture resembles coarse crumbs. Sprinkle topping evenly over apple mixture. Cook, uncovered, on high for 7 to 9 minutes or till heated through. Serve warm with whipped dessert topping, if desired. Makes 8 servings.

Gingerbread-Pudding Cake

This dessert pleases both fruit and cake lovers.

1 cup all-purpose flour
½ teaspoon baking powder
½ teaspoon ground ginger *or*
    1 teaspoon grated fresh
    gingerroot
½ teaspoon ground cinnamon
¼ cup butter *or* margarine
½ cup packed brown sugar
2 egg yolks
¼ cup molasses
½ cup milk
1 21-ounce can cherry, apple,
    raisin, peach, blueberry,
    pineapple, *or* lemon pie
    filling
¼ cup water
1 tablespoon lemon juice
2 egg whites
    Vanilla ice cream
    (optional)

■ In a small mixing bowl stir together flour, baking powder, ginger or gingerroot, and cinnamon. In a small mixer bowl beat butter or margarine with an electric mixer on medium speed for ½ minute. Add brown sugar and beat till fluffy. Add egg yolks and molasses. Beat till combined. Add flour mixture and milk alternately to beaten mixture, beating on low speed after each addition just till combined. Set aside.

■ In an 8x8x2-inch baking dish combine pie filling, water, and lemon juice. Cook, uncovered, on 100% power (high) for 4 to 5 minutes or till hot and bubbling at corners, stirring once.

■ Meanwhile, using clean beaters, beat egg whites with an electric mixer on high speed till stiff peaks form (tips stand straight). Fold egg whites into batter. Spoon batter atop hot pie filling.

■ Cook, uncovered, on high for 9 to 11 minutes or till done, giving the dish a quarter-turn every 3 minutes. (To check doneness, scratch the slightly wet surface with a wooden toothpick. If done, a cooked texture will have formed underneath, as in photo 4, page 71.) Serve warm with vanilla ice cream, if desired. Makes 8 servings.

Low-wattage oven: For *fruit mixture,* cook on high for 5 to 7 minutes. For *cake topping,* cook on high for 12 to 14 minutes.

Coconut-Topped Grapefruit

This citrus fix-up switch-hits as a dessert or a brunch first course.

2 medium grapefruit *or* large
    oranges
2 tablespoons brown sugar,
    sugar, *or* maple syrup
⅛ teaspoon ground nutmeg *or*
    ginger
2 tablespoons toasted coconut

■ Halve grapefruit or oranges crosswise and loosen sections, if desired. Remove the white membranes from the centers. Place grapefruit or orange halves in microwave-safe serving dishes.

■ In a small bowl combine brown sugar, sugar, or maple syrup with nutmeg or ginger. Spoon mixture over citrus halves and sprinkle with coconut. Cook, uncovered, on 100% power (high) for 2 to 4 minutes or till citrus halves are warm. Makes 4 servings.

Steaming Fresh Fruit

Prick skins or peel **apples, peaches,** and **pears.** Place in a 1-quart casserole (1½-quart for 4 fruits). Add 2 tablespoons water (omit water for pears). Cook, covered, on 100% power (high) for specified time, rearranging and spooning liquid over fruit once during cooking.

Fruit	Amount	Cooking time
Apples, cored	1 medium	1½ to 2½ minutes
	2 medium	2½ to 3½ minutes
	4 medium (1 pound)	4 to 6 minutes
Peaches or nectarines, halved and seeded	1 medium	45 to 60 seconds
	2 medium	1½ to 3 minutes
	4 medium (1 pound)	3 to 5 minutes
Pears, cored and quartered	1 medium	1 to 2 minutes
	2 medium	2 to 3 minutes
	4 medium (1¼ pounds)	3 to 5 minutes

Defrosting Frozen Fruit

Place **frozen fruit** in a 1½-quart casserole or baking dish. Cook, covered, on 100% power (high) for the time specified or till no ice remains, stirring once to break up fruit. Drain, if desired.

Fruit	Amount	Defrosting time
Unsweetened berries	One 10-ounce package	1 to 2½ minutes
	One 16-ounce package	4 to 6 minutes
Berries (in quick-thaw pouch)	One 10-ounce package	2½ to 3½ minutes
Melon balls	One 16-ounce package	4 to 6 minutes
Peach slices	One 16-ounce package	4 to 6 minutes
Sliced rhubarb	One 16-ounce package	5 to 7 minutes

Rehydrating Dried Fruit

Place **dried fruit** in a 1-quart casserole. Add an equal amount of warm water. Cook, covered, on 100% power (high) for time specified or till boiling, stirring once. Drain.

Fruit	Amount	Cooking time
Dried apples, currants, raisins, figs, mixed fruit, peaches, or prunes	1 cup	3 to 5 minutes
Dried apricots	1 cup	2 to 3 minutes
Currants or raisins	½ cup	1½ to 2½ minutes
Mixed dried fruit	½ cup	2½ to 3 minutes

Nutrition Analysis

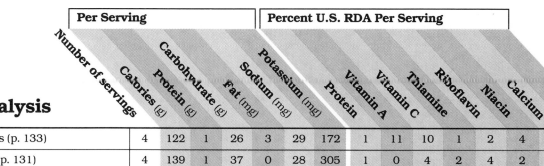

	Number of servings	Calories	Protein (g)	Carbohydrate (g)	Fat (g)	Sodium (mg)	Potassium (mg)	Protein	Vitamin A	Vitamin C	Thiamine	Riboflavin	Niacin	Calcium	Iron
		Per Serving						**Percent U.S. RDA Per Serving**							
Anytime Glazed Peaches (p. 133)	4	122	1	26	3	29	172	1	11	10	1	2	4	1	1
Apple-Raisin Compote (p. 131)	4	139	1	37	0	28	305	1	0	4	2	4	2	2	5
Caramel-Apple Streusel (p. 136)	8	213	2	42	5	75	117	2	3	2	3	4	2	3	4
Chocolate-Raisin-Stuffed Apples (p. 128)	4	171	1	37	4	1	274	2	2	10	3	2	1	2	4
Choose-a-Fruit Cobbler (p. 134)	6	262	4	48	8	112	214	6	29	4	10	7	5	7	8
Choose-a-Fruit Crumble w/ Chocolate Topping (p. 136)	4	175	1	39	3	100	147	1	8	12	6	6	6	1	3
w/ Coconut Topping (p. 136)	4	164	1	31	5	78	167	1	3	5	2	3	2	1	2
w/ Granola Topping (p. 136)	4	222	3	37	9	32	236	4	3	8	10	4	2	2	5
w/ Oat Topping (p. 136)	4	267	3	42	11	63	224	5	6	8	9	3	3	3	6
Coconut-Topped Grapefruit (p. 137)	4	75	1	17	1	3	199	1	3	69	3	1	2	2	2
Cream-Cheese-Stuffed Peaches (p. 130)	4	131	2	17	7	47	151	2	9	6	2	3	2	2	1
Gingerbread-Pudding Cake (p. 137)	8	348	4	66	8	110	278	6	11	7	9	10	6	9	13
Glazed Peaches (p. 133)	4	122	1	26	3	29	172	1	11	10	1	2	4	1	1
Pineapple-Berry Compote (p. 131)	2	167	1	30	6	64	201	1	6	26	8	2	2	3	3
Raisin-Stuffed Apples (p. 128)	4	164	1	37	3	2	283	2	2	17	4	2	1	2	3
Spicy Poached Fruit (p. 130)	4	142	1	37	1	3	268	1	1	25	3	4	1	3	4
Spicy Wine-Poached Fruit (p. 130)	4	173	1	42	1	2	238	1	1	18	3	4	1	3	4
Walnut Bananas Foster (p. 133)	4	389	5	52	18	123	585	7	12	20	7	16	3	12	6

MEAT

Microwave-cooked meats can be timesaving, attractive, and flavorful. How? Just match the right cut of meat with the right micro-cooking technique. You'll get tender, juicy results every time.

The right cut
We found the best meats to micro-cook are the less-tender beef cuts, such as chuck pot roasts, stew meat, or rolled rump roasts. Small cuts of lamb, pork, and ham also work well, as do some sausages, ground meats, and bacon. Large pieces (over 3 pounds) and cuts that are usually broiled cook best conventionally.

Sizing it up
When selecting meat to cook in the microwave, choose pieces that are even in shape, size, and thickness. When pieces are not the same thickness, the thinner, less-dense parts cook faster. That means you'll have to trim off thick areas or tuck under thin portions.

It's a good idea to trim off any fat, because it attracts microwaves and may cause meat near it to overcook. Bones have the opposite effect; they shield microwaves. Meat near large bones may cook slower. Prevent the meat from undercooking by removing large bones or turning the meat over.

Less power to meat
In meat micro-cooking, the highest power setting isn't necessarily the best. We found high power works well for ground meats, bacon, sausages, and small cuts of ham and lamb. Other cuts of beef and pork, though, are more tender and evenly done if cooked on lower power levels.

Lower power levels also come in handy for thawing meats. The medium-low or defrost settings will defrost meats quickly (see our defrosting and cooking charts at the end of the chapter).

To cover or not to cover
When it comes to covering up, follow these guidelines. Cover most meats loosely with waxed paper during cooking to prevent

Mexican Beef Salad
(see recipe, page 154)

spattering. One exception to this rule is pork. It should be tightly covered with plastic wrap or a lid so it cooks evenly to the well-done stage. Cover high-fat meats, such as bacon or sausages, with microwave-safe paper towels to absorb grease. And, if you're planning to cook a high-fat meat for longer than 5 minutes, choose a baking dish that can withstand the high temperature of the fat.

Making meats look good

Because microwave-cooked meats don't brown as well as conventionally cooked meats, we looked for ways to add color. Some of our recipes call for browning chops and meat strips in a special microwave browning dish. In other recipes, we brush larger cuts with soy sauce or Kitchen Bouquet for a rich brown color.

Judging doneness

How do you know when micro-cooked meats are done? Just begin at our minimum timing and follow these doneness guidelines. Check the meat's color. Pork and ground beef should have no pink remaining. Then check for tenderness. Finally, with larger cuts, use a temperature probe or microwave thermometer to test for the correct temperature. (Be sure to check the meat in several places to make sure it is done throughout.)

To prevent some meat portions from cooking before others, turn over large cuts, rearrange pieces, or stir mixtures, according to the directions we give in each recipe. If thinner portions of meat do finish cooking before the rest, shield them with small pieces of foil so they won't overcook. (Check your owner's manual first to see whether you can use foil in your microwave oven.)

One final hint: When you check the meat, you may find a lot of liquid accumulating in the baking dish. These juices lengthen the cooking time, so spoon them off occasionally.

Citrus-Stuffed Pork Chops
(see recipe, page 148)

Dilled Ham and Spinach
(see recipe, page 155)

Simmering a pot roast

Beef Roast with Dill Sauce

The beef chuck arm roast is easy to spot. It's oval with a round bone.

1 2½- to 3-pound beef chuck
   arm roast (cut 2 inches
   thick)
½ cup water
½ teaspoon salt
½ teaspoon dried dillweed
¼ teaspoon garlic powder
¼ teaspoon pepper
2 medium onions, sliced and
   separated into rings
1 10-ounce package frozen
   brussels sprouts
2 tablespoons all-purpose
   flour
1 8-ounce carton dairy sour
   cream
1 teaspoon sugar
½ teaspoon caraway seed

■ Trim excess fat from beef (see photo 1). In a 3-quart casserole combine water, salt, dillweed, garlic powder, and pepper. Add trimmed beef roast. Turn to coat meat on all sides.

■ Cook beef, covered, on 100% power (high) for 5 minutes or till liquid is boiling. Cook, covered, on 50% power (medium) for 40 minutes. Turn meat over (see photo 2). Add sliced onions. Cook, covered, on medium for 20 minutes more. Turn meat over.

■ Halve any large brussels sprouts, then add to the casserole. Cook the mixture, covered, on medium for 17 to 20 minutes or till meat and vegetables are tender.

■ Remove meat and slice. Transfer meat and vegetables to a serving platter, reserving any cooking liquid. Cover to keep meat warm while preparing sauce.

■ For sauce, skim fat from the reserved cooking liquid. Measure liquid. Add water, if necessary, to equal 1 cup total. In a 4-cup measure stir flour into sour cream (see photo 3). Stir in reserved cooking liquid, sugar, and caraway.

■ Cook sour cream mixture, uncovered, on high for 2 to 4 minutes or till thickened and bubbly, stirring every minute till slightly thickened, then every 30 seconds. Cook, uncovered, for 30 seconds more. Season to taste with salt and pepper. Spoon some of the sour cream sauce over beef and vegetables (see photo 4). Pass remaining sauce. Makes 8 to 10 servings.

Low-wattage oven: Not recommended.

1

Use a sharp knife to trim the fat from the meat. Because fat cooks faster than lean, trimming the fat helps the meat cook evenly.

2

Use tongs to turn the beef roast over at the intervals directed in the recipe. This keeps the meat from drying out on top.

3

For the sauce, stir flour into the dairy sour cream before cooking. The flour keeps the sour cream from curdling as it heats.

4

Serve the beef and vegetables topped with the sour cream sauce. As you can see, the meat browns nicely after lengthy cooking in the microwave oven.

Country-Apple Pot Roast

A homey one-dish meal for a cool day.

1 3- to 3½-pound rolled beef
    rump roast
1 tablespoon minced dried
    onion
1 teaspoon dried rosemary,
    crushed
1 teaspoon instant beef
    bouillon granules
½ teaspoon dry mustard
½ teaspoon ground cinnamon
¼ teaspoon pepper
3 stalks celery, cut into 1-inch
    pieces
2 medium sweet potatoes,
    cut into 1-inch cubes
½ of a 6-ounce can (⅓ cup)
    frozen apple juice
    concentrate, thawed
¼ cup red currant jelly
2 medium apples, cored and
    sliced into ½-inch rings
2 tablespoons cornstarch

■ Refer to photos, page 143. Trim fat from meat. In a 3-quart casserole combine onion, rosemary, beef bouillon granules, dry mustard, cinnamon, pepper, and 1 cup *water*. Add meat, celery, and sweet potatoes. Cook, covered, on 100% power (high) about 5 minutes or till liquid is boiling. Cook, covered, on 50% power (medium) for 30 minutes.

■ Turn meat over. Combine apple juice concentrate and jelly. Pour over meat and vegetables. Cook, covered, on medium for 30 minutes more, spooning cooking liquid over meat and vegetables every 10 minutes.

■ Add apple rings and cook, covered, on medium for 8 to 10 minutes more or till meat and apple rings are tender. Remove meat and slice. Transfer meat, vegetables, and apple rings to a serving platter, reserving cooking liquid. Cover to keep warm.

■ For sauce, strain and skim fat from pan juices. Measure juices. Add water, if necessary, to equal 1½ cups total. Combine cornstarch and 2 tablespoons cold *water*. Stir into juice mixture. Cook, uncovered, on high for 1½ to 3 minutes or till thickened and bubbly, stirring every 30 seconds. Spoon some sauce over meat. Pass remaining. Serves 10 to 12.

Low-wattage oven: Not recommended.

TIP Searching for the Perfect Roast

With just a little know-how, you can micro-cook beef chuck and rump roasts with mouth-watering results. Start by choosing a roast with a uniform shape and thickness so it will cook evenly. Flat roasts, such as a beef chuck arm pot roast, are the ideal shape.

Look for a roast with good marbling (even amounts of fat spread throughout the meat). If one area has heavier marbling, it will cook faster than the rest of the roast.

In general, boneless roasts cook more evenly than roasts with a bone, because large bones shield the meat from the microwaves.

Italian-Style Pot Roast

1   3-pound boneless beef chuck
    arm pot roast (cut 2
    inches thick)
1   8-ounce can pizza sauce *or*
    tomato sauce
½   cup dry red *or* white wine
3   medium carrots, cut into
    1½-inch chunks
1   4-ounce can mushroom
    stems and pieces, drained
¼   cup cold water
2   tablespoons cornstarch
¼   cup sliced pimiento-stuffed
    olives
2   tablespoons snipped parsley

■ Trim fat from meat (see photo 1, page 143). In a 3-quart casserole combine pizza sauce or tomato sauce and wine. Add meat. Turn to coat with sauce. Cook, covered, on 100% power (high) for 5 minutes or till sauce is boiling. Cook, covered, on 50% power (medium) for 30 minutes.

■ Turn meat over (see photo 2, page 143). Add carrots and mushrooms. Cook, covered, on medium for 45 to 55 minutes more or till meat and carrots are tender, turning meat over after 20 minutes. Remove meat and slice. Transfer meat and vegetables to a serving platter, reserving cooking liquid. Cover to keep warm.

■ For sauce, skim fat from cooking liquid. Measure and add water, if necessary, to equal 2 cups total. Combine water and cornstarch. Stir into cooking liquid. Cook, uncovered, on high for 3 to 5 minutes or till thickened and bubbly, stirring every minute. Stir in olives and parsley. Pour some sauce over meat. Pass remaining. Makes 8 to 10 servings.

Low-wattage oven: Not recommended.

Fruit and Veal Sauté

This easy main dish cooks in about 15 minutes.

1   pound veal cutlets,
    cut ½ inch thick
2   medium pears *or* 1 large
    papaya
    Lemon juice
1   tablespoon cooking oil
2   teaspoons cornstarch
⅔   cup pear *or* papaya nectar
2   tablespoons sliced green
    onion
1   teaspoon instant beef
    bouillon granules
½   teaspoon dried mint,
    crushed

■ Cut veal into 4 serving-size portions. Sprinkle with salt and pepper and set aside. Peel papaya. Cut unpeeled pears or peeled papaya in half lengthwise and remove cores or seeds. Cut fruit crosswise into ¼-inch-thick slices and brush with lemon juice. Set aside.

■ Meanwhile, preheat a 10-inch microwave browning dish on 100% power (high) for 5 minutes. Add cooking oil and swirl to coat the dish (see photo 1, page 153). Add veal to the browning dish. Cook veal, uncovered, on high for 3 to 5 minutes or till no pink remains, turning veal over after 2 minutes. Remove veal and set aside, reserving drippings in the browning dish.

■ Stir cornstarch into drippings. Stir in pear or papaya nectar, green onion, beef bouillon granules, and mint. Cook, uncovered, on high for 2 to 4 minutes or till mixture is thickened and bubbly, stirring every minute. Add pear or papaya slices and cooked veal to the browning dish. Cook, covered, on high for 1 to 3 minutes more or till fruit is heated through. Makes 4 servings.

Low-wattage oven: If the browning dish fits into your oven, preheat it on high for 7 minutes.

Cooking pork ribs

Orange-Ginger Spareribs

Don't use metal twists in your oven. Close cooking bags with string or a strip cut from the end of the cooking bag.

3 pounds pork spareribs *or* pork loin back ribs
1 tablespoon cornstarch
1 cup water
½ cup orange marmalade
¼ cup soy sauce
¼ teaspoon garlic powder
¼ teaspoon ground ginger
⅛ teaspoon ground Szechuan pepper *or* red pepper
Orange slices (optional)
Fresh coriander (optional)

■ Cut spareribs into 3-rib portions (see photo 1). Sprinkle cornstarch into a 24x19-inch oven cooking bag (see photo 2). Place ribs in the bag and place bag in a 3-quart casserole. Add water (see photo 3). Close bag loosely with a string or a ½-inch strip cut from the open end of the bag. Cut six ½-inch slits in the top of the bag (see photo 4).

■ Cook ribs on 50% power (medium) for 40 minutes, turning bag over and giving the dish a half-turn once during cooking (see photo 5). Meanwhile, for glaze, combine marmalade, soy sauce, garlic powder, ginger, and pepper.

■ Carefully drain meat. Pour soy-marmalade mixture over meat in bag and retie the end. Cook on medium for 10 to 15 minutes more or till meat is tender and no pink remains, turning the bag once to distribute glaze (see photo 6).

■ Cut the bag open and transfer ribs to a serving platter. Spoon some glaze over ribs before serving. Garnish with orange slices and fresh coriander, if desired. Makes 4 servings.

Low-wattage oven: Not recommended.

TIP **Pork in the Microwave**

For safety's sake, we've taken a few extra steps with pork to make sure it's micro-cooked all the way through. We've cooked the meat covered, either in a cooking bag or a tightly covered casserole, so the steam surrounds the meat and does not escape.

We recommend cooking pork slowly, usually on medium or medium-low power. That way, the heat has time to penetrate to the center, cooking the meat evenly to the well-done stage. When you think it's done, check your pork in several spots for any pinkness—a sign of uncooked meat. Or, check larger cuts of meat by inserting a meat thermometer or temperature probe in two or three different places. The internal temperature at each spot should be 170°.

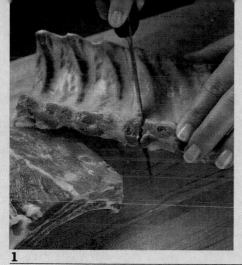

1

Using a sharp knife, cut the pork spareribs into 3-rib portions. The ribs cook more evenly if cut into equal-size pieces.

2

Sprinkle the cornstarch into a cooking bag, as shown. Shake to coat the inside of the bag. The starch prevents the bag from exploding during cooking.

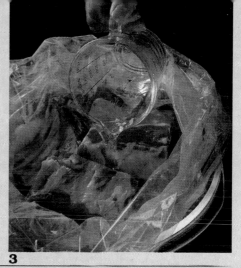

3

Add the ribs, then place the bag in a 3-quart casserole. Pour water over the ribs, as shown. The water creates steam, which helps the pork cook more evenly.

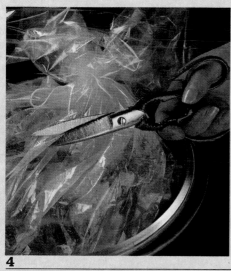

4

Using kitchen shears, cut six ½-inch slits in the closed cooking bag, as shown. The slits vent the steam that builds up as the pork ribs cook.

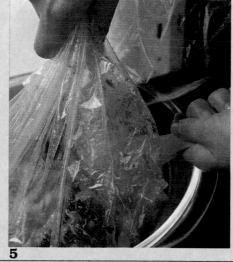

5

Turn the cooking bag over once during cooking. This repositions the ribs and helps them cook more evenly.

6

The spareribs are done when the meat is tender and no pink remains. Cut near the bone to check for pinkness, as shown.

Peppy Barbecue-Style Pork Ribs

Country-style ribs are the meatiest pork ribs you can buy.

3 pounds pork country-
    style ribs
1 tablespoon cornstarch
1 15-ounce can tomato sauce
1 medium onion, chopped
    (½ cup)
2 cloves garlic, minced
¼ cup packed brown sugar
¼ cup vinegar
2 tablespoons Worcestershire
    sauce
1 teaspoon prepared
    horseradish
½ teaspoon dry mustard

■ Refer to photos, page 147. Cut ribs into serving-size portions. Sprinkle cornstarch into a 16x10-inch oven cooking bag. Place ribs in the bag and place bag in a 3-quart casserole.

■ For sauce, combine tomato sauce, onion, garlic, brown sugar, vinegar, Worcestershire sauce, horseradish, and dry mustard. Pour sauce over ribs. Close bag loosely with a string or a ½-inch strip cut from the open end of the bag. Cut six ½-inch slits in the top of the bag.

■ Cook ribs on 50% power (medium) for 20 minutes. Snip off the top of the cooking bag. Carefully transfer contents from the bag to the casserole. Cook, covered, on medium for 20 to 25 minutes more or till tender and no pink remains, stirring once.

■ Transfer ribs to a serving platter. Skim fat from pan juices and serve with ribs. Makes 4 servings.

Low-wattage oven: Not recommended.

Citrus-Stuffed Pork Chops

Remember to shred the peel before juicing the orange. (Pictured on pages 140–141.)

2 pork loin chops, cut
    1¼ inches thick
    (about 1½ pounds total)
¼ teaspoon finely shredded
    orange peel (set aside)
½ cup orange juice
⅓ cup chopped apple
2 tablespoons fine dry bread
    crumbs
1 tablespoon chopped almonds
    or pecans
⅛ teaspoon ground cinnamon
1 tablespoon cooking oil
1 teaspoon cornstarch
½ teaspoon instant beef
    bouillon granules

■ Trim fat from chops (see photo 1, page 143). Cut a pocket in each chop by cutting from fat side almost to bone edge. Sprinkle the cavity with salt and pepper. For filling, in a small mixing bowl combine *1 tablespoon* of the orange juice, apple, crumbs, almonds or pecans, and cinnamon. Spoon about *half* of the filling into *each* chop.

■ Meanwhile, preheat a 10-inch microwave browning dish on 100% power (high) for 5 minutes. Add cooking oil. Swirl to coat the dish (see photo 1, page 153). Add the stuffed chops and cook, covered, on high for 4 minutes, turning chops over once.

■ Cook, covered, on 50% power (medium) for 9 to 11 minutes or till chops are tender and no pink remains (see photo 3, opposite), giving the dish a half-turn and turning chops over once during cooking.

■ For sauce, in a 1-cup measure combine reserved peel, remaining juice, cornstarch, and bouillon granules. Cook, uncovered, on high for 1 to 2 minutes, stirring every 30 seconds. Serve over chops. Makes 2 servings.

Low-wattage oven: Not recommended.

Tomato-Topped Pork Chops

Here's a chop recipe that doesn't require a browning dish.

2 pork loin chops, cut ¾ inch thick (about 1 pound total)
½ of a medium onion, sliced and separated into rings
1 tablespoon butter or margarine
4 whole black peppers, crushed
¼ teaspoon salt
¼ teaspoon caraway seed
1 medium tomato, seeded and chopped

■ Trim fat from chops (see photo 1, page 143). Sprinkle chops with salt. In an 8x8x2-inch baking dish arrange chops with meatiest portions facing the outside of the dish. Cover with vented clear plastic wrap (see photo 1, below). Cook on 30% power (medium-low) for 10 minutes.

■ Give the dish a half-turn and turn chops over (see photo 2, below). Cover and cook on medium-low for 10 to 12 minutes more or till chops are tender and no pink remains (see photo 3, below). Transfer chops to a serving platter. Cover to keep warm. Drain juices from the baking dish.

■ In the same dish combine onion rings, butter or margarine, crushed pepper, salt, and caraway seed. Cover and cook on 100% power (high) for 3 to 5 minutes or till onion is tender. Stir in tomato. Cook, covered, for 30 to 60 seconds more or till heated through. Top chops with onion mixture. Makes 2 servings.

Low-wattage oven: Not recommended.

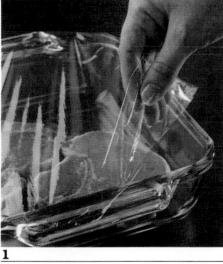

1

Cover the chops with microwave-safe clear plastic wrap or lid to hold in the steam and promote even cooking. While a tight cover is essential for pork, too tight a cover will trap steam and may make the wrap explode. To prevent this, vent the wrap by turning back a small portion at one corner, as shown.

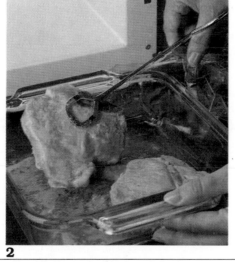

2

The heat of the dish cooks the chops faster on the bottom. For that reason, it's important to turn the chops over, as shown.

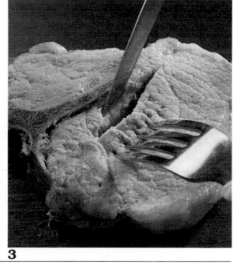

3

To check for doneness, use a sharp knife to cut into the chop in several places, particularly near the bone. The chops should be tender and show no pink inside, as shown.

Pineapple-Cashew Lamb Chops

Pineapple-Cashew Lamb Chops

Lamb, like beef, is a meat that's tender and safe to eat while it's still a little pink, so cook until it's done the way you want.

¾ cup quick-cooking rice
¾ cup water
1 8¼-ounce can crushed
    pineapple
¼ cup chopped cashews *or*
    peanuts
¼ cup sliced green onions
    Dash ground cloves
4 lamb leg sirloin chops, cut
    ¾ inch thick (1¼ pounds
    total)
1 tablespoon soy sauce
2 teaspoons cornstarch
    Green onion brush (optional)

■ In a 1-quart casserole combine uncooked rice and water. Cover and cook on 100% power (high) for 3 to 5 minutes or till water is boiling. Let stand, covered, for 5 minutes.

■ Meanwhile, drain crushed pineapple over a 1-cup measure. Measure juice. Add water, if necessary, to equal ⅓ cup. Set juice aside. In an 8x8x2-inch baking dish combine drained pineapple, cashews or peanuts, *half* of the green onions, and cloves. Stir in the hot cooked rice. Spread in the baking dish.

■ Trim fat from lamb (see photo 1, page 143). Sprinkle with salt and pepper. Arrange chops atop rice mixture with the meatiest portions facing the outside of the dish. Cover with waxed paper. Cook on high for 8 to 11 minutes or till done, turning chops over and rearranging once.

■ Meanwhile, for sauce, stir remaining green onions, soy sauce, and cornstarch into reserved pineapple juice. Cook, uncovered, on high for 1½ to 2½ minutes or till thickened and bubbly, stirring every 30 seconds. Serve sauce over meat. If desired, garnish with a green onion brush. Makes 4 servings.

Peach-Glazed Ham Slice

Count 'em—only five ingredients in this speedy recipe.

1 8¾-ounce can peach slices,
    drained
2 tablespoons honey
2 tablespoons lemon juice
¼ teaspoon ground cinnamon
1 1½- to 2-pound fully cooked
    ham slice, boned and cut
    1¼ inches thick

■ For glaze, in a blender container combine peach slices, honey, lemon juice, and cinnamon. Cover and blend till smooth.

■ Place ham in a 10x6x2-inch baking dish. Cover with waxed paper. Cook on 100% power (high) for 8 to 10 minutes or till heated through, turning ham over and brushing with glaze after 5 minutes.

■ In a 2-cup measure cook remaining glaze, uncovered, on high for 1 to 2 minutes or till heated through. Spoon over ham. Makes 6 to 8 servings.

Low-wattage oven: For *ham*, cook for 14 to 16 minutes on high, turning and brushing with glaze after 8 minutes.

Stir-frying in a browning dish

Beef and Pea Pod Stir-Fry

Wispy bean threads balloon into crunchy, transparent sticks after you deep-fry them.

¾ pound beef top round steak
or 1 pound lamb leg sirloin chops
3 tablespoons soy sauce
2 tablespoons red wine vinegar
1 tablespoon grated gingerroot
or ½ teaspoon ground ginger
1 clove garlic, minced
1 tablespoon cooking oil
3 green onions, bias-sliced into ½-inch lengths
2 tablespoons cold water
4 teaspoons cornstarch
1 6-ounce package frozen pea pods
½ cup quartered cherry tomatoes
½ of an 8-ounce can (⅓ cup) sliced water chestnuts, drained
Hot cooked rice *or* deep-fried bean threads

■ Partially freeze beef or lamb. Thinly slice meat across the grain into bite-size strips.

■ For marinade, in a medium mixing bowl combine soy sauce, vinegar, gingerroot, and garlic. Stir in the strips of meat. Cover and let stand at room temperature for 30 minutes. Drain meat, reserving marinade.

■ Meanwhile, preheat a 10-inch microwave browning dish on 100% power (high) for 5 minutes. Add cooking oil. Swirl to coat the dish (see photo 1). Add the marinated strips of meat. Cook, uncovered, on high for 2 to 3 minutes or till meat is tender, stirring every minute (see photo 2).

■ Use a slotted spoon to remove meat from the dish, reserving juices (see photo 3). Set meat aside.

■ In a 1-cup measure combine reserved juices and reserved marinade. Add water, if necessary, to equal ¾ cup total. Stir in green onions. Return mixture to the browning dish. Cook, covered, on high for 1 to 2 minutes or till green onions are crisp-tender.

■ Stir together 2 tablespoons cold water and cornstarch. Stir cornstarch mixture into the green onion mixture. Cook, uncovered, on high for 2 to 4 minutes or till mixture is thickened and bubbly, stirring every minute till slightly thickened, then every 30 seconds.

■ Stir in cooked meat, pea pods, cherry tomatoes, and water chestnuts (see photo 4). Cook, uncovered, on high for 2 to 4 minutes or till heated through. Serve over hot cooked rice or bean threads (see large photo). Makes 4 servings.

Low-wattage oven: If the browning dish fits into your oven, preheat it on high for 7 minutes.

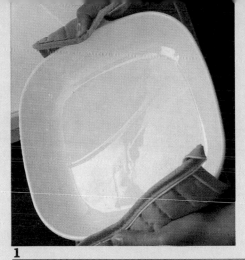

1
Preheat the 10-inch microwave browning dish on high so it's hot for stir-frying the beef. Add the cooking oil and swirl to coat.

2
As the meat strips cook, stir every minute to brown all sides. Be sure to use hot pads because the dish will be hot.

3
When the meat is tender and brown, use a slotted spoon to remove it from the dish. You'll use the meat juices, reserved marinade, and water to cook the green onions in the dish.

4
After thickening the marinade mixture, add the cooked meat, pea pods, cherry tomatoes, and water chestnuts, as shown above. Cook, uncovered, till heated through. Serve over hot cooked rice, as shown at right.

Mexican Beef Salad

For a rich color, add Kitchen Bouquet. (Pictured on pages 140–141.)

¾ pound beef top round steak
½ teaspoon unseasoned instant
  meat tenderizer
3 tablespoons cooking oil
¼ teaspoon Kitchen Bouquet
  (optional)
3 tablespoons vinegar
½ teaspoon salt
¼ teaspoon ground cumin
¼ teaspoon dried oregano,
  crushed
⅛ teaspoon garlic powder
⅛ teaspoon ground red pepper
1 16-ounce can yellow hominy,
  drained
1 small onion, sliced and
  separated into rings
1 green pepper, sliced into
  rings
⅓ cup sliced pitted ripe olives
4 cups torn lettuce
½ cup halved cherry tomatoes
  Lettuce leaves
½ cup finely shredded
  Monterey Jack cheese
  (2 ounces)

■ Partially freeze meat. Slice meat across the grain into bite-size strips. Sprinkle meat tenderizer over meat. In a 1½-quart casserole combine beef and *1 tablespoon* of the cooking oil. Stir in Kitchen Bouquet, if desired. Cover with waxed paper. Cook on 100% power (high) for 3 to 5 minutes or till meat is done, stirring every 2 minutes. Remove meat and set aside, reserving drippings.

■ Add remaining cooking oil to drippings. Stir in vinegar, salt, cumin, oregano, garlic powder, and red pepper. Cook, uncovered, on high about 30 seconds or till bubbly. Add meat, hominy, onion, green pepper, and olives. Toss gently to coat. Cover and chill for 3 to 24 hours.

■ Before serving, in a medium mixing bowl combine meat mixture, torn lettuce, and cherry tomatoes. Toss gently to coat. Spoon mixture onto lettuce-lined plates. Sprinkle with cheese. Makes 4 to 6 servings.

Low-wattage oven: For *meat strips,* cook on high for 5 to 7 minutes.

Herbed Lamb Kabobs

Kabobs in the microwave? Use wooden instead of metal skewers.

¼ cup dry white wine
3 tablespoons cooking oil
1½ teaspoons snipped fresh
  mint *or* ½ teaspoon dried
  mint, crushed
½ teaspoon dried thyme,
  crushed
½ teaspoon dried basil,
  crushed
¼ teaspoon salt
1 pound boneless lamb, cut
  into 1-inch cubes
1 medium green pepper, cut
  into 1-inch squares

■ In a medium mixing bowl combine wine, cooking oil, mint, thyme, basil, and salt. Add lamb cubes. Cover and marinate in the refrigerator for at least 6 hours.

■ Drain meat, reserving marinade. On four 8-inch-long wooden skewers, alternately thread lamb cubes and green pepper squares. Place the skewers lengthwise in a 10x6x2-inch baking dish and cover with waxed paper. Cook on 100% power (high) for 3 minutes. Rearrange, moving the center skewers to the outside. Cook, covered, on 50% power (medium) for 4 to 6 minutes more or till lamb is done. Makes 4 servings.

Low-wattage oven: Cook on high for 7 minutes total, rearranging the skewers after 5 minutes.

Dilled Ham and Spinach

If you don't have Gouda, try teaming Swiss or mozzarella cheese with the ham and spinach. (Pictured on pages 140–141.)

1 tablespoon butter *or* margarine
2 tablespoons fine dry bread crumbs
1 tablespoon grated Parmesan cheese
1 teaspoon dried parsley flakes
1 tablespoon butter *or* margarine
1 tablespoon all-purpose flour
¼ teaspoon dried dillweed
¼ teaspoon pepper
½ cup milk
¼ cup shredded Gouda cheese (1 ounce)
1 tablespoon dry white wine
1 10-ounce package frozen chopped spinach, thawed and well drained
6 ounces fully cooked ham, cut into thin strips

■ For topping, in a custard cup cook 1 tablespoon butter or margarine on 100% power (high) for 30 to 40 seconds or till melted. Stir in bread crumbs, Parmesan cheese, and parsley flakes. Set aside.

■ In a 2-cup measure cook 1 tablespoon butter or margarine, uncovered, on high for 30 to 40 seconds or till melted. Stir in flour, dillweed, and pepper. Stir in milk. Cook, uncovered, on high for 1 to 2 minutes or till thickened and bubbly, stirring every 30 seconds. Stir in cheese and wine.

■ Stir about *half* of the hot mixture into spinach. Spread spinach mixture in two 14-ounce au gratin dishes. Cook, uncovered, on high for 2 to 4 minutes or till heated through.

■ Top with ham and the remaining cheese mixture. Cook, uncovered, on high for 1½ to 3½ minutes or till heated through, rearranging once. Sprinkle with crumb topping. Makes 2 servings.

Low-wattage oven: For *ham mixture,* cook on high about 5 minutes.

Ham-Stuffed Peppers

¼ cup chopped onion
¼ cup chopped celery
1 clove garlic, minced
1 tablespoon butter *or* margarine
1 7½-ounce can tomatoes, cut up
½ teaspoon sugar
   Few dashes bottled hot pepper sauce
   Dash ground cloves
½ cup quick-cooking rice
2 medium green peppers
2 tablespoons water
1 cup ground fully cooked ham
¾ cup shredded Swiss cheese (3 ounces)

■ For filling, in a 1-quart casserole combine onion, celery, garlic, and butter or margarine. Cook, covered, on 100% power (high) for 2 to 3 minutes or till tender. Stir in *undrained* tomatoes, sugar, hot pepper sauce, and cloves. Cook, covered, on high for 2 to 3 minutes or till bubbly and heated through. Add uncooked rice and let stand, covered, for 5 minutes.

■ Meanwhile, cut green peppers in half lengthwise and remove seeds. Place pepper halves, cut side down, in an 8x8x2-inch baking dish. Add water. Cover with vented clear plastic wrap. Cook on high for 3 to 5 minutes or till crisp-tender. Drain, cut side down, on paper towels.

■ Stir ham and ⅔ *cup* of the cheese into rice mixture. Spoon filling into pepper halves. Arrange pepper halves in the 8x8x2-inch baking dish. Cover with waxed paper. Cook on high for 3 to 5 minutes or till filling is heated through, giving the dish a half-turn once. Sprinkle remaining cheese on top. Makes 4 servings.

Low-wattage oven: For *pepper shells,* cook on high for 6 to 8 minutes.

Technique:
Shaping a meat loaf

Apricot Meat Ring

1 beaten egg
⅓ cup dried currants *or* raisins
¼ cup fine dry bread crumbs
¼ cup milk
½ teaspoon salt
¼ teaspoon ground cinnamon
¼ teaspoon pepper
1 pound ground beef
1 8¾-ounce can unpeeled
   apricot halves
2 teaspoons cornstarch
1 teaspoon lemon juice
1 tablespoon snipped parsley

■ In a medium mixing bowl combine beaten egg, currants or raisins, fine dry bread crumbs, milk, salt, cinnamon, and pepper. Add ground beef and mix well.

■ In a 9-inch pie plate shape meat mixture into a 6-inch ring, 2 inches wide (see photo 1). Cover with waxed paper. Cook on 100% power (high) for 8 to 10 minutes or till no pink remains and meat is well-done (170°), giving the dish a quarter-turn every 3 minutes (see photo 2).

■ Transfer the meat ring to a serving platter (see photo 3). Cover to keep warm while preparing fruit sauce.

■ For sauce, drain apricot halves, reserving syrup. Chop apricot halves and set aside. Add water to reserved syrup, if necessary, to equal ⅔ cup total. Stir cornstarch and lemon juice into syrup mixture.

■ Cook cornstarch mixture, uncovered, on high for 2 to 3 minutes or till thickened and bubbly, stirring every 30 seconds. Stir in the chopped apricots and snipped parsley. Cook, uncovered, for 30 seconds more. Spoon sauce over meat (see photo 4). Makes 4 servings.

Low-wattage oven: For *meat ring,* cook on high for 10 to 12 minutes.

TIP Meat Loaf Toppings

Custom-design a meat loaf to suit your family's taste. Start with ours but omit the currants or raisins and cinnamon. Then, instead of the apricot sauce, spread a little chili sauce, barbecue sauce, pizza sauce, or enchilada sauce on top of the meat after cooking.
   Or, make a cheesy loaf. Arrange cheese slices or sprinkle grated Parmesan cheese over the just-cooked meat. Let the loaf stand a few minutes so the cheese has a chance to melt.

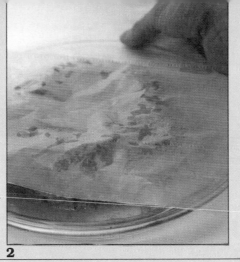

1

In a 9-inch pie plate shape the ground-meat mixture into a 6-inch ring that's 2 inches wide. Ring shapes cook better than loaves in a microwave oven.

2

During cooking, turn the waxed-paper-covered ring partway around as directed. Turning the dish assures that no spot cooks more than another.

3

Once you've checked the meat ring in several places to be sure no pink remains, transfer it to a serving platter. Because of the unattractive juices that accumulate, you won't want to cook and serve your meat ring in the same dish.

4

To serve, spoon the apricot sauce over the meat ring. Garnish the platter with additional apricot pieces and a parsley sprig.

Herbed Bulgur Meat Ring

What's bulgur? It's precooked cracked wheat.

⅔ cup water
¼ cup bulgur
1 beaten egg
¼ cup fine dry bread crumbs
¼ cup shredded carrot
2 tablespoons snipped parsley
½ teaspoon salt
½ teaspoon dried marjoram, crushed
½ teaspoon dried thyme, crushed
⅛ teaspoon pepper
1 pound lean ground beef
 Plain yogurt
 Snipped parsley

■ In a medium microwave-safe mixing bowl combine water and bulgur. Cook, uncovered, on 100% power (high) for 1½ to 2½ minutes or till boiling. Let stand for 5 to 10 minutes to cool slightly.

■ Stir in egg, bread crumbs, carrot, parsley, salt, marjoram, thyme, and pepper. Add ground beef and mix well. In a 9-inch pie plate shape meat mixture into a 6-inch ring, 2 inches wide (see photo 1, page 157).

■ Cover with waxed paper. Cook on high for 8 to 10 minutes or till no pink remains and meat is well-done (170°), giving the dish a quarter-turn every 3 minutes (see photo 2, page 157). Transfer the ring to a serving platter (see photo 3, page 157). Serve with yogurt. Garnish with additional parsley. Makes 4 servings.

Low-wattage oven: For *meat ring,* cook on high for 10 to 12 minutes.

Corned Beef 'n' Kraut Wedges

To test the meat, insert a microwave meat thermometer before cooking or an instant-read thermometer after cooking.

2 beaten eggs
1 16-ounce can sauerkraut, rinsed, drained, and snipped
1½ cups soft rye bread crumbs (2 slices)
1 5-ounce can (⅔ cup) evaporated milk
¼ cup chopped onion
1 teaspoon Dijon-style mustard
⅛ teaspoon pepper
1 pound lean ground beef
1 12-ounce can corned beef, flaked
 Swiss cheese slices
 Celery leaves
 Catsup (optional)

■ In a large mixing bowl combine eggs, sauerkraut, bread crumbs, milk, onion, mustard, and pepper. Add ground beef and corned beef. Mix well. Spread mixture in an 8x1½-inch round baking dish. Invert the mixture onto a 10-inch-round microwave-safe plate. Remove the baking dish.

■ Cover with waxed paper. Cook on 100% power (high) for 20 to 24 minutes or till well-done (170°), giving the dish a quarter-turn every 8 minutes (see photo 2, page 157). (Be sure to do the temperature test, because, with the corned beef, the meat will be pink even when done.)

■ Transfer meat to a serving platter. Garnish with triangles or strips of Swiss cheese and celery leaves. Cut meat into wedges to serve. Serve with catsup, if desired. Makes 8 servings.

Mediterranean Meatballs

Mint and cinnamon add a Mediterranean accent.

1 beaten egg
¾ cup soft bread crumbs
¼ cup finely chopped onion
2 tablespoons milk
1 teaspoon snipped fresh mint
    or ¼ teaspoon dried mint,
    crushed
¼ teaspoon salt
⅛ teaspoon pepper
¾ pound ground beef *or* lamb
½ cup chopped onion
1 clove garlic, minced
1 tablespoon cooking oil
1 7½-ounce can tomatoes,
    cut up
½ cup tomato sauce
2 tablespoons snipped parsley
½ teaspoon instant beef
    bouillon granules
½ teaspoon ground cinnamon
    Hot cooked rice

■ In a medium mixing bowl combine egg, bread crumbs, ¼ cup finely chopped onion, milk, mint, salt, and pepper. Add ground meat and mix well. Shape into 6 meatballs (see photo 1, page 27).

■ Arrange meatballs in an 8x8x2-inch baking dish. Cover with waxed paper. Cook on 100% power (high) for 5 to 7 minutes or till no pink remains, rearranging and turning meatballs over once (see photo 3, page 27). Drain meatballs on paper towels (see photo 4, page 27).

■ In a 1½-quart casserole combine ½ cup onion, garlic, and cooking oil. Cook, covered, on high for 2 to 4 minutes or till tender. Stir in *undrained* tomatoes, tomato sauce, parsley, bouillon granules, and cinnamon. Cook, covered, on high for 2 to 3 minutes or till heated through, stirring once.

■ Add meatballs. Cook, uncovered, on high for 1 to 2 minutes more or till meatballs are warm, stirring once. Serve over rice. Garnish with fresh mint, if desired. Makes 3 servings.

Sauerbraten-Style Meatballs

The crushed gingersnaps and splash of vinegar give these meatballs a genuine German flavor.

1 beaten egg
¼ cup finely crushed
    gingersnaps
¼ cup finely chopped onion
2 teaspoons Worcestershire
    sauce
¼ teaspoon garlic powder
¼ teaspoon pepper
1 pound ground beef
1 15-ounce can tomato sauce
⅓ cup finely crushed
    gingersnaps
2 tablespoons brown sugar
2 tablespoons vinegar
6 cups chopped cabbage
½ cup chopped green pepper
2 tablespoons water

■ In a medium mixing bowl combine egg, ¼ cup crushed gingersnaps, onion, Worcestershire sauce, garlic powder, and pepper. Add meat and mix well. Shape into 24 meatballs (see photo 1, page 27).

■ Arrange meatballs in an 8x8x2-inch baking dish. Cover with waxed paper. Cook on 100% power (high) for 5 to 7 minutes or till no pink remains, rearranging and turning meatballs over once (see photo 3, page 27). Drain meatballs on paper towels (see photo 4, page 27).

■ Meanwhile, for sauce, in a medium mixing bowl combine tomato sauce, ⅓ cup gingersnaps, brown sugar, and vinegar. Set aside.

■ In a 2-quart casserole combine cabbage, green pepper, and water. Cover and cook on high for 8 to 10 minutes or till crisp-tender. Drain. Stir sauce into the cabbage. Add the meatballs. Cook, uncovered, on high for 7 to 10 minutes or till hot, stirring twice. Makes 6 servings.

Preparing patties

Peanutty Rice-Stuffed Burgers

Pictured on the cover.

¼ cup quick-cooking rice
¼ cup water
2 tablespoons sliced green onion
⅛ teaspoon salt
⅛ teaspoon dried thyme, crushed
½ cup shredded cheddar cheese (2 ounces)
2 tablespoons chopped peanuts
1 beaten egg
½ cup soft rye *or* whole wheat bread crumbs
¼ cup milk
2 tablespoons snipped parsley
2 teaspoons Worcestershire sauce
¼ teaspoon salt
⅛ teaspoon pepper
1 pound ground beef
4 hamburger buns, split (optional)
  Lettuce leaves (optional)
  Tomato slices (optional)

■ For burger filling, in a 1-quart casserole combine uncooked rice, water, sliced green onion, ⅛ teaspoon salt, and thyme. Cook, covered, on 100% power (high) for 1 to 2 minutes or till boiling.

■ Let filling stand, covered, about 5 minutes or till rice absorbs the water. Add shredded cheddar cheese and chopped peanuts. Toss gently to mix, then set aside.

■ Meanwhile, in a medium mixing bowl combine beaten egg, rye or whole wheat bread crumbs, milk, snipped parsley, Worcestershire sauce, ¼ teaspoon salt, and pepper. Add ground beef and mix well.

■ Shape meat mixture into eight ¼-inch-thick patties. Place *four* patties on waxed paper, then spoon about *3 tablespoons* of the filling onto the center of *each* patty. Place the remaining patties atop filling (see photo 1). Press edges to seal patties (see photo 2).

■ Arrange patties in an 8x8x2-inch baking dish. Cover with waxed paper. Cook patties on high for 8 to 10 minutes or till no pink remains. After 4 minutes, drain off fat (see photo 3). At the same time, give the baking dish a half-turn and turn the patties over (see photo 4).

■ Drain patties on paper towels. If desired, serve burgers on hamburger buns with lettuce and tomato slices (see large photo). Makes 4 servings.

1

After spooning the hot rice filling onto the four meat patties, top with the remaining patties, as shown. The hot filling helps cook each burger's center quickly, before the outside overcooks.

2

Using your fingertips, press the edges of each stuffed burger to seal the filling inside. If not well sealed, the seams of the burger will split and the rice filling will leak during cooking.

3

To focus the microwaves on the meat, not on the juices, and to speed cooking, remove the juices with a baster or spoon as they collect during cooking.

4

Burgers cook more evenly if, during cooking, you give the baking dish a half-turn, then flip each patty over, as shown above. When they're done, serve the stuffed burgers with your favorite condiments, as shown at right.

The Better Burger

Vary the flavor by trying different salad dressing mixes.

1 beaten egg
¼ cup fine dry bread crumbs
¼ cup water
½ of a 0.7-ounce package
    (about 2½ teaspoons) dry
    Italian salad dressing mix
1 pound ground beef
4 hamburger buns, split
    Onion slices (optional)
    Tomato slices (optional)
    Lettuce leaves (optional)

■ In a medium mixing bowl combine egg, bread crumbs, water, and dry salad dressing mix. Add ground beef and mix well. Shape meat mixture into four ¾-inch-thick patties.

■ Arrange beef patties in an 8x8x2-inch baking dish. Cover with waxed paper. Cook on 100% power (high) for 6 to 8 minutes or till no pink remains. After 3 minutes, drain fat (see photo 3, page 161). At the same time, give the dish a half-turn and turn the meat patties over (see photo 4, page 161). Toast hamburger buns. Serve patties on buns with onion slices, tomato slices, and lettuce, if desired. Makes 4 servings.

Oriental Sloppy Joes

½ pound ground beef
¼ cup chopped onion
1 clove garlic, minced
1 16-ounce can chop suey
    vegetables
¼ teaspoon ground ginger
2 tablespoons cold water
2 tablespoons soy sauce
1 teaspoon cornstarch
4 hamburger buns, split,
    toasted, and buttered
4 green *or* red sweet pepper
    rings (optional)

■ In a 1-quart casserole crumble beef. Add onion and garlic. Cook, covered, on 100% power (high) for 2½ to 3½ minutes or till no pink remains and onion is tender, stirring once. Drain off fat.

■ Drain, rinse, and snip chop suey vegetables. Add vegetables and ginger to beef mixture. Combine water, soy sauce, and cornstarch. Stir into beef mixture. Cook, uncovered, on high for 3 to 5 minutes or till thickened and bubbly, stirring every minute till slightly thickened, then every 30 seconds. Serve beef-vegetable mixture in buttered hamburger buns with pepper rings, if desired. Makes 4 servings.

Low-wattage oven: For *beef-vegetable mixture,* cook for 7 to 9 minutes.

If your ground meat is frozen, thaw it in minutes. Heat 1 pound, covered, on 30% power (medium-low) for 7 to 8 minutes or till no longer icy. Break up the meat about halfway through the defrosting time, as shown. For more defrosting information, turn to page 170.

Peppery Tacos

For extra zip, drizzle tacos with hot-style taco sauce.

½ pound ground beef, pork,
    or raw turkey
⅓ cup sliced green onions
1 clove garlic, minced
¼ cup chili salsa
2 tablespoons chopped canned
    green chili peppers
⅛ teaspoon salt
    Several dashes bottled
      hot pepper sauce
6 taco shells
1½ cups finely shredded lettuce
1 cup shredded mozzarella *or*
    cheddar cheese (4 ounces)
1 medium tomato, seeded,
    chopped, and drained
    Taco sauce

■ In a 1-quart casserole crumble meat. Add green onions and garlic. Cook, covered, on 100% power (high) for 2½ to 3½ minutes or till no pink remains and onion is tender, stirring once. Drain off fat.

■ Stir chili salsa, chopped chili peppers, salt, hot pepper sauce, and ⅛ teaspoon *pepper* into meat mixture. Spoon about ¼ *cup* of the meat mixture into *each* taco shell.

■ Arrange tacos upright in an 8x8x2-inch baking dish. Cook, uncovered, on high about 1 minute or till hot. Top with shredded lettuce, mozzarella or cheddar cheese, and tomato. Pass taco sauce. Makes 3 servings.

Curried Lamb Sandwiches

Serve the lamb filling Middle Eastern-style in pita bread halves or American-style in hamburger buns.

1 pound ground lamb *or* beef
1 large onion, sliced and
    separated into rings
1 clove garlic, minced
2 apples, cored and finely
    chopped
¼ cup raisins
1 tablespoon water
1 to 2 teaspoons curry powder
2 tablespoons all-purpose
    flour
2 tablespoons snipped parsley
1 8-ounce carton plain yogurt
    or dairy sour cream
4 *or* 5 large pita bread rounds,
    halved crosswise, *or*
    hamburger buns, split
    Lettuce leaves *or* alfalfa
      sprouts
    Avocado slices (optional)
    Plain yogurt *or* dairy sour
      cream (optional)

■ In a 2-quart casserole crumble lamb or beef. Add onion and garlic. Cook, covered, on 100% power (high) for 4 to 6 minutes or till no pink remains and onion is tender, stirring once. Drain off fat.

■ Stir in chopped apples, raisins, water, curry powder, ¼ teaspoon *salt*, and ¼ teaspoon *pepper*. Cook, covered, on high for 2 to 3 minutes or till apples are crisp-tender.

■ Stir flour and parsley into yogurt or sour cream. Add to meat mixture. Cook, uncovered, on high for 2 to 3 minutes or till thickened and bubbly, stirring every 30 seconds. Cook for 30 seconds more.

■ To serve, line pita halves or hamburger buns with lettuce or sprouts. Spoon in the meat mixture. If desired, garnish with avocado slices and additional yogurt or sour cream. Makes 4 or 5 servings.

Low-wattage oven: For *apple mixture,* cook on high for 4½ to 5½ minutes. For *yogurt mixture,* cook on high for 4 to 5 minutes, stirring every minute.

Making a ground-meat casserole

Spaghetti Pie

1 pound ground beef
1 medium onion, chopped
(½ cup)
¼ cup chopped green pepper
1 clove garlic, minced
1 7½-ounce can tomatoes,
cut up
1 6-ounce can tomato paste
1 tablespoon all-purpose flour
1 teaspoon dried basil,
crushed
½ teaspoon fennel seed,
crushed
2 well-beaten eggs
⅓ cup grated Parmesan cheese
2 tablespoons butter *or*
margarine
3 cups hot cooked spaghetti
(6 ounces uncooked)
1 cup cream-style cottage
cheese, drained
½ cup shredded mozzarella
cheese (2 ounces)

■ In a 1½-quart casserole crumble beef. Add onion, green pepper, and garlic. Cook, covered, on 100% power (high) for 4 to 6 minutes or till no pink remains and vegetables are tender, stirring once. Drain off fat.

■ Stir in *undrained* tomatoes, tomato paste, flour, basil, and fennel seed (see photo 1). Cook, uncovered, on high for 6 to 8 minutes or till bubbly, stirring every 3 minutes. Cook for 1 minute more. Cover and set aside.

■ For crust, in a medium mixing bowl combine eggs, Parmesan cheese, and butter or margarine. Stir in hot cooked spaghetti. Turn the spaghetti mixture into a lightly greased 10-inch pie plate. Form the spaghetti mixture into a crust (see photo 2).

■ Cover the spaghetti crust with vented clear plastic wrap. Cook on 50% power (medium) for 5 to 7 minutes or till crust is just set, giving the dish a half-turn once.

■ Spread cottage cheese over the bottom of the spaghetti crust (see photo 3). Fill pie with meat mixture (see photo 4). Cover with vented clear plastic wrap. Cook on medium for 3 to 5 minutes or till heated through, giving the dish a half-turn once. Sprinkle with mozzarella cheese. Let stand for 5 minutes. Cut into wedges to serve (see large photo). Makes 6 servings.

Low-wattage oven: Not recommended.

1

Add the tomatoes, tomato paste, flour, basil, and fennel to the hot cooked meat and vegetables. Combining cold foods with hot foods shortens the cooking time.

2

It's easy to shape a pasta crust. With the back of a spoon, press the spaghetti-egg mixture evenly against the bottom and sides of a 10-inch pie plate.

3

When the spaghetti shell is just set, remove the cover and spread the drained cottage cheese evenly over the hot crust, as shown.

4

Fill the pasta pie with the hot tomato-meat mixture. Assembling the pie with as many warm ingredients as possible cuts the final heating time. Let the finished pie stand for 5 minutes so it can set and the cheese can melt. Cut the pie into wedges to serve.

Beef, Beans, and Dumplings

We've sprinkled the dumplings with Parmesan and parsley for color.

½ pound ground beef
½ pound bulk pork sausage
1 medium onion, chopped
   (½ cup)
1 clove garlic, minced
1 15½-ounce jar spaghetti
   sauce with mushrooms
1 15-ounce can pinto beans
⅓ cup beer *or* water
2 tablespoons canned chopped
   green chili peppers
¼ teaspoon pepper
1 package (6) refrigerated
   biscuits, quartered
2 tablespoons grated
   Parmesan cheese
2 tablespoons snipped parsley

■ In a 2-quart casserole crumble ground beef and sausage. Add onion and garlic. Cook, covered, on 100% power (high) for 4 to 6 minutes or till no pink remains and onion is tender, stirring once. Drain off fat.

■ Stir in spaghetti sauce, *undrained* pinto beans, beer or water, green chili peppers, and pepper. Cook, covered, on high for 7 to 9 minutes or till heated through, stirring once.

■ For dumplings, arrange biscuit pieces around the outer edges of the casserole, leaving the center open. Sprinkle biscuits with Parmesan cheese and parsley. Cook, uncovered, on high for 2 to 3 minutes or till biscuits are done, giving the dish a half-turn after 1½ minutes. Serve in bowls. Makes 6 servings.

Ranch-Style Meatball Bake

1 beaten egg
½ cup instant mashed potato
   flakes
¼ cup bottled barbecue sauce
1 teaspoon minced dried onion
   Several dashes bottled hot
   pepper sauce
1 pound ground beef
1 16-ounce can tomatoes,
   cut up
1 15-ounce can pinto beans
⅓ cup bottled barbecue sauce
1 teaspoon chili powder
   Corn bread *or* hot cooked
   rice
½ cup shredded smoked
   cheddar cheese *or* cheddar
   cheese (2 ounces)

■ In a medium mixing bowl combine egg, potato flakes, ¼ cup barbecue sauce, dried onion, and bottled hot pepper sauce. Add meat and mix well. Shape into 24 meatballs (see photo 1, page 27).

■ Arrange meatballs in an 8x8x2-inch baking dish. Cover with waxed paper. Cook on 100% power (high) for 5 to 7 minutes or till no pink remains, rearranging and turning meatballs over once (see photo 3, page 27). Drain meatballs on paper towels (see photo 4, page 27).

■ In a 2-quart casserole stir together *undrained* tomatoes, *undrained* pinto beans, ⅓ cup barbecue sauce, and chili powder. Cook, uncovered, on high for 9 to 11 minutes or till bubbly, stirring once.

■ Stir in meatballs. Cook, uncovered, on high for 5 to 7 minutes or till heated through. Serve over corn bread or rice. Sprinkle each serving with cheese. Makes 6 servings.

Zucchini and Pork Casserole

A meal of its own, except for dessert.

¾ pound ground pork *or* beef
1 medium onion, chopped
(½ cup)
1 medium zucchini, halved
lengthwise and sliced
¼ inch thick
1 tablespoon all-purpose flour
½ teaspoon dried oregano,
crushed
¼ teaspoon ground allspice
¼ teaspoon pepper
1 8-ounce can tomato sauce
1 8-ounce can whole kernel
corn, drained
½ cup shredded cheddar
cheese (2 ounces)

■ In a 1½-quart casserole crumble meat. Add onion and cook, covered, on 100% power (high) for 4 to 6 minutes or till no pink remains and onion is tender, stirring once. Add zucchini slices and cook, covered, for 2 to 4 minutes more or till zucchini is crisp-tender, stirring once. Drain.

■ Stir flour, oregano, allspice, and pepper into tomato sauce. Stir tomato sauce mixture and corn into meat-zucchini mixture. Cook, covered, on high for 5 to 7 minutes or till thickened and bubbly, stirring every 2 minutes. Sprinkle with shredded cheddar cheese. Makes 4 servings.

Cheesy Broccoli-and-Beef Bake

⅔ cup elbow macaroni
½ pound ground beef
1 medium onion, chopped
(½ cup)
1 clove garlic, minced
1 15½-ounce jar spaghetti
sauce
½ teaspoon dried oregano,
crushed
¼ teaspoon pepper
1 cup shredded Monterey
Jack cheese (4 ounces)
1 10-ounce package frozen
cut broccoli, thawed
and drained

■ Cook macaroni according to package directions. Drain and set aside.

■ Meanwhile, in a 2-quart casserole crumble beef. Add onion and garlic. Cook, covered, on 100% power (high) for 2½ to 3½ minutes or till no pink remains and onion is tender, stirring once. Drain off fat.

■ Stir in spaghetti sauce, oregano, and pepper. Set aside *¼ cup* of the shredded cheese for the top of the casserole. Stir remaining cheese, drained macaroni, and cut broccoli into meat mixture.

■ Cover and cook on high for 8 to 10 minutes or till heated through, stirring once. Top with reserved cheese and let stand till cheese is melted. Makes 4 servings.

Mexican-Style Manicotti

Mexican-Style Manicotti

Cook the beef filling in your microwave while the manicotti shells simmer on the stove.

6 manicotti shells
½ pound lean ground beef
¾ cup refried beans
½ cup finely chopped celery
½ teaspoon ground cumin
1 12-ounce can whole kernel corn with sweet peppers, drained
1 8-ounce bottle picante sauce
½ cup dairy sour cream
¼ cup sliced green onions
¼ cup chopped pitted ripe olives
¼ cup chopped tomato

■ Cook manicotti shells according to package directions. Drain.

■ Meanwhile, in a 1½-quart casserole crumble ground beef. Cook, covered, on 100% power (high) for 2½ to 3½ minutes or till no pink remains. Drain off fat. Stir in refried beans, celery, and cumin. Fill cooked manicotti shells with meat mixture.

■ Arrange the stuffed shells in a 10x6x2-inch baking dish. Pour corn and picante sauce over shells. Cover with vented clear plastic wrap. Cook the stuffed shells on high for 8 to 10 minutes or till mixture is heated through, giving the dish a half-turn once.

■ Spoon sour cream over casserole. Sprinkle with green onions, ripe olives, and chopped tomato. Makes 3 servings.

Low-wattage oven: For *stuffed shells,* cook on high about 15 minutes, giving the dish a half-turn twice.

Saucy Sausage And Noodles

3 ounces medium noodles
1 pound bulk pork sausage
1 medium onion, chopped (½ cup)
1 10¾-ounce can condensed cream of celery soup
½ cup plain yogurt
½ cup milk
1 2½-ounce jar sliced mushrooms, drained
¼ teaspoon dried basil, crushed
1 10-ounce package frozen mixed vegetables, thawed and drained
1 3-ounce can french-fried onions

■ Cook noodles according to package directions, *except* omit salt. Drain the noodles.

■ Meanwhile, in a 2-quart casserole crumble sausage. Add onion and cook, covered, on 100% power (high) for 6 to 8 minutes or till no pink remains and onion is tender, stirring once. Drain off fat.

■ In a medium mixing bowl stir together condensed soup, yogurt, milk, mushrooms, and basil. Stir into sausage mixture. Stir in drained noodles and mixed vegetables.

■ Cook, covered, on high for 10 to 12 minutes or till heated through, stirring every 3 minutes. Top with french-fried onions and cook for 1 minute more. Makes 6 servings.

Defrosting Meat

Forget to take meat out of the freezer for dinner? Never fear, your microwave oven is here! It makes short work of thawing meat.

Place unwrapped frozen meat in a casserole or baking dish. Cover with the lid or vented heavy-duty clear plastic wrap. Micro-cook on 30% power (medium-low) for the time specified at right.

After *half* of the defrosting time, turn over large pieces of meat or stir meatballs or cubes, separating pieces. Stir ground meats twice. If some parts of steaks or roasts are thawing faster than others, shield the thawed portions with small pieces of foil. (Check your owner's manual to see if you can use foil in your microwave oven.)

When thawed, the meat should yield to moderate pressure applied with a fork. The center should be slightly icy, but not hard, and the edges uncooked.

Let meat stand, covered, to finish defrosting. Allow 10 minutes for roasts and 5 minutes for steaks, chops, and burgers. Loose ground meat, meatballs, and cubed meat do not need to stand.

Meat	Cut	Time per pound
Beef	Roasts	5 to 6 minutes
	Steaks	7 to 8 minutes
	¾-inch cubes	5 to 6 minutes
	Ribs	6 to 7 minutes
	Ground	7 to 8 minutes
	¾-inch-thick patties	6 to 7 minutes
	Meatballs	7 to 8 minutes
Pork	Roasts	7 to 8 minutes
	Steaks and chops	7 to 8 minutes
	¾-inch cubes	6 to 7 minutes
	Ribs	6 to 7 minutes
	Bacon, sliced	3 to 4 minutes
	Bulk sausages	6 to 7 minutes
	Ground	7 to 8 minutes
	¾-inch-thick patties	6 to 7 minutes
	Meatballs	7 to 8 minutes
	Frankfurters	4 to 5 minutes
Lamb	Roasts	5 to 6 minutes
	Chops	7 to 8 minutes
	¾-inch cubes	5 to 6 minutes
	Riblets	6 to 7 minutes
	Ground	7 to 8 minutes
	¾-inch-thick patties	6 to 7 minutes
	Meatballs	7 to 8 minutes

Cooking Meat

To cook **lamb** and **veal,** preheat a 10-inch microwave browning dish on 100% power (high) for 5 minutes. Trim fat from lamb chops. Pound veal between two pieces of clear plastic wrap till ¼ inch thick. Add 1 tablespoon cooking oil to browning dish. Swirl to coat dish. Cook, covered, on high for the time specified or till tender, turning meat over once.

Meat	Amount	Cooking time
Veal round steak	Four 4-ounce pieces	3 to 5 minutes
Lamb chops	Four 3-ounce chops	3 to 5 minutes

For **beef, pork,** or **lamb cubes,** cut meat into ¾-inch cubes. Place in a 1½-quart casserole. (Add ½ cup water to the beef.) Cover and cook on the suggested power level for the cooking time specified or till tender and no pink remains, stirring every 10 minutes (stirring every 5 minutes for lamb and pork).

Meat	Amount	Power	Cooking time
Beef stew meat*	1 pound	100% (high)	5 minutes
		50% (medium)	40 minutes
Lamb cubes*	1 pound	100% (high)	5 minutes
		50% (medium)	3 to 5 minutes
Pork cubes*	1 pound	50% (medium)	10 to 15 minutes

To heat boneless **ham** that's fully cooked, place the meat in an 8x8x2-inch baking dish. (Add ½ cup water to canned ham.) Cover with waxed paper. Cook on the suggested power level for the cooking time specified or till heated through, turning meat occasionally. If necessary, shield any parts that are overcooking with small pieces of foil. (Check your owner's manual to see if you can use foil in your microwave oven.)

Meat	Amount	Power	Cooking time
1-inch sliced ham	One 2-pound	100% (high)	8 to 10 minutes
Canned ham*	One 3-pound	100% (high)	5 minutes
		50% (medium)	40 to 50 minutes
	One 5-pound	100% (high)	7 minutes
		50% (medium)	50 to 60 minutes

For **bacon,** place on a rack or paper plate. Cover with microwave-safe paper towels. Cook on 100% power (high) for time specified or till done.

Meat	Amount	Cooking time
Bacon	2 slices	1½ to 2 minutes
	4 slices	2½ to 3½ minutes
	6 slices	4 to 5 minutes

*Note: Timings are for 600- to 700-watt microwave ovens and may be longer in low-wattage ovens.

Cooking Meat *(continued)*

Here are the basics for **meat loaf, burgers,** or **meatballs.** Combine 1 beaten egg, ¼ cup fine dry bread crumbs, ¼ cup milk, and desired seasonings. Add 1 pound ground beef and mix well. Shape as indicated.

Arrange shaped meat in an 8x8x2-inch baking dish. Cover with waxed paper. Cook on 100% power (high) for the time specified or till no pink remains, giving the dish a half-turn and turning patties or meatballs over once.

Meat	Amount	Cooking time
Meat ring	One 6-inch	6 to 8 minutes
Patties	Four ¾-inch-thick	6 to 8 minutes
Meatballs	Twenty-four 1-inch	4 to 6 minutes

For **ground meat,** crumble meat in a 1½-quart casserole. Cover and cook on 100% power (high) for the time specified or till no pink remains, stirring once or twice. Drain off fat.

Meat	Amount	Cooking time
Ground beef	1 pound	4 to 6 minutes
Ground pork	1 pound	6 to 8 minutes

To heat **frankfurters,** arrange them in an 8x8x2-inch baking dish. Cover with waxed paper. Cook on 100% power (high) for time specified or till heated through.

Meat	Amount	Cooking time
Frankfurters	1 link	15 to 30 seconds
	2 links	30 to 60 seconds

Nutrition Analysis

	Number of servings	Per Serving						Percent U.S. RDA Per Serving							
		Calories	Protein (g)	Carbohydrate (g)	Fat (g)	Sodium (mg)	Potassium (mg)	Protein	Vitamin A	Vitamin C	Thiamine	Riboflavin	Niacin	Calcium	Iron
Apricot Meat Ring (p. 156)	4	306	27	22	12	402	446	41	20	31	9	17	28	6	22
Beef and Pea Pod Stir-Fry (p. 152)	4	177	19	11	7	818	378	29	5	24	8	11	20	4	16
Beef, Beans, and Dumplings (p. 166)	6	354	20	40	12	1179	400	31	3	13	23	15	21	10	22
Beef Roast with Dill Sauce (p. 142)	8	229	25	8	11	281	360	38	9	36	6	15	18	6	18
Better Burger, The (p. 162)	4	362	29	29	14	921	348	45	2	1	18	21	34	7	26
Cheesy Broccoli-and-Beef Bake (p. 167)	4	399	26	36	16	936	376	40	30	56	18	21	21	30	21
Citrus-Stuffed Pork Chops (p. 148)	2	551	50	17	31	249	794	77	1	43	71	34	53	4	14
Corned Beef 'n' Kraut Wedges (p. 158)	8	261	26	8	13	807	304	41	3	10	7	19	22	9	23
Country-Apple Pot Roast (p. 144)	10	240	22	21	7	109	418	34	47	10	6	11	21	3	18
Curried Lamb Sandwiches (p. 163)	4	490	29	73	10	85	553	45	5	21	28	24	25	20	23
Dilled Ham and Spinach (p. 155)	2	401	29	17	24	1450	754	45	187	46	52	30	22	36	24
Fruit and Veal Sauté (p. 145)	4	300	22	20	15	139	357	34	0	5	5	14	23	2	16
Ham-Stuffed Peppers (p. 155)	4	237	16	19	11	596	447	25	22	133	27	13	13	22	10
Herbed Bulgur Meat Ring (p. 158)	4	266	26	13	11	395	350	41	20	5	9	16	29	4	24
Herbed Lamb Kabobs (p. 154)	4	156	19	2	7	85	294	30	3	56	9	13	21	1	10
Italian-Style Pot Roast (p. 145)	8	251	24	8	12	367	301	36	65	8	5	14	21	3	20
Mediterranean Meatballs (p. 159)	3	451	31	42	17	684	776	47	28	28	21	20	38	8	32
Mexican Beef Salad (p. 154)	4	335	22	18	20	872	517	34	22	68	14	18	21	16	24
Mexican-Style Manicotti (p. 169)	3	543	27	29	20	1401	954	42	28	20	33	26	33	14	29
Orange-Ginger Spareribs (p. 146)	4	651	41	30	41	1168	501	63	1	0	37	32	40	7	17
Oriental Sloppy Joes (p. 162)	4	250	18	28	7	983	322	27	1	2	14	17	59	4	18
Peach-Glazed Ham Slice (p. 151)	6	197	24	10	6	1367	377	37	4	46	57	14	24	1	10
Peanutty Rice-Stuffed Burgers (p. 160)	4	347	32	12	19	456	499	49	37	39	12	22	33	19	28
Peppery Tacos (p. 163)	3	575	31	45	31	893	544	48	18	32	18	25	25	39	24
Peppy Barbecue-Style Pork Ribs (p. 148)	4	841	55	27	56	820	1198	85	22	11	53	44	57	11	27
Pineapple-Cashew Lamb Chops (p. 151)	4	291	22	32	8	304	360	33	1	8	18	13	26	3	14
Ranch-Style Meatball Bake (p. 166)	6	284	24	21	11	416	640	37	24	19	11	15	24	11	23
Saucy Sausage and Noodles (p. 169)	6	374	14	29	23	1005	427	22	49	11	31	17	17	11	10
Sauerbraten-Style Meatballs (p. 159)	6	239	19	22	8	506	783	29	18	64	10	14	24	7	20
Spaghetti Pie (p. 164)	6	423	32	33	18	676	677	50	34	34	27	27	32	21	26
Tomato-Topped Pork Chops (p. 149)	2	469	49	4	27	439	765	76	13	15	69	32	52	3	14
Zucchini and Pork Casserole (p. 167)	4	298	27	16	14	516	692	41	20	17	33	21	29	14	11

PIES

If you love pie—whether lemon meringue or pecan—you'll find your microwave oven to be a cool alternative to conventional baking. But before you start rolling the crust, you'll need to know some of our special microwave-pie tricks.

First comes the shell
Our Test Kitchen found micro-cooked pastry is less flaky than conventionally cooked pastry. So, to lighten our recipe, we added baking powder.

Like conventional pastry, microwave pastry has a tendency to bubble. Pricking the shell with a fork before cooking lets the steam escape.

For crisp pastry, we recommend cooking the filling separately, then pouring it into a cooled, baked pie shell. One exception is our Maple-Pecan Pie, where the nutty filling is baked in the cooked shell. We also leave that shell unpricked so the filling won't run through the holes and make the crust soggy.

Remember, a microwave piecrust is done when the surface is dry and bubbly from tiny air bubbles, not when it's brown. Sometimes brown spots appear in the crust before it is done. If that happens, turn the pie plate more often and shield the spots with small pieces of foil. (First, check your owner's manual to see if you can use foil or metal in your microwave oven.)

Choose-a-Fruit Pie
(see recipe, page 178)

Mix-and-match shells and fillings

Because micro-cooked pastry does not brown, we've created a variety of colorful flavored crusts. Choose from whole wheat, coffee, pecan, spice, lemon, cheddar, or chocolate. Then mix and match the crusts with different fillings.

Pie toppings

As you might have guessed, double-crust pies don't crisp in the microwave oven's moist heat. So we've come up with lots of ways to add a top crust of sorts to one-crust pies. Try sprinkling them with streusel toppings or dolloping them with whipped cream, meringue, or ice cream.

Lemon Meringue Pie
(see recipe, page 179)

175

Preparing a pie pastry

Pastry for One-Crust Pie

The pie plate gets hot, so keep your pot holders nearby.

1¼ cups all-purpose flour
¼ teaspoon baking powder
¼ teaspoon salt
⅓ cup shortening
1 tablespoon butter *or* margarine
3 to 4 tablespoons cold water

■ In a mixing bowl stir together flour, baking powder, and salt. Cut in shortening and butter or margarine till pieces are the size of small peas. Sprinkle *1 tablespoon* of the water over part of the mixture. Toss with a fork. Push to side of bowl. Repeat till all is moistened. Form into a ball.

■ On a lightly floured surface flatten dough. Roll dough from center to edges, forming a circle 12 inches in diameter. Transfer and fit pastry into a 9-inch pie plate (see photo 1). *Do not stretch pastry.* Trim ½ inch beyond edges. Fold under and flute edges (see photo 2).

■ Prick pastry at ½-inch intervals with a fork. Prick continuously at bottom bend of dish (see photo 3). Cook, uncovered, on 100% power (high) for 5 to 7 minutes or till dry and air bubbles form, giving dish a quarter-turn once. Cool on a rack (see photo 4). Makes one 9-inch shell.

Low-wattage oven: Cook 8 minutes, giving dish a quarter-turn twice.

Coffee Pastry: Prepare Pastry for One-Crust Pie as above, *except* dissolve 1 teaspoon instant *coffee crystals* in the cold water.

Whole Wheat Pastry: Prepare Pastry for One-Crust Pie as above, *except* reduce flour to ¾ cup. Add ½ cup *whole wheat flour*.

Lemon Pastry: Prepare Pastry for One-Crust Pie as above, *except* add 1 tablespoon *sugar* and ½ teaspoon finely shredded *lemon peel* to flour. Substitute 1 tablespoon *lemon juice* for 1 tablespoon water.

Pecan Pastry: Prepare Pastry for One-Crust Pie as above, *except* add ¼ cup ground *pecans* after cutting in shortening and butter.

Cheddar Pastry: Prepare Pastry for One-Crust Pie as above, *except* add ½ cup shredded *cheddar cheese* after cutting in butter.

Spiced Pastry: Prepare Pastry for One-Crust Pie as above, *except* add 1 tablespoon *sugar*, 1 teaspoon ground *cinnamon*, and ¼ teaspoon ground *nutmeg* to the flour mixture.

Chocolate Pastry: Prepare Pastry for One-Crust Pie as above, *except* add 2 tablespoons *sugar* and 2 tablespoons *unsweetened cocoa powder* to the flour mixture.

1

Roll dough on a lightly floured surface, forming a circle 12 inches in diameter. To transfer, gently wrap the dough around a rolling pin. If you're using a pastry cloth, lift the dough with the cloth, as shown. Unroll the pastry over the pie plate and ease it into the pie plate, being careful not to stretch or tear the pastry.

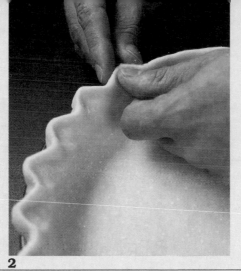

2

Trim the pastry to ½ inch beyond the rim. Fold under the edge. Pinch the dough with the thumb of one hand against the thumb and forefinger of your other hand to form a high fluted edge, as shown. Hook the edges over the rim of the plate to keep the pastry in place during cooking.

3

Prick the bottom and sides of the shell with a fork at ½-inch intervals. Then prick continuously around the bend at the bottom of the plate, as shown. This lets the steam escape during cooking so the pastry won't puff.

4

The crust is done when the surface is dry and the texture is slightly bumpy from tiny air bubbles. When done, cool the shell on a wire rack, as shown above. With nothing added, microwave plain pastry looks paler than conventional. But add different flavors and you'll get different colors, as shown right.

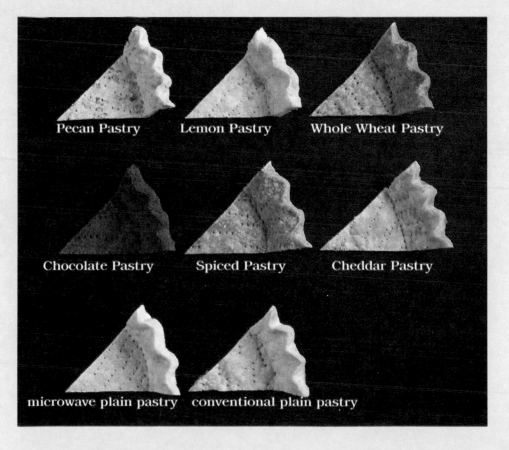

Pecan Pastry   Lemon Pastry   Whole Wheat Pastry

Chocolate Pastry   Spiced Pastry   Cheddar Pastry

microwave plain pastry   conventional plain pastry

Choose-a-Fruit Pie

The cherry version is pictured on pages 174–175.

Pastry for One-Crust Pie
(see recipe, page 176)
Desired fruit filling* *or* one
21-ounce can pie filling
¼ cup all-purpose flour
¼ cup quick-cooking rolled
oats
3 tablespoons brown sugar
½ teaspoon ground cinnamon
⅛ teaspoon ground ginger
⅛ teaspoon ground nutmeg
3 tablespoons butter *or*
margarine

■ For pastry, refer to photos, page 177. Set aside. Cook desired filling as directed below. (Or, in a 2-cup measure cook canned filling, uncovered, on 100% power [high] 4 to 5 minutes or till bubbly, stirring once.)

■ For topping, stir together flour, oats, brown sugar, cinnamon, ginger, and nutmeg. Cut in butter or margarine till crumbly. Turn hot filling into cooled crust. Sprinkle with topping. Cook, uncovered, on high for 2 to 3 minutes or till topping looks set and filling is bubbly. Cool on a wire rack. Serve warm or cool. Makes 8 servings.

*Fruit filling: Choose from 6 cups peeled, cored, and thinly sliced fresh *apples or pears;* 5 cups peeled, pitted, and sliced fresh *peaches or apricots, or* sliced *rhubarb;* 4 cups fresh *or* frozen pitted tart *red cherries,* frozen unsweetened *blueberries, boysenberries, or blackberries, or* frozen lightly sweetened *raspberries.*

In a 2-quart casserole combine ⅔ cup *sugar* (1 cup for rhubarb or cherries) and 3 tablespoons *cornstarch.* Stir in desired fruit and 1 tablespoon *lemon juice* (omit juice for rhubarb or cherries). Cook, covered, on high till fruit is tender and mixture is bubbly, stirring every 2 minutes till slightly thickened, then every minute. Allow 5 to 7 minutes for apples, peaches, and apricots; 8 to 10 minutes for pears and berries; 10 to 13 minutes for rhubarb and cherries.

Note: Timings for fruit fillings are for 625- to 700-watt microwave ovens and may be longer in low-wattage ovens.

Peach Glacé Pie

Crumb Crust (see recipe,
page 182)
4 cups sliced peaches
or nectarines
1 tablespoon lemon juice
⅓ cup sugar
2 tablespoons cornstarch
⅛ teaspoon ground ginger
1 cup orange juice
½ cup water
Whipped cream *or* ice
cream (optional)

■ Prepare crust. Set aside. Toss fruit with lemon juice to prevent cut edges from darkening. Set aside.

■ In a 4-cup measure combine sugar, cornstarch, and ginger. Stir in orange juice and water. Cook, uncovered, on 100% power (high) for 4 to 6 minutes or till thickened and bubbly, stirring every minute. Cook, uncovered, for 30 seconds more. Cool slightly, about 5 minutes. Arrange about *half* of the fruit in the chilled crust. Spoon about *half* of the thickened mixture on top. Add remaining fruit and thickened mixture. Chill for at least 2 hours but not more than 24 hours. Before serving, set pie plate on a hot, damp towel to loosen crust. If desired, serve with whipped cream or ice cream. Makes 8 servings.

Lemon Meringue Pie

Pictured on pages 174–175.

Pecan Pastry for One-
  Crust Pie (see recipe,
  page 176)
1½ cups sugar
  3 tablespoons all-purpose
    flour
  3 tablespoons cornstarch
1½ cups water
  2 egg yolks
  2 tablespoons butter *or*
    margarine
  1 teaspoon finely shredded
    lemon *or* lime peel
⅓ cup lemon *or* lime juice
  Meringue Topping

Meringue Topping: In a
small mixer bowl combine
2 *egg whites,* ½ teaspoon
vanilla, and ⅛ teaspoon
cream of tartar. Beat with an
electric mixer on medium
speed till soft peaks form
(tips curl). Add ¼ cup *sugar,*
1 tablespoon at a time,
beating on high speed till stiff
glossy peaks form (tips stand
straight) and sugar is
dissolved.

■ For pastry, refer to photos, page 177. Set aside. For filling, in a 2-quart casserole combine sugar, flour, and cornstarch. Stir in water. Cook, uncovered, on 100% power (high) for 4 to 6 minutes or till mixture begins to bubble on edges, stirring every 2 minutes. Cook for 2 to 4 minutes more or till thickened and bubbly over entire surface, stirring every minute. Cook for 1 minute more.

■ Beat yolks slightly. Gradually stir *1 cup* of the hot mixture into yolks (see photo 2, page 217). Return yolk mixture to the casserole. Cook, uncovered, on high for 2 to 3 minutes or till bubbly around the edges, stirring once. Add butter or margarine, stirring just till melted. Gently stir in lemon or lime peel and juice. Set aside.

■ Prepare Meringue Topping. Pour hot filling into cooled pastry shell. Dollop meringue into 8 mounds around edges (see photo 1, below). Cook, uncovered, on high 1½ to 2½ minutes or till knife inserted into meringue comes out clean (see photo 2, below), giving the dish a half-turn once. Cool on a wire rack. Makes 8 servings.

Low-wattage oven: For *filling* to bubble on edges, cook on high for 8 to 10 minutes, stirring every 2 minutes. Continue cooking till thickened and bubbly over entire surface, stirring every minute.

1

Dollop mounds of meringue into a ring around the edges of the pie, leaving the center open so the meringue will cook evenly.

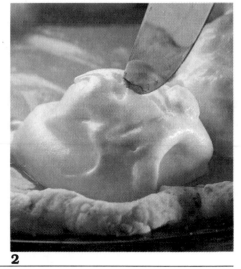

2

To test for doneness, insert a knife into the center of a mound. The knife will come out clean if the meringue is done.

Cooking an unpricked crust

Maple-Pecan Pie

Add the pecan halves to the filling before the last minute of cooking.

Pecan Pastry for One-Crust
  Pie (see recipe, page 176)
1½ cups dry beans *or* long
  grain rice
¼ cup butter *or* margarine
3 eggs
¾ cup packed brown sugar
½ cup light corn syrup
¼ cup maple syrup *or*
  maple-flavored syrup
1 cup toasted pecan halves

■ For pastry, refer to photos, page 177. *Do not prick or cook.* Line unpricked, uncooked crust with cheesecloth, then top with beans or rice (see photo 1, opposite). Tie corners to form a bag. Cook, uncovered, on 100% power (high) for 4 minutes, giving the dish a quarter-turn twice. Remove cheesecloth and beans. Cook, uncovered, on high for 1 to 2 minutes or till surface is dry and bubbles form. Cool on a wire rack.

■ In a 1-cup measure cook butter or margarine, uncovered, on high for 45 to 60 seconds or till melted. Beat eggs till well mixed. Gradually stir butter or margarine into eggs. Add sugar, corn syrup, and maple syrup or maple-flavored syrup. Mix well.

■ Reserve *2 tablespoons* of the mixture. Turn remaining mixture into crust (see photo 2, opposite). Cook, uncovered, on 50% power (medium) for 11 to 14 minutes or till set halfway to center, giving the dish a quarter-turn every 4 minutes. Sprinkle pecans on top (see photo 3, opposite). Pour reserved mixture over nuts (see photo 4, opposite). Cook, uncovered, on 100% power (high) about 1 minute or till pie bubbles from the edges to about 2 inches from the center. Cool the pie on a wire rack. Serve cool (see large photo, opposite). Makes 10 servings.

Low-wattage oven: For *pie before adding nuts,* cook on high 8 minutes.

TIP **Thawing Frozen Whipped Topping**

Did you forget to thaw the frozen whipped dessert topping for your cream or fruit pie? Don't worry, your microwave will thaw it quickly. Place the container of frozen topping in your microwave oven. Cook, uncovered, on 30% power (medium-low) till softened. Allow 45 to 60 seconds for a 4-ounce container and 1 to 1½ minutes for an 8-ounce container.

1
Leave the shell unpricked. Line the uncooked shell with 4 thicknesses of 16-inch-square cheesecloth. Top with dry beans or rice. Tie the corners of the cheesecloth together to make a bag. Keep the beans or rice evenly distributed. The weight keeps the crust from shrinking and prevents large bubbles from forming.

2
Measure 2 tablespoons of the syrup mixture and set aside. Pour the remaining mixture into the cooled pie shell.

3
Cook on medium power until the filling is set halfway to the center. (Jiggle the pie plate to see if the filling is set.) Sprinkle the toasted pecans over the top.

4
Pour the reserved 2 tablespoons of syrup mixture over the pecan halves, as shown. Cook for 1 minute more or until the filling bubbles from the edges to about 2 inches from the center.

Layered Cream-and-Pumpkin Pie

For a cream pie, fill our Crumb Crust with one of our Vanilla Pudding flavors (page 216) or a prepared 6-serving-size package of pudding mix.

Crumb Crust
½ cup milk
1 envelope unflavored gelatin
3 egg yolks
⅓ cup sugar
1¼ cups canned pumpkin
½ teaspoon ground cinnamon
¼ teaspoon ground ginger
¼ teaspoon ground nutmeg
3 egg whites
¼ cup sugar
1 cup whipping cream
½ teaspoon vanilla

■ Prepare Crumb Crust as directed below and chill. In a medium microwave-safe mixing bowl combine milk and gelatin. Let stand for 5 minutes to soften gelatin.

■ Meanwhile, in a small mixer bowl beat egg yolks with an electric mixer on high speed about 4 minutes or till thick and lemon colored. Gradually beat in ⅓ cup sugar. Set aside. Wash beaters.

■ Cook gelatin mixture, uncovered, on 100% power (high) for 50 to 60 seconds or till gelatin is dissolved (*do not boil*), stirring after 30 seconds. Gradually stir gelatin mixture into yolk mixture. Return to the bowl.

■ Cook, uncovered, on high for 1½ to 2½ minutes or till slightly thickened and hot, stirring every 30 seconds. Stir in pumpkin, cinnamon, ginger, and nutmeg. Chill for 45 minutes to 1 hour or till mixture is the consistency of corn syrup, stirring occasionally.

■ Remove pumpkin mixture from refrigerator. Immediately beat egg whites in a large mixer bowl with an electric mixer on medium speed till soft peaks form (tips curl). Gradually add ¼ cup sugar, beating till stiff peaks form (tips stand straight). When pumpkin mixture is partially set (consistency of unbeaten egg whites), fold the mixture into egg whites.

■ In a small mixer bowl combine *½ cup* of the whipping cream and vanilla. Beat till soft peaks form. Spoon *half* of the pumpkin mixture into crust, then spoon the whipped cream evenly over the pumpkin layer. Top with remaining pumpkin mixture. Chill about 6 hours or till firm.

■ Before serving, set pie plate on a hot, damp towel to loosen crust. Beat remaining whipping cream till soft peaks form, then dollop atop pie. Makes 8 servings.

Low-wattage oven: For *gelatin mixture,* cook on high for 1½ to 2 minutes or till gelatin is dissolved (*do not boil*), stirring every 30 seconds.

Crumb Crust: In a mixing bowl combine 1¼ cups finely crushed *graham crackers* and ¼ cup *sugar*. Stir in 6 tablespoons melted *butter or margarine* and toss to thoroughly combine. Turn into a 9-inch pie plate and spread evenly. Press on bottom and sides to form a firm, even crust. Chill about 1 hour or till firm before filling.

Cooking Convenience Piecrusts

Prepare pastry according to directions. Place in a 9-inch pie plate and flute edges. Prick generously with a fork. Cook, uncovered, on 100% power (high) for specified time, giving the dish a quarter-turn every 2 minutes. Cool on a wire rack.

Pastry	Cooking time
Folded refrigerated unbaked piecrust	5 to 6 minutes
Pie pastry from stick or mix	7 to 9 minutes

Nutrition Analysis

	Number of servings	Per Serving						Percent U.S. RDA Per Serving							
		Calories	Protein (g)	Carbohydrate (g)	Fat (g)	Sodium (mg)	Potassium (mg)	Protein	Vitamin A	Vitamin C	Thiamine	Riboflavin	Niacin	Calcium	Iron
Cheddar Pastry (p. 176)	8	186	4	15	12	135	26	6	3	0	8	6	5	6	5
Chocolate Pastry (p. 176)	8	173	2	19	10	101	28	4	1	0	8	5	5	1	6
Choose-a-Fruit Pie (p. 178)	8	361	3	56	15	137	148	5	5	4	12	6	7	2	8
Coffee Pastry (p. 176)	8	157	2	15	10	91	19	3	1	0	8	4	5	1	5
Layered Cream-and-Pumpkin Pie (p. 182)	8	365	6	35	24	306	214	9	66	4	3	13	4	7	6
Lemon Meringue Pie (p. 179)	8	421	4	65	17	136	75	7	5	6	12	8	6	2	8
Lemon Pastry (p. 176)	8	165	2	17	10	91	21	3	1	0	8	5	5	1	5
Maple-Pecan Pie (p. 180)	10	421	5	49	24	158	196	7	6	0	15	8	5	6	15
Pastry for One-Crust Pie (p. 176)	8	157	2	15	10	91	19	3	1	0	8	4	5	1	5
Peach Glacé Pie (p. 178)	8	224	2	34	10	177	202	3	12	26	3	6	5	1	3
Pecan Pastry (p. 176)	8	183	2	15	13	91	41	4	1	0	10	5	5	1	5
Spiced Pastry (p. 176)	8	165	2	17	10	91	21	3	1	0	8	5	5	1	5
Whole Wheat Pastry (p. 176)	8	154	2	14	10	91	39	3	1	0	8	3	5	1	4

POULTRY

Match poultry with the microwave oven and you've got an unbeatable team. Whether whole or cut up, birds attract microwaves for extra fast and flavorful cooking. On the next few pages, we'll show you everything that you need to know about micro-cooking poultry—whether you're defrosting a turkey, cooking a Cornish hen, or poaching a chicken breast.

Cooking whole birds

In recipe testing, we looked for ways to make poultry as succulent as possible. For the best quality, we recommend micro-cooking only birds under 6 pounds. We found larger birds cooked unevenly, drying out in some areas while undercooking in others.

We also noticed that the weight and size of birds affect the cooking times, so make sure your bird fits within the weight range given in our recipes. If your bird is on the light side, expect the timing to be shorter. If it's heavier, look to the longer cooking time.

We feel medium power gives the juiciest, tenderest, and most evenly cooked birds. Cornish hens are the exception; they're small enough to cook on high. With all birds, if the wing tips and legs start cooking before the rest, shield them with foil. (Check your owner's manual about using metal in your oven.)

As the poultry juices collect during cooking, spoon them off. Otherwise, they'll draw microwaves away from the bird and lengthen the cooking time.

Is it done?

Because microwaves cook in an uneven pattern, check the bird in several places to be sure it is thoroughly done. The drumstick should move easily in its socket and the juices should run clear. If you're using a temperature probe, it should register between 180° and 185°. Just as in conventional cooking, let whole birds stand a few minutes for easier carving.

Pineapple-Stuffed Cornish Hen
(see recipe, page 188)

Cooking poultry parts

You'll need to use a few different techniques when you're cooking parts instead of a whole bird. First, make sure the parts fit into the baking dish and that the dish fits into the microwave oven. The pieces should lie in a single layer with meaty sides toward the edges of the dish.

For even cooking, leave a little space between the pieces. If the dish is too crowded, leave out the neck, back, or wings.

Cover the poultry parts during cooking so fat won't spatter. For unskinned pieces, use waxed paper; it will prevent the skin from stewing. For skinned pieces, use a lid or vented clear plastic wrap to keep the skinless surfaces from drying.

Because microwaves penetrate poultry parts easily, cook them on high power. When no pink remains and the juices run clear, the parts are done.

A bird by any other color

In the microwave's moist heat, poultry skin does not crisp and brown as it does when cooked conventionally. Some whole birds do brown slightly with longer cooking. But in most recipes you'll get a golden brown surface only if you brush the skin with melted butter or margarine, soy sauce, Kitchen Bouquet, or Worcestershire sauce. Some of our recipes also ask you to cover the poultry with crumbs or brown it in a browning dish.

Defrosting chicken

The microwave oven offers a quick way to thaw all sizes of birds. Larger birds require some standing time between defrosting cycles, but smaller birds and parts can be defrosted all at once. Turn to our chart on page 211 for more information.

To fry or not to fry?

Due to the high temperatures required for deep-fat frying and the difficulty of heating oil evenly, you should continue to fry poultry as usual—on your range-top, not in your microwave oven.

Chicken and Broccoli Stir-Fry
(see recipe, page 206)

Turkey Breast with Ham-Tomato Sauce
(see recipe, page 189)

Technique:
Stuffing a whole bird

Chicken Véronique

Pictured on the cover.

⅓ cup chicken broth
¼ cup thinly sliced green onion
2 tablespoons snipped parsley
2 tablespoons dry white wine
¼ teaspoon salt
⅛ teaspoon pepper
½ cup quick-cooking rice
½ cup red *or* green grapes, halved and seeded
1 2½- to 3-pound broiler-fryer chicken
2 tablespoons butter *or* margarine
¼ teaspoon Kitchen Bouquet

■ For stuffing, in a 1-quart casserole combine broth, green onion, parsley, white wine, salt, and pepper. Cook, uncovered, on 100% power (high) for 2 to 3 minutes or till boiling. Stir in uncooked rice. Cover and let stand for 5 to 10 minutes or till broth is absorbed. Stir in grapes.

■ Meanwhile, rinse chicken. Pat dry. Spoon some of the stuffing loosely into neck cavity. Pull neck skin to back and secure with a wooden skewer or toothpick. Spoon remaining stuffing loosely into body cavity (see photo 1). Tie legs to tail. Twist wing tips under back. Place chicken, breast side down, on a rack in a 12x7½x2-inch baking dish.

■ In a custard cup cook 2 tablespoons butter or margarine, uncovered, on high for 40 to 50 seconds or till melted. Stir in Kitchen Bouquet. Brush some of the mixture onto chicken. Cover with waxed paper (see photo 2). Cook on 50% power (medium) for 45 to 60 minutes or till done, turning bird breast side up, brushing with butter mixture, and, if desired, inserting a temperature probe after 20 minutes (see photo 3).

■ When done, the drumstick should move easily in its socket. The meat temperature should be 180° to 185° and stuffing should be 165°. The juices should run clear and no pink should remain. Cover with foil (see photo 4). Let stand 15 minutes before carving (see photo 5). Serves 6.

Low-wattage oven: If the 12x7½x2-inch baking dish will not fit, use an 8x8x2-inch baking dish. For *chicken,* cook on high for 28 to 33 minutes.

To thaw a frozen bird, follow the directions on page 211. If the wing and leg tips begin to cook, shield with small pieces of foil, as shown. Be sure that the foil does not touch any other metal.

1
Stuff the bird while the stuffing is hot. A cold stuffing takes longer to cook and may not get hot enough in the center to be safe to eat. After filling the neck cavity, spoon the hot stuffing loosely into the body cavity, as shown.

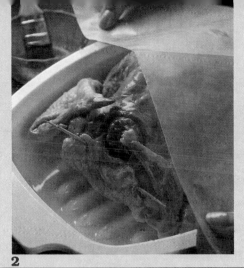

2
Place the bird, breast side down, on a microwave-safe rack in the baking dish. The rack prevents the chicken from stewing in its own juices. To prevent spattering, cover the bird loosely with waxed paper, as shown. If covered too tightly, the skin will stew.

3
After turning the bird breast side up, insert a temperature probe, if you like. Place it in the center of the inside thigh muscle, making sure the point does not touch bone or fat.

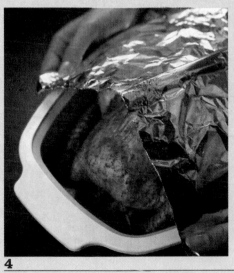

4
After checking the bird in several spots to make sure it is done, cover it with foil, as shown, to hold the heat. Let the bird stand for 15 minutes before carving.

5
When you carve the chicken, you will find it moist, tender, and juicy. The juices are clear, no pink remains, and the drumstick moves easily in its socket.

Pineapple-Stuffed Cornish Hen

Pictured on pages 184–185.

1 1- to 1½-pound Cornish game hen
1 8-ounce can crushed pineapple (juice pack)
⅓ cup chopped water chestnuts
¼ cup shredded carrot
  Dash salt
  Soy sauce
  Orange juice
1 teaspoon cornstarch
¼ teaspoon grated gingerroot
  Fresh thyme (optional)

■ Refer to photos, page 187. Thaw hen, if frozen (see chart, page 211). For stuffing, drain pineapple, reserving juice. Set aside. In a 2-cup measure combine ¼ *cup* of the pineapple, water chestnuts, carrot, and salt. Cover with vented clear plastic wrap. Cook on 100% power (high) for 3 to 5 minutes or till carrot is tender.

■ Meanwhile, rinse hen and pat dry. Spoon stuffing loosely into the body cavity. Tie legs to tail. Twist wing tips under back. Place hen, breast side down, on a rack in an 8x8x2-inch baking dish. Brush with soy sauce.

■ Cover hen with waxed paper. Cook on high for 10 to 13 minutes or till done, turning bird breast side up, brushing with additional soy sauce, and, if desired, inserting a temperature probe after 6 minutes. When the hen is done, the drumstick should move easily in its socket. The temperature of the bird should be 180° to 185° and the stuffing should be 165°. The juices should run clear and no pink should remain. Cover with foil. Let stand while preparing sauce.

■ For sauce, in a 1-cup measure combine reserved pineapple and juice. Add orange juice, if necessary, to equal ⅔ cup total. Stir in cornstarch and gingerroot. Cook, uncovered, on high for 2 to 3 minutes or till thickened and bubbly, stirring every minute. Transfer hen to a serving platter and garnish with thyme, if desired. Pass sauce. Makes 2 servings.

Cherry-Glazed Cornish Hens

The cranberry-flavored cherry glaze makes these hens shine.

2 1- to 1½-pound Cornish game hens
¼ cup cherry preserves
¼ cup cranberry juice cocktail
1½ teaspoons cornstarch
1 teaspoon soy sauce
¼ teaspoon finely shredded orange peel

■ Refer to photos, page 187. Thaw hens, if frozen (see chart, page 211). For glaze, in a 1-cup measure combine cherry preserves, cranberry juice cocktail, cornstarch, soy sauce, and orange peel. Cook, uncovered, on 100% power (high) for 1 to 2 minutes or till thickened and bubbly, stirring once. Set aside.

■ Rinse hens and pat dry. Season cavities of hens with salt and pepper. Tie legs to tail. Twist wing tips under back. Place hens, breast side down, on a rack in an 8x8x2-inch baking dish. Cover with waxed paper. Cook on high for 13 to 18 minutes or till done, turning hens breast side up, brushing with glaze, and, if desired, inserting a temperature probe after 8 minutes. When the hens are done, the drumsticks should move easily in their sockets. The temperature should be 180° to 185°. The juices should run clear and no pink should remain. Brush with remaining glaze. Cut in half to serve. Makes 4 servings.

Turkey Breast with Ham-Tomato Sauce

A turkey breast is a nifty alternative to a whole bird, because there's little or no leftover turkey. (Pictured on pages 184–185.)

1 3- to 4-pound turkey
   breast half
¼ cup chopped onion
1 clove garlic, minced
1 tablespoon butter *or*
   margarine
1 16-ounce can tomatoes,
   cut up
½ cup cubed fully cooked ham
2 tablespoons snipped parsley
1 teaspoon dried basil,
   crushed
½ teaspoon sugar
⅓ cup dry white wine
1 tablespoon cornstarch
   Parsley sprigs

■ See photos, page 187. Rinse breast. Pat dry. Place on a rack in a 12x7½x2-inch baking dish. Cover with waxed paper. Cook on 50% power (medium) 40 to 55 minutes or till done, turning over every 15 minutes. If desired, insert a temperature probe after 30 minutes and shield with foil. When done, temperature should be 185°, juices should run clear, and no pink should remain. Cover and let stand 15 minutes.

■ For sauce, in a 4-cup measure combine onion, garlic, and butter or margarine. Cover with vented clear plastic wrap. Cook on 100% power (high) for 1 to 2 minutes or till tender. Stir in *undrained* tomatoes, ham, parsley, basil, and sugar. Combine wine and cornstarch. Stir into tomato mixture. Cook, uncovered, on high for 4 to 6 minutes or till thickened and bubbly, stirring every minute. Cook 1 minute more. Slice turkey and place on platter. Trim with parsley. Pass sauce. Makes 8 to 12 servings.

Low-wattage oven: Not recommended.

Herb-Buttered Chicken

The butter pulls double-duty, adding both flavor and color.

1 tablespoon butter *or*
   margarine
½ teaspoon salt
½ teaspoon dried dillweed,
   basil, sage, *or* tarragon,
   crushed
½ teaspoon paprika
¼ teaspoon dry mustard
¼ teaspoon Worcestershire
   sauce
1 2½- to 3-pound broiler-fryer
   chicken

■ Refer to photos, page 187. In a custard cup cook butter or margarine, uncovered, on 100% power (high) for 30 to 40 seconds or till melted. Stir in salt, herb, paprika, dry mustard, and Worcestershire sauce. Set aside.

■ Rinse bird and pat dry. Tie legs to tail and twist wing tips under back. Place bird, breast side down, on a rack in a 12x7½x2-inch baking dish. Brush on herb butter. Cover with waxed paper. Cook on 50% power (medium) for 32 to 37 minutes, turning breast side up, brushing with butter, and, if desired, inserting a temperature probe after 10 minutes.

■ When the chicken is done, the drumstick should move easily in its socket. The temperature should be 180° to 185°. The juices should run clear and no pink should remain. Cover with foil. Let stand for 10 minutes before carving. Makes 6 servings.

Low-wattage oven: If the baking dish will not fit into your oven, use an 8x8x2-inch baking dish. For *chicken,* cook on high for 20 to 25 minutes.

Cooking cut-up chicken

Herbed Chicken And Peas

This whole recipe cooks in one dish. (Pictured on pages 6–7.)

4 slices bacon
1 2½- to 3-pound broiler-fryer
  chicken, cut up
1 medium onion, chopped
  (½ cup)
1 clove garlic, minced
2 tablespoons dry white wine
½ teaspoon dried basil,
  crushed
½ teaspoon dried thyme,
  crushed
¼ teaspoon salt
1 10-ounce package frozen
  peas
2 medium tomatoes, cut into
  wedges
2 tablespoons snipped parsley
  Hot cooked brown rice *or*
  rice (optional)

■ In a 12x7½x2-inch baking dish arrange bacon. Cover with paper towels. Cook on 100% power (high) for 4 to 6 minutes or till crisp (see photo 1). Remove and drain on paper towels. Crumble and set aside.

■ Rinse chicken and pat dry. In the same baking dish arrange chicken pieces, skin side down, with the meaty portions toward the edges of the dish (see photo 2). Cover with waxed paper. Cook on high for 5 minutes.

■ Combine onion, garlic, wine, basil, thyme, and salt. Drain juices from chicken. Give dish a half-turn, turn pieces skin side up, and rearrange, putting cooked portions toward the center (see photo 3). Pour onion mixture over top. Cover with waxed paper. Cook on high for 5 minutes.

■ Give the dish a half-turn. Add peas (see photo 4). Cook, covered, on high for 5 minutes. Add tomato wedges, parsley, and bacon pieces. Cook, covered, for 3 to 5 minutes more or till chicken and peas are done (see large photo). Serve with rice, if desired. Makes 6 servings.

Low-wattage oven: If the dish will not fit into your oven, use an 8x8x2-inch baking dish. For *bacon,* cook on high for 6 to 8 minutes. For *chicken,* if too crowded, omit neck, back, or wings.

TIP **Cooking Poultry in Low-Wattage Ovens**

Because of the lower cooking power in low-wattage ovens (400 to 550 watts), some whole birds and poultry parts may take a little longer to cook. The chart on page 212 points out which do. Also, many low-wattage ovens have smaller cavities, so you may need to use a dish smaller than the one specified in a recipe. If all the pieces of a cut-up broiler-fryer chicken won't fit in a single layer in the largest dish that fits into your oven, then leave out the neck, wings, or back. Refrigerate or freeze any extra pieces for soup or stock.

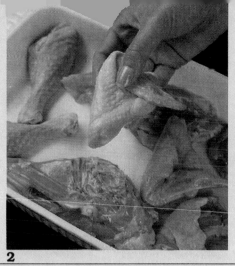
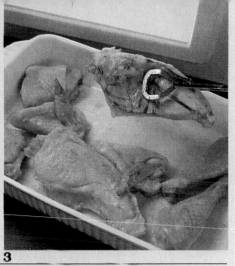

1
Cook the bacon in a single layer in the baking dish. Be sure to cover the bacon with microwave-safe paper towels to prevent spattering and help absorb the fat.

2
Arrange the chicken pieces in the same baking dish that was used to cook the bacon. Place the chicken pieces with the skin side down, putting the meaty chicken portions toward the edges of the dish, as shown.

3
Partway through cooking, turn the chicken pieces so the skin side is up. At the same time, rearrange the pieces so the less-cooked parts are near the edges of the dish, where they'll cook faster.

4
Sprinkle the frozen peas over the chicken. Later add the tomato wedges, parsley, and bacon pieces. When the chicken is done just right, the peas and tomatoes will be perfectly cooked, too.

Spiced Chicken And Pea Pods

This Oriental-flavored dish brings together three microwave winners: poultry, fruit, and vegetables.

1 11-ounce can mandarin
   orange sections
2 tablespoons dry sherry
2 tablespoons soy sauce
1 tablespoon cornstarch
¼ teaspoon ground ginger
⅛ teaspoon aniseed, crushed
   Dash ground red pepper
   Dash ground cloves
1 2½- to 3-pound broiler-fryer
   chicken, cut up
   Soy sauce
1 6-ounce package frozen
   pea pods
½ cup broken walnuts

■ Refer to photos, page 191. For glaze, drain oranges over a 2-cup measure, reserving liquid. Set fruit aside. If necessary, add water to reserved liquid to equal ½ cup total. Add sherry, 2 tablespoons soy sauce, cornstarch, ginger, aniseed, red pepper, and cloves. Cook, uncovered, on 100% power (high) for 3 to 5 minutes or till thickened and bubbly, stirring every minute till slightly thickened, then every 30 seconds.

■ Rinse chicken. Pat dry. In a 12x7½x2-inch baking dish arrange pieces, skin side down, with meaty portions toward edges. Brush with soy sauce. Cover with waxed paper. Cook on high for 5 minutes. Give dish a half-turn, turn pieces skin side up, and rearrange, putting cooked portions toward center. Brush with soy sauce. Cook, covered, 5 minutes. Drain.

■ Meanwhile, run hot water over frozen pea pods in a colander till separated. Add pea pods, walnuts, and orange sections to chicken. Pour glaze over all. Cover with waxed paper. Cook on high for 3 to 5 minutes more or till chicken and pea pods are done. Makes 6 servings.

Low-wattage oven: If the dish will not fit, use an 8x8x2-inch baking dish. For *chicken,* if too crowded, omit neck, back, or wings.

Chicken Cacciatore

The simmering herb-tomato sauce helps the chicken cook evenly.

1 2½- to 3-pound broiler-fryer
   chicken, cut up
1 medium green pepper,
   seeded and chopped
1 medium onion, sliced and
   separated into rings
1 16-ounce can tomatoes,
   cut up
1 6-ounce can tomato paste
⅓ cup dry red wine
1 tablespoon quick-cooking
   tapioca
2 bay leaves
2 cloves garlic, minced
½ teaspoon dried basil,
   crushed
¼ teaspoon fennel seed
¼ teaspoon pepper
   Hot cooked spaghetti
   Grated Parmesan cheese

■ Remove skin from chicken, if desired. Rinse and pat dry. Arrange chicken pieces in a 3-quart casserole, with meaty portions toward the edges of the dish. Add chopped green pepper and onion rings. In a small mixing bowl combine *undrained* tomatoes, tomato paste, wine, tapioca, bay leaves, garlic, basil, fennel seed, and pepper. Pour over chicken.

■ Cover and cook on 100% power (high) for 20 to 25 minutes or till chicken and vegetables are done, giving the dish a half-turn and stirring the mixture after 10 minutes.

■ Remove chicken and bay leaves. Skim fat from sauce, if necessary. Serve chicken and sauce over spaghetti. Sprinkle with Parmesan cheese. Makes 6 servings.

Low-wattage oven: Cook on high for 30 to 35 minutes.

Spiced Chicken and Pea Pods

Hot Barbecue-Style Chicken

Cook this spicy chicken entirely in your microwave or finish it off on your grill, following the tip, below.

½ cup catsup
¼ cup maple-flavored syrup
1 tablespoon prepared mustard
1 tablespoon Worcestershire sauce
1 teaspoon lemon juice
¼ teaspoon chili powder
1 clove garlic, minced
 Several dashes bottled hot pepper sauce
1 2½- to 3-pound broiler-fryer chicken, cut up

■ For sauce, in a 2-cup measure combine catsup, maple-flavored syrup, mustard, Worcestershire sauce, lemon juice, chili powder, garlic, and hot pepper sauce. Cook, uncovered, on 100% power (high) for 2 to 3 minutes or till bubbly, stirring once. Set aside.

■ Rinse chicken and pat dry. In a 12x7½x2-inch baking dish arrange chicken pieces, skin side down, with the meaty portions toward the edges of the dish (see photo 2, page 191). Cover with waxed paper. Cook on high for 10 minutes, giving the dish a half-turn after 5 minutes.

■ Drain off fat. Brush chicken with sauce. Turn chicken pieces skin side up and rearrange, putting cooked portions toward the center (see photo 3, page 191). Brush again with sauce. Cook, covered with waxed paper, for 2 to 5 minutes more or till no pink remains.

■ Cook any remaining sauce, uncovered, on high for 1 to 2 minutes or till heated through. Pass sauce with chicken. Makes 6 servings.

Low-wattage oven: If the baking dish will not fit, use an 8x8x2-inch baking dish. For *chicken,* omit neck, back, or wings, then cook on high for 15 to 18 minutes.

TIP Microwave-Grilled Chicken

If you like the charcoal flavor of outdoor cooking, but hate the wait, use your microwave oven to speed up the process. Micro-cook the chicken just until it starts to cook on the outside, then transfer it to the grill to bask in the glow of the coals. Just think, if you're cooking for a crowd, you can have one batch of chicken micro-cooking while you're grilling another.

For Hot Barbecue-Style Chicken, cook the chicken for 10 minutes on 100% power (high) as directed in the recipe above, then grill over *medium* coals for another 10 to 15 minutes or till done.

Another way to get great grilled flavor in a flash is to grill a lot of chicken when the coals are fired up, then refrigerate or freeze some to reheat in the microwave oven later.

Easy Chicken Marengo

Keep these ingredients on hand for when you need a quick-fix dish.

1   2½- to 3-pound broiler-fryer
      chicken, cut up
1   10¾-ounce can condensed
      golden mushroom soup
1   8-ounce can tomato sauce
1   cup frozen small whole
      onions
1   3-ounce can sliced
      mushrooms, drained
¼   cup water
1   teaspoon dried parsley flakes
½   teaspoon sugar
½   teaspoon dried oregano,
      crushed
½   teaspoon lemon juice
⅛   teaspoon garlic powder
½   cup sliced pitted ripe olives
      Hot cooked couscous *or* rice

■ Rinse chicken and pat dry. In a 12x7½x2-inch baking dish arrange chicken pieces, skin side down, with the meaty portions toward the edges of the dish (see photo 2, page 191). Cover with waxed paper. Cook on 100% power (high) for 12 to 15 minutes or till no pink remains. After 5 minutes, give the dish a half-turn, turn pieces skin side up, and rearrange, putting cooked portions toward the center (see photo 3, page 191). Drain fat from chicken and set chicken aside.

■ Meanwhile, for sauce, in a 4-cup measure combine condensed mushroom soup, tomato sauce, onions, mushrooms, water, parsley, sugar, oregano, lemon juice, and garlic powder. Cook, uncovered, on high for 5 to 7 minutes or till hot, stirring once. Stir in olives.

■ Pour the sauce over the chicken in the baking dish. Cook, uncovered, on high for 2 to 3 minutes or till heated through. Serve over couscous or rice. Makes 6 servings.

Low-wattage oven: If the baking dish will not fit, use an 8x8x2-inch baking dish. For *chicken,* if too crowded, omit neck, back, or wings, then cook on high for 15 to 18 minutes.

Caper-Sauced Chicken

Great news: Fix this company-special dish in less than 30 minutes.

1   2½- to 3-pound broiler-fryer
      chicken, cut up
1   8-ounce carton dairy sour
      cream
2   tablespoons all-purpose
      flour
½   cup milk
1   tablespoon capers, drained
½   teaspoon dried dillweed
¼   teaspoon salt
      Hot cooked spaetzle, *or*
      whole wheat *or* spinach
      noodles
      Paprika

■ Remove skin from chicken, if desired. Rinse and pat dry. In a 12x7½x2-inch baking dish arrange chicken with the meaty portions toward the edges of the dish (see photo 2, page 191). Cover with waxed paper. Cook on 100% power (high) for 12 to 15 minutes or till no pink remains. After 5 minutes, give the dish a half-turn, turn pieces skin side up, and rearrange, putting cooked portions toward the center (see photo 3, page 191). Drain fat from chicken and set chicken aside.

■ Meanwhile, for sauce, in a 4-cup measure stir together sour cream and flour. Stir in milk, capers, dillweed, and salt. Cook, uncovered, on high for 3 to 4 minutes or till thickened and bubbly, stirring every minute till slightly thickened, then every 30 seconds.

■ Pour sauce over chicken in the baking dish. Cook, uncovered, on high for 2 to 3 minutes more or till heated through. Serve over spaetzle or noodles. Sprinkle with paprika. Makes 6 servings.

Low-wattage oven: If the dish will not fit, use an 8x8x2-inch baking dish. For *chicken,* if too crowded, omit neck, back, or wings, then cook on high for 15 to 18 minutes.

Technique:

Coating chicken pieces

Herbed Parmesan Drumsticks

For six servings, double all of the ingredients and cook the drumsticks in two batches.

⅓ cup herb-seasoned stuffing mix
¼ cup grated Parmesan cheese
1 tablespoon dried parsley flakes
¼ teaspoon garlic powder
2 tablespoons butter *or* margarine
6 chicken drumsticks (1¼ to 1½ pounds)

■ For coating, in a plastic bag crush herb-seasoned stuffing mix. In a small mixing bowl combine crushed stuffing mix, Parmesan cheese, parsley flakes, and garlic powder. Set aside.

■ In a custard cup cook butter or margarine, uncovered, on 100% power (high) for 40 to 50 seconds or till melted.

■ Rinse drumsticks and pat dry. On waxed paper brush drumsticks with melted butter or margarine. Dip each drumstick into Parmesan cheese mixture, coating the meatier side and leaving the other side uncoated (see photo 1). In an 8x8x2-inch baking dish arrange drumsticks, coated side up, on a rack, with meaty ends toward the edges of the dish (see photo 2). Sprinkle with any remaining crumb mixture.

■ Cover with paper towels (see photo 3). Cook on high for 7 to 9 minutes or till no pink remains (see photo 4), giving the dish a half-turn after 5 minutes. Makes 3 servings.

Low-wattage oven: For *chicken,* cook on high for 10 to 13 minutes.

1

Brush the drumsticks with the melted butter. Then dip the meatier side of each drumstick into the crumb mixture, leaving the other side uncoated. If you coat both sides, the crumb coating on the bottom will get soggy.

2

Arrange the drumsticks, coated side up, on a microwave-safe rack in the baking dish. Place the meaty ends toward the edges of the dish so they'll finish cooking at the same time as the thin ends in the center.

3

Before cooking, cover the chicken with microwave-safe paper towels. The paper prevents the chicken from spattering during cooking and absorbs moisture so the coating will stay dry.

4

The drumsticks are done when no pink remains and the juices near the meaty parts of the chicken are clear, as shown.

Coated Chicken Dijon

1 tablespoon butter *or*
  margarine
¼ cup fine dry seasoned bread
  crumbs
1 tablespoon dried parsley
  flakes
½ teaspoon paprika
2 whole medium chicken
  breasts (12 ounces each),
  skinned and halved
  lengthwise
1 tablespoon Dijon-style
  mustard

■ For coating, in a 1-cup measure cook butter or margarine, uncovered, on 100% power (high) for 30 to 40 seconds or till melted. In a small mixing bowl combine bread crumbs, parsley flakes, and paprika. Toss with melted butter.

■ Rinse chicken pieces and pat dry. On waxed paper brush pieces with mustard. Dip each piece into crumb mixture, coating the meatier side and leaving the other side uncoated (see photo 1, page 197). In an 8x8x2-inch baking dish arrange pieces, coated side up, on a rack, with the meaty portions toward the edges of the dish (see photo 2, page 197).

■ Cover with paper towels (see photo 3, page 197). Cook on high for 8 to 10 minutes or till no pink remains (see photo 4, page 197), giving the dish a half-turn every 3 minutes. Makes 4 servings.

Low-wattage oven: For *chicken,* cook on high for 11 to 13 minutes.

Curried Peanut-Coated Chicken

Try this flavorful coated chicken and you'll find out why the curry-peanut combo is so popular in East Indian cooking.

¼ cup crushed wheat crackers
2 tablespoons finely chopped
  peanuts
¼ teaspoon curry powder
¼ teaspoon paprika
⅛ teaspoon pepper
  Dash onion powder
1 2½- to 3-pound broiler-fryer
  chicken, cut up
2 tablespoons milk

■ For coating, combine crushed crackers, peanuts, curry powder, paprika, pepper, and onion powder.

■ Rinse chicken and pat dry. (Refrigerate neck, back, and wings for another use.) On waxed paper brush pieces with milk. Dip each piece into peanut mixture, coating the meatier side and leaving the other side uncoated (see photo 1, page 197). In a 12x7½x2-inch baking dish arrange pieces, coated side up, on a rack, with the meaty portions toward the edges of the dish (see photo 2, page 197).

■ Cover the coated chicken with paper towels (see photo 3, page 197). Cook on 100% power (high) for 11 to 14 minutes or till no pink remains (see photo 4, page 197), giving the dish a half-turn every 4 minutes. Makes 6 servings.

Low-wattage oven: If dish will not fit, use an 8x8x2-inch baking dish.

Herb-Marinated Chicken

The cooking oil in the marinade helps the chicken brown as it cooks.

1   2½- to 3-pound broiler-fryer chicken, cut up
1   medium onion, chopped (½ cup)
¼   cup vinegar
2   tablespoons cooking oil
2   tablespoons snipped parsley
2   cloves garlic, minced
1   tablespoon Worcestershire sauce
1   teaspoon dried dillweed *or* tarragon, crushed
3   whole black peppers, cracked

■ Rinse chicken. Place in a plastic bag that's set in a 12x7½x2-inch baking dish. For marinade, in a 2-cup measure combine onion, vinegar, cooking oil, parsley, garlic, Worcestershire sauce, herb, and peppers. Pour marinade over chicken and close bag (see photo, below). Marinate in the refrigerator for 6 to 24 hours.

■ Drain chicken, reserving marinade. In the same baking dish arrange chicken, skin side down, with meaty portions toward the edges of the dish (see photo 2, page 191). Cover with waxed paper. Cook on 100% power (high) for 12 to 15 minutes or till no pink remains (see photo 4, page 197). After 5 minutes, brush with marinade. At the same time, give the dish a half-turn, turn chicken pieces skin side up, and rearrange, putting cooked portions toward center (see photo 3, page 191). Drain chicken before serving. Makes 6 servings.

Low-wattage oven: If the dish will not fit, use an 8x8x2-inch baking dish. For *chicken,* if too crowded, omit neck, back, or wings, then cook on high for 15 to 18 minutes.

Marinate and cook in the same baking dish. Begin by rinsing the chicken pieces and placing them in a plastic bag that's set in the baking dish. Then pour the marinade over the chicken. Close the bag and marinate in the refrigerator for 6 to 24 hours.

Stuffing a chicken breast

Chicken à l'Oscar

The classic Oscar combines crabmeat, asparagus, and béarnaise sauce.

1 cup fresh *or* frozen cut
   asparagus
2 tablespoons water
2 whole medium chicken
   breasts (12 ounces each)
1 6-ounce can crabmeat,
   drained, flaked, and
   cartilage removed
¼ teaspoon dried dillweed
¼ teaspoon pepper
1 tablespoon butter *or*
   margarine
1 tablespoon snipped chives
2 teaspoons all-purpose flour
1 cup milk
¾ teaspoon finely shredded
   lemon peel
  Lemon wedges (optional)
  Fresh dill (optional)

■ Place asparagus in an 8x8x2-inch baking dish. Add water. Cover with vented clear plastic wrap. Cook on 100% power (high) for 2½ to 3½ minutes or till tender. Drain.

■ Rinse chicken and pat dry. Skin and bone breasts, halving lengthwise (see photo 1). Place 1 chicken piece between 2 pieces of clear plastic wrap. Working from center to edges, pound lightly with a meat mallet to form a rectangle about ¼ inch thick. Repeat with remaining chicken.

■ For filling, in a mixing bowl combine crabmeat, dillweed, and pepper. Toss to mix. Spoon *one-fourth* of the filling onto *each* breast half. Arrange cooked asparagus across chicken breasts. Roll up each breast half, jelly-roll style (see photo 2). Secure with wooden toothpicks or skewers, if necessary (see photo 3).

■ Arrange chicken rolls, seam side down, in the same baking dish used for the asparagus. Cover with vented clear plastic wrap. Cook on high for 6 to 8 minutes or till chicken is done, giving the dish a half-turn and rearranging the rolls after 4 minutes (see photo 4).

■ For sauce, in a 2-cup measure combine butter or margarine and chives. Cook, uncovered, on high for 30 to 40 seconds or till butter is melted. Stir in flour. Add milk. Cook, uncovered, for 3 to 5 minutes or till thickened and bubbly, stirring every minute till slightly thickened, then every 30 seconds. Stir in lemon peel. Serve over chicken. If desired, garnish with lemon wedges and dill (see large photo). Makes 4 servings.

Low-wattage oven: For *chicken,* cook on high for 9 to 11 minutes.

TIP **Skinning Chicken for Fewer Calories**

Since most of the fat in chicken is located in or directly under the skin, you can save calories by removing the skin before microwave cooking. Cover the skinned chicken with vented microwave-safe clear plastic wrap to trap the steam and assure that the chicken won't dry or stick to the dish. The plastic wrap also speeds cooking.

1

To bone a chicken breast, first remove the skin. Then cut through the meat to the bone near the center of the back, as shown. Starting from that bone, cut meat away from ribs, using a sawing motion and pressing the flat side of the knife against the ribs. As you cut, gently pull meat up and away. Repeat for the other side.

2

Top each pounded chicken breast half with some of the crabmeat filling and asparagus. Roll up each as you would a jelly roll.

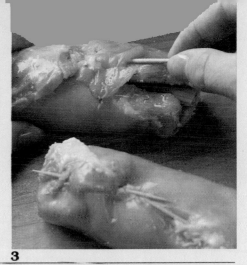

3

To help the rolls keep their shape, hold them together with wooden toothpicks or skewers, as shown. Be sure to use wood, because metal skewers might cause sparks in your microwave oven.

4

After part of the cooking time, give the dish a half-turn and rearrange the chicken rolls, as shown above. Continue cooking till no pink remains. If you like, serve the chicken rolls with rice and garnish with lemon wedges and fresh dill, as shown at right.

Ham-and-Swiss-Stuffed Chicken Breasts

Choose a delicate herb mustard to let the cheesy flavor come through.

2 whole medium chicken
   breasts (12 ounces each)
2 thin slices fully cooked ham,
   halved (2 ounces)
2 slices Swiss cheese, halved
   (2 ounces)
2 teaspoons herb mustard
1 tablespoon butter *or*
   margarine
3 tablespoons fine dry
   seasoned bread crumbs

■ Rinse chicken and pat dry. Skin and bone chicken breasts, halving lengthwise (see photo 1, page 201). Place 1 chicken piece between 2 pieces of clear plastic wrap. Working from center to edges, pound lightly with a meat mallet to form a rectangle about ¼ inch thick. Repeat with remaining chicken. Place 1 ham piece and 1 cheese piece on each breast half trimming to fit. Spread each with some of the mustard. Roll up each breast half jelly-roll style (see photo 2, page 201). Secure with wooden toothpicks or skewers, if necessary (see photo 3, page 201).

■ In a custard cup cook butter or margarine, uncovered, on 100% power (high) for 30 to 40 seconds or till melted. Stir in bread crumbs. On waxed paper coat all but one side of the rolls with the crumb mixture. Arrange chicken, uncoated side down, on a rack in an 8x8x2-inch baking dish. Cover with paper towels. Cook on high for 6 to 8 minutes or till chicken is done, giving the dish a half-turn and rearranging rolls after 4 minutes (see photo 4, page 201). Makes 4 servings.

Low-wattage oven: For *chicken,* cook on high for 9 to 11 minutes.

Breast of Chicken In Thyme Sauce

1 tablespoon butter *or*
   margarine
1 clove garlic, minced
½ teaspoon dried thyme,
   crushed
2 whole medium chicken
   breasts (12 ounces each)
1 cup sliced fresh mushrooms
¼ cup sliced green onion
⅔ cup light cream
2 teaspoons cornstarch
1 tablespoon dry sherry
   (optional)
   Hot cooked spinach noodles

■ In a 10x6x2-inch baking dish combine butter or margarine, garlic, and thyme. Cook, uncovered, on 100% power (high) for 30 to 40 seconds or till butter is melted. Set aside.

■ Rinse chicken and pat dry. Skin and bone chicken, halving lengthwise (see photo 1, page 201). Sprinkle with salt and pepper. Arrange chicken in the same dish as butter mixture, with meaty portions toward edges. Tuck under thin portions for more even thickness. Add mushrooms and green onion. Cover with vented clear plastic wrap. Cook on high for 4 to 6 minutes or till no pink remains (see photo 4, page 197), giving the dish a half-turn and rearranging and turning chicken over after 3 minutes. Remove chicken and set aside, reserving juices in dish.

■ For sauce, combine cream and cornstarch, then stir into juices. Cook, uncovered, on high for 3 to 5 minutes or till thickened and bubbly, stirring every minute till slightly thickened, then every 30 seconds. Stir in sherry, if desired. Return chicken to sauce. Cook, uncovered, for 30 to 60 seconds or till warm. Serve over spinach noodles. Makes 4 servings.

Low-wattage oven: For *chicken,* cook on high for 7 to 9 minutes.

Cucumber Chicken Breasts

A creamy light-tasting entrée.

3 whole medium chicken
    breasts (12 ounces each)
    Salt
    Paprika
½ of a medium cucumber,
    seeded and cut into
    matchstick-size pieces
    (1 cup)
⅓ cup finely chopped celery
2 tablespoons water
½ cup dairy sour cream
¼ cup creamy cucumber salad
    dressing

■ Rinse chicken and pat dry. Skin and bone chicken breasts, halving lengthwise (see photo 1, page 201). Sprinkle with salt and paprika.

■ In a 10x6x2-inch baking dish arrange chicken with meaty portions toward the edges of the dish. Tuck under thin portions for more even thickness. Cover with vented clear plastic wrap. Cook on 100% power (high) for 6 to 8 minutes or till no pink remains (see photo 4, page 197), giving the dish a half-turn and rearranging and turning chicken over after 3 minutes. Remove chicken. Cover to keep warm. Discard juices.

■ For sauce, add cucumber, celery, and water to the baking dish. Cook, covered, on high for 2 to 3 minutes or till vegetables are tender, stirring once. Stir sour cream and salad dressing into the dish. Cook, uncovered, on high about 1 minute or till heated through (*do not boil*).

■ Add chicken. Cook, uncovered, for 1 to 2 minutes more or till chicken is heated through (*do not boil*). Makes 6 servings.

Low-wattage oven: For *vegetables,* cook on high for 6 to 8 minutes.

Curry-Glazed Chicken Breasts

Curry powder, mustard, and honey blend for a glistening golden glaze.

2 slices bacon
2 whole medium chicken
    breasts (12 ounces each)
4 teaspoons prepared mustard
1 tablespoon honey
½ teaspoon curry powder
¼ teaspoon salt
    Hot cooked rice (optional)

■ In an 8x8x2-inch baking dish arrange bacon slices. Cover with paper towels. Cook on 100% power (high) for 1½ to 2½ minutes or till done. Remove bacon and drain on paper towels. Crumble and set aside.

■ Rinse chicken and pat dry. Skin and bone chicken breasts, halving lengthwise (see photo 1, page 201). Drain fat from the baking dish. Arrange chicken pieces in the dish with meaty portions toward the edges. Tuck under thin portions for more even thickness. Cover with vented clear plastic wrap. Cook on high for 2 minutes.

■ Meanwhile, for glaze, in a small mixing bowl combine mustard, honey, curry powder, and salt. Brush some of the glaze onto chicken. Give the dish a half-turn and rearrange and turn the chicken over. Brush some more glaze onto chicken. Cook, covered, on high for 2 to 4 minutes more or till no pink remains (see photo 4, page 197).

■ Transfer chicken to a serving platter. Stir mustard glaze and spoon over chicken. Top with crumbled bacon. Serve with rice, if desired. Makes 4 servings.

Spicy Cheddar-Sauced
Chicken Breasts

Spicy Cheddar-Sauced Chicken Breasts

Cheese spread makes a super easy sauce.

2 whole medium chicken
    breasts (12 ounces each)
½ cup cheese spread with
    jalapeño peppers
⅛ teaspoon ground cumin *or*
    allspice
¼ cup sliced pitted ripe olives
1 tablespoon chopped
    pimiento (optional)

■ Rinse chicken and pat dry. Remove skin and cut breasts in half lengthwise. In an 8x8x2-inch baking dish arrange chicken, bone side up, with meaty portions toward the edges of the dish. Cover with vented clear plastic wrap. Cook on 100% power (high) for 8 to 10 minutes or till no pink remains (see photo 4, page 197), giving the dish a half-turn and rearranging and turning chicken over after 5 minutes. Transfer chicken to a platter, reserving 1 tablespoon cooking liquid. Cover to keep warm.

■ For sauce, in a 2-cup measure combine reserved cooking liquid, cheese spread, and cumin or allspice. Cook, uncovered, on high about 1 minute or till heated through. Pour sauce over chicken. Top with sliced olives and chopped pimiento, if desired. Makes 4 servings.

Low-wattage oven: For *chicken,* cook on high for 11 to 13 minutes.

Pepper Chicken With Papaya

Jazz up everyday chicken with papaya or nectarines.

2 whole medium chicken
    breasts (12 ounces each)
1 medium green pepper, cut
    into ¾-inch pieces
1 medium papaya, peeled and
    sliced, *or* 2 medium
    nectarines, sliced
    Unsweetened pineapple juice
1 tablespoon cornstarch
1 tablespoon water
1 teaspoon instant chicken
    bouillon granules
⅛ teaspoon ground ginger
    Several dashes ground red
    pepper
    Hot cooked bulgur *or* rice

■ Rinse chicken and pat dry. Remove skin and cut breasts in half lengthwise. Sprinkle with salt and pepper, if desired. In a 12x7½x2-inch baking dish arrange chicken, bone side up, with meaty portions toward the edges of the dish. Cover with vented clear plastic wrap. Cook on 100% power (high) for 4 minutes. Give the dish a half-turn and rearrange and turn chicken over. Add green pepper. Cook chicken mixture, covered, for 2 minutes more.

■ Arrange papaya or nectarine slices around chicken. Cook, covered, on high for 6 to 8 minutes more or till chicken and fruit are done (see photo 4, page 197). Transfer chicken, green pepper, and fruit to a serving platter, reserving juices. Cover chicken to keep warm.

■ For sauce, pour juices into a 2-cup measure. Add enough pineapple juice to equal 1 cup total. Stir together cornstarch, water, bouillon granules, ginger, and red pepper. Stir into juice mixture. Cook, uncovered, on high for 3 to 5 minutes or till thickened and bubbly, stirring every minute till slightly thickened, then every 30 seconds. Pour sauce over chicken. Serve with bulgur or rice. Makes 4 servings.

Low-wattage oven: If the dish will not fit, use a 10x6x2-inch baking dish. For *chicken,* cook on high for 10 to 12 minutes after adding fruit.

Chicken and Broccoli Stir-Fry

Use a browning dish instead of a wok to stir-fry in the microwave oven. (Pictured on pages 184–185.)

3 tablespoons dry sherry
3 tablespoons soy sauce
1 whole large chicken breast (1 pound)
1 tablespoon cooking oil
2 tablespoons water
1½ cups small broccoli flowerets
1 medium carrot, thinly bias sliced (½ cup)
2 cloves garlic, minced
½ teaspoon grated gingerroot
¼ cold water
1 tablespoon cornstarch
4 ounces tofu (fresh bean curd), drained and cut into ¾-inch cubes
½ cup fresh bean sprouts
Hot cooked rice (optional)

■ Refer to photos, page 153. For marinade, in a bowl combine sherry and soy sauce. Rinse chicken and pat dry. Skin and bone breast, halving lengthwise (see photo 1, page 201). Cut into bite-size strips. Add to marinade. Let stand for 15 minutes. Drain chicken, reserving marinade.

■ Meanwhile, preheat a 10-inch browning dish on 100% power (high) 5 minutes. Add oil, swirling to coat dish. Add chicken. Cook, uncovered, on high for 2 to 3 minutes or till done. Remove chicken and set aside.

■ Add reserved marinade and 2 tablespoons water to dish. Add broccoli, carrot, garlic, and gingerroot. Cook, covered, on high 3 to 5 minutes or till crisp-tender, stirring once. Remove with slotted spoon. Reserve liquid.

■ Combine ¼ cup water and cornstarch, then stir into liquid in dish. Cook, uncovered, on high 2 to 3 minutes or till thickened and bubbly, stirring after 1 minute, then every 30 seconds. Stir in chicken, vegetables, tofu, and sprouts. Cook, covered, 2 to 3 minutes more or till heated through, stirring once. Serve over rice, if desired. Serves 3.

Low-wattage oven: If browning dish will fit, preheat on high 7 minutes.

Sweet-and-Sour Chicken with Grapes

2 whole medium chicken breasts (12 ounces each)
2 medium carrots, thinly sliced (1 cup)
3 green onions, bias-sliced into 1-inch pieces
1 clove garlic, minced
1 tablespoon water
½ cup chicken broth
3 tablespoons honey
2 tablespoons vinegar
2 tablespoons soy sauce
4 teaspoons cornstarch
1 cup red *or* green seedless grapes, halved
Hot cooked rice
¼ cup sliced almonds, toasted (optional)

■ Rinse chicken and pat dry. Skin and bone breasts, halving lengthwise (see photo 1, page 201). Cut into ¾-inch pieces. Set aside.

■ In a 2-quart casserole combine carrots, green onions, garlic, and water. Cook, covered, on 100% power (high) for 3 to 4 minutes or till vegetables are crisp-tender. Add chicken. Cook, covered, on high for 4 to 6 minutes or till chicken is just done, stirring once. Drain.

■ Meanwhile, in a 1-cup measure combine the chicken broth, honey, vinegar, soy sauce, and cornstarch. Stir into chicken mixture. Cook, uncovered, on high for 4½ to 6½ minutes or till thickened and bubbly, stirring every minute till slightly thickened, then every 30 seconds. Stir in grapes. Serve over rice. Sprinkle with almonds, if desired. Serves 4.

Herbed Turkey Ring

A tangy cranberry sauce caps this ground-turkey ring.

1 beaten egg
¼ cup quick-cooking rolled
    oats
¼ cup finely chopped onion
¼ cup finely chopped celery
2 tablespoons milk
½ teaspoon salt
½ teaspoon ground sage
¼ teaspoon dried thyme,
    crushed
¼ teaspoon pepper
1 pound ground raw turkey
½ cup cranberry-orange sauce
1 tablespoon orange juice

■ In a medium mixing bowl combine egg, oats, onion, celery, milk, salt, sage, thyme, and pepper. Add turkey. Mix well. In a 9-inch pie plate shape mixture into a 6-inch ring, 2 inches wide (see photo 1, page 157). Cover with waxed paper. Cook on 100% power (high) for 7 to 9 minutes or till no pink remains, giving the dish a half-turn after 4 minutes (see photo 2, page 157). Let stand, covered, for 10 minutes.

■ Meanwhile, for sauce, in a 1-cup measure combine cranberry-orange sauce and orange juice. Cook, uncovered, on high for 1 to 2 minutes or till heated through. Transfer the turkey ring to a serving platter (see photo 3, page 157). Spoon sauce over. Makes 5 servings.

Low-wattage oven: For *turkey ring,* cook on high for 11 to 13 minutes, turning the dish every 3 minutes.

Quick Turkey Burgers

1 beaten egg
¾ cup soft bread crumbs
    (1 slice)
1 2-ounce can chopped
    mushrooms, drained
2 tablespoons sliced green
    onion
2 tablespoons orange juice
½ teaspoon Worcestershire
    sauce
¼ teaspoon salt
¼ teaspoon poultry seasoning
⅛ teaspoon pepper
1 pound ground raw turkey
    Whole wheat hamburger
        buns, toasted and buttered
    Lettuce leaves
    Whole cranberry sauce

■ In a medium mixing bowl combine egg, bread crumbs, mushrooms, green onion, orange juice, Worcestershire sauce, salt, poultry seasoning, and pepper. Add turkey and mix well.

■ Shape into four ½-inch-thick patties. Place patties in an 8x8x2-inch baking dish. Cover with waxed paper. Cook on 100% power (high) for 6 to 8 minutes or till no pink remains, giving the dish a quarter-turn and rearranging and turning patties over after 3 minutes (see photo 4, page 161). Serve burgers in toasted buns with lettuce leaves and cranberry sauce. Makes 4 servings.

Low-wattage oven: Cook on high for 9 to 11 minutes, rearranging and turning patties over after 4 minutes.

Creating a chicken casserole

Cheesy Chicken-Stuffed Shells

The beer-cheese sauce will remind you of Welsh rarebit.

½ cup frozen peas
2 tablespoons chopped onion
1 tablespoon butter *or* margarine
2 tablespoons chopped pimiento, drained
4 teaspoons cornstarch
2 teaspoons prepared mustard
1 cup beer *or* chicken broth
1 cup shredded American cheese (4 ounces)
1½ cups diced cooked chicken *or* turkey
4 ounces large shell macaroni (about 12 shells), cooked and drained

■ For sauce, in a 4-cup measure combine peas, onion, and butter or margarine. Cook, uncovered, on 100% power (high) for 2 to 3 minutes or till onion is tender.

■ Stir in pimiento, cornstarch, and mustard. Add beer or chicken broth (see photo 1). Cook, uncovered, on high for 2 to 3 minutes or till thickened and bubbly, stirring after 1 minute, then every 30 seconds. Add shredded American cheese, then stir till melted.

■ For filling, stir ½ *cup* of the sauce into chicken or turkey. Fill the cooked macaroni shells with the chicken-cheese mixture (see photo 2). Arrange the stuffed shells in an 8x8x2-inch baking dish (see photo 3).

■ Pour the remaining sauce over shells (see photo 4). Cover with vented clear plastic wrap (see photo 5). Cook on high for 3 to 5 minutes or till heated through. Makes 4 servings.

Low-wattage oven: For *stuffed shells,* cook on high for 5 to 7 minutes.

TIP **Quick-Cooking Chicken**

If a recipe calls for cooked chicken or turkey and you don't have any on hand, just cook some chicken breasts according to the directions given on page 212. One 12-ounce whole chicken breast will yield about ¾ cup cut-up cooked meat.

1

After adding cornstarch to the cooked vegetables, stir in the beer or chicken broth all at once. The heat from the cooked vegetables will warm the liquid and shorten the thickening time.

2

To make the filling, stir ½ cup of the cheese sauce into the chicken or turkey. Then spoon a generous 2 tablespoons of filling into each cooked macaroni shell.

3

After filling the macaroni shells with the chicken and cheese mixture, place them in an 8x8x2-inch microwave-safe baking dish. Arrange them attractively, because you'll serve them at the table right from this dish.

4

Pour the remaining cheese sauce over the shells. Cooking the filled shells in the sauce helps heat them more quickly and evenly.

5

Cover the baking dish with vented clear plastic wrap. To vent, turn back one corner so some of the steam can escape. The steam that remains will prevent the pasta from drying.

Country-Apple Chicken

½ cup thinly sliced carrot
⅓ cup chopped onion
2 tablespoons butter *or* margarine
1 large tart red apple, peeled, cored, and thinly sliced (1½ cups)
1½ cups light cream *or* milk
2 tablespoons all-purpose flour
1½ cups diced cooked chicken *or* turkey
¼ cup snipped parsley
2 tablespoons frozen apple juice concentrate, thawed
1 tablespoon brandy (optional)
¼ teaspoon ground nutmeg
Hot cooked rice
Paprika *or* snipped parsley

■ In a 1½-quart casserole combine carrot, onion, and butter or margarine. Cook, covered, on 100% power (high) for 3 minutes. Add apple slices. Cook, covered, on high for 1 to 3 minutes more or till onion and apple slices are tender. Using a slotted spoon, remove apple mixture and set aside, reserving juices in the casserole.

■ Stir together cream or milk and flour. Stir into reserved juices. Cook, uncovered, on high for 4 to 7 minutes or till thickened and bubbly, stirring every minute till slightly thickened, then every 30 seconds.

■ Stir in apple mixture, chicken or turkey, parsley, apple juice concentrate, brandy (if desired), and nutmeg. Cover and cook on high for 2 to 3 minutes or till heated through. Serve over hot cooked rice. Sprinkle with paprika or snipped parsley. Makes 4 servings.

Turkey au Gratin

Use your temperature probe to measure the heat of the milk, if you like.

1 stalk celery, sliced (½ cup)
1 medium onion, chopped (½ cup)
2 tablespoons butter *or* margarine
2 cups milk
1 cup quick-cooking rice
1½ cups diced cooked turkey *or* chicken
1 10¾-ounce can condensed cream of mushroom soup
1 cup herb-seasoned stuffing mix
1 cup shredded cheddar cheese (4 ounces)
1 4-ounce can green chili peppers, rinsed, seeded, and chopped (optional)

■ In a 2-quart casserole combine celery, onion, and butter or margarine. Cook, covered, on 100% power (high) for 2 to 3 minutes or till onion is tender. Add milk. Cook, covered, on high for 4 to 6 minutes or till steaming and foamy but not boiling (about 180°). Stir in uncooked rice. Let stand, covered, for 2 minutes.

■ Stir in turkey or chicken, condensed soup, stuffing mix, *half* of the cheese, and chili peppers (if desired). Cook, covered, on high for 5 to 7 minutes or till heated through, stirring once. Sprinkle with remaining cheese. Let stand till cheese is melted. Makes 6 servings.

Low-wattage oven: For *turkey or chicken mixture,* cook on high for 7 to 9 minutes.

Defrosting Poultry

If you've got a frosty bird on your hands, turn to your microwave for some defrosting help.

For **whole birds,** place the unwrapped bird, breast side down, in a baking dish. Remove the metal clamp, if present, and the giblets packet as soon as you can.

For **poultry parts,** place the unwrapped pieces in a baking dish.

For both, defrost on 30% power (medium-low) for the time specified below. After half of the defrosting time, turn the whole bird breast side up. Or, separate, rearrange, and turn poultry parts over, putting icy parts near the edges. If some areas thaw faster, shield with small pieces of foil. (Check your owner's manual to see if you can use foil.)

When you notice poultry starting to cook on the edges, remove it from the microwave and let it stand in cold water for the specified time. (Some whole birds and roasts need additional defrosting time after standing, as indicated.†) Poultry should be completely thawed before cooking. It should feel soft and moist, but still cold.

Bird	Amount	Defrosting time	Standing time
Roasting chicken, whole	One 3½- to 4-pound bird	25 to 30 minutes	30 minutes
Broiler-fryer chicken, whole	One 2½- to 3-pound bird	20 to 25 minutes	30 minutes
Broiler-fryer chicken, cut up	One 2½- to 3-pound bird	15 to 17 minutes*	
Chicken breasts, whole	Two 12-ounce breasts	12 to 14 minutes	15 minutes
Chicken drumsticks	2 drumsticks	3 to 5 minutes	
	6 drumsticks	8 to 10 minutes	
¾-inch chicken pieces	1 pound	8 to 12 minutes	
Turkey, whole	One 10-pound bird	30 minutes*	30 minutes†
	One 8-pound bird	25 minutes*	30 minutes†
Turkey breast half	One 3- to 4-pound half	20 to 25 minutes	45 minutes
Turkey roast, boneless	One 3- to 3½-pound roast	20 to 25 minutes*	15 minutes†
Turkey drumstick	One 1-pound drumstick	7 to 9 minutes	
Turkey breast tenderloins	Four 4-ounce steaks	8 to 10 minutes	
Ground raw turkey	1 pound	10 to 12 minutes	5 minutes
Cornish game hen, whole	One 1- to 1½-pound bird	8 to 10 minutes	30 minutes
	Two 1- to 1½-pound birds	12 to 15 minutes	30 minutes
Domestic duckling, whole	One 4- to 5-pound bird	25 minutes	30 minutes†

*Note: Timings are for 600- to 700-watt microwave ovens and may be longer in low-wattage ovens. Large birds may not fit in small ovens.
†Note: After standing, defrost these birds for additional time: 10-pound turkey, 30 minutes; 8-pound turkey, 20 minutes; 3- to 4-pound turkey roast, 10 to 15 minutes; 4- to 5-pound duckling, 25 to 30 minutes. Turn halfway through both defrosting cycles.

Cooking Poultry

To cook a **whole bird,** rinse and pat the bird dry. Tie the legs to the tail and twist the wing tips under the back. Place the bird, breast side down, on a microwave-safe rack in a baking dish. Brush with melted butter or margarine. Cover loosely with waxed paper. Micro-cook on the specified power level for specified time or till done. After half of the cooking time, turn the bird breast side up and brush with additional butter or margarine. (If desired, insert a temperature probe in the thigh at this time, making sure it does not touch the bone.)

The bird is done when the drumsticks move easily in their sockets and the bird's temperature registers 185° in several spots. The juices should run clear and no pink should remain. If the wing and leg tips or other areas are done before the rest, shield the cooked areas with small pieces of foil. (Check your owner's manual to see if you can use foil in your microwave.) Let cooked birds weighing more than 2 pounds stand, covered with foil, for 15 minutes before carving.

Bird	Amount	Power	Cooking time
Broiler-fryer chicken	One 2½- to 3-pound bird	50% (medium)	32 to 37 minutes*
Cornish game hen	One 1- to 1½-pound bird	100% (high)	7 to 10 minutes
	Two 1- to 1½-pound birds	100% (high)	13 to 18 minutes

To cook **poultry parts,** rinse and pat dry. Arrange in a baking dish with meaty portions toward edges of dish, tucking under thin boneless portions. Cover with waxed paper. (Or, for skinless poultry, cover with a lid or vented clear plastic wrap.) Cook on specified power and time till done, rearranging, stirring, or turning pieces over after half of the cooking time. Shield with foil as needed.

Part	Amount	Power level	Cooking time
Broiler-fryer chicken, cut up	One 2½- to 3-pound bird	100% (high)	12 to 17 minutes*
Chicken breasts, halved	Two 16-ounce breasts	100% (high)	8 to 11 minutes*
	Two 12-ounce breasts	100% (high)	8 to 10 minutes
Chicken breasts, whole	Two 12-ounce breasts	100% (high)	13 to 15 minutes
	One 12-ounce breast	100% (high)	5 to 7 minutes*
Chicken drumsticks	2 drumsticks	100% (high)	3 to 5 minutes*
	6 drumsticks	100% (high)	7 to 9 minutes*
¾-inch chicken pieces	1 pound	100% (high)	3 to 5 minutes
Turkey breast half	One 3- to 4-pound half	50% (medium)	40 to 55 minutes*
Turkey roast, boneless	One 3- to 3½-pound roast	50% (medium)	50 to 60 minutes*
Turkey drumstick	One 1-pound drumstick	100% (high)	7 to 9 minutes
Turkey breast tenderloins	Four 4-ounce steaks	100% (high)	6 to 8 minutes
Ground raw turkey	1 pound	100% (high)	5 to 7 minutes*

Note: Timings are for 600- to 700-watt microwave ovens and may be longer in low-wattage ovens. For the smaller ovens, if chicken pieces are too crowded in the dish, omit neck, back, or wings.

Nutrition Analysis

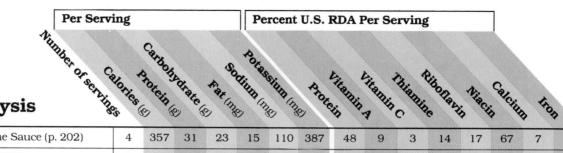

	Number of servings	Per Serving						Percent U.S. RDA Per Serving							
		Calories	Protein (g)	Carbohydrate (g)	Fat (g)	Sodium (mg)	Potassium (mg)	Protein	Vitamin A	Vitamin C	Thiamine	Riboflavin	Niacin	Calcium	Iron
Breast of Chicken in Thyme Sauce (p. 202)	4	357	31	23	15	110	387	48	9	3	14	17	67	7	12
Caper-Sauced Chicken (p. 195)	6	342	31	23	13	183	340	48	8	1	14	15	63	9	10
Cheesy Chicken-Stuffed Shells (p. 208)	4	378	26	29	15	289	262	40	11	4	22	17	40	23	11
Cherry-Glazed Cornish Hens (p. 188)	4	310	37	17	9	198	337	57	1	12	6	14	59	2	10
Chicken à l'Oscar (p. 200)	4	251	35	6	9	435	454	54	18	15	10	15	64	11	9
Chicken and Broccoli Stir-Fry (p. 206)	3	248	29	12	8	1116	593	45	148	53	11	12	61	10	14
Chicken Cacciatore (p. 192)	6	316	33	33	5	451	785	50	26	54	19	15	70	9	19
Chicken Véronique (p. 186)	6	220	27	10	7	229	272	42	5	4	7	6	60	2	7
Coated Chicken Dijon (p. 198)	4	200	27	4	7	290	237	42	7	1	4	6	59	2	6
Country-Apple Chicken (p. 210)	4	486	20	44	26	72	451	30	107	10	15	13	35	12	12
Cucumber Chicken Breasts (p. 203)	6	226	27	3	11	186	292	42	4	3	5	8	59	4	6
Curried Peanut-Coated Chicken (p. 198)	6	174	27	3	5	97	251	42	2	0	6	7	61	2	6
Curry-Glazed Chicken Breasts (p. 203)	4	182	28	5	5	319	249	43	0	2	6	6	60	2	6
Easy Chicken Marengo (p. 195)	6	343	30	35	9	849	487	46	8	10	16	10	68	6	15
Ham-and-Swiss-Stuffed Chicken Breasts (p. 202)	4	263	34	4	11	396	278	52	5	5	11	10	61	15	6
Herb-Buttered Chicken (p. 189)	6	173	26	0	7	284	223	40	5	0	4	6	58	2	5
Herbed Chicken and Peas (p. 190)	6	217	30	9	6	271	408	47	14	16	16	10	64	4	12
Herbed Parmesan Drumsticks (p. 196)	3	317	31	12	16	526	269	47	9	1	8	17	30	15	11
Herbed Turkey Ring (p. 207)	5	198	22	17	4	313	359	34	2	8	14	18	28	7	26
Herb-Marinated Chicken (p. 199)	6	151	26	1	4	69	228	40	1	1	4	6	57	2	5
Hot Barbecue-Style Chicken (p. 194)	6	201	27	15	3	363	330	41	8	4	6	7	60	3	7
Pepper Chicken with Papaya (p. 205)	4	496	35	80	4	162	789	54	34	100	24	13	77	7	28
Pineapple-Stuffed Cornish Hen (p. 188)	2	336	38	23	10	184	547	58	79	16	11	15	61	4	12
Quick Turkey Burgers (p. 207)	4	327	31	33	7	530	473	47	3	31	20	21	35	7	20
Spiced Chicken and Pea Pods (p. 192)	6	249	29	11	9	411	398	45	11	46	12	9	61	4	10
Spicy Cheddar-Sauced Chicken Breasts (p. 205)	4	273	34	1	14	591	274	52	9	1	4	12	59	22	7
Sweet-and-Sour Chicken with Grapes (p. 206)	4	364	31	52	4	686	520	47	203	6	16	10	69	4	14
Turkey au Gratin (p. 210)	6	426	23	39	20	952	371	35	9	4	14	22	19	29	13
Turkey Breast with Ham-Tomato Sauce (p. 189)	8	321	40	5	14	314	641	61	9	15	13	14	48	5	15

PUDDINGS AND CUSTARDS

Is it possible to cook delicate puddings and custards in the microwave oven? You bet! These delectable desserts cook just as easily in your microwave as they do in your conventional oven or on your range-top.

Pudding proficiency

Before you tackle pudding and custard making in your microwave, we'd like to share a few pertinent points with you.

First, small amounts cook faster and more evenly. That's why our recipes make less than 4 cups.

Second, puddings and custards usually contain egg yolks. Thickening without overcooking the egg can be tricky, so we ask you to beat the yolks well and add them after the milk is steaming hot. That way, they cook in less time and are less likely to curdle.

Third, these delicate desserts cook more evenly in the round dishes we call for in our recipes. A square or rectangular dish would not work well for puddings or custards, because the food in the corners would cook faster than the food in the center.

And, when it comes to power levels, we found medium works best for large baked custards, and that high power is fine for small baked custards and for puddings that can be stirred.

A real bonus of microwave-cooked puddings and custards is that they need only occasional stirring. Just think, you won't have to hover over a hot range-top.

Bread Pudding
(see recipe, page 223)

When is it done?

As a rule, stirred custards and puddings will thicken in the microwave oven the same as in conventional cooking. When cooked, they'll coat a metal spoon.

But telling when a microwave-baked custard is done is another story. In microwave cooking, a baked custard's edges cook before its center is completely set. A small baked custard is ready when its edges are set but its center quivers like soft-set gelatin. A large baked custard is ready when a knife inserted 1 or 2 inches from the edge comes out clean, as shown on page 223. Baked custards will continue to set during the standing time.

Mocha Mousse
(see recipe, page 219)

Creamy Cheesecake Ring
(see recipe, page 224)

215

Preparing a pudding

Vanilla Pudding

See the Mocha Pudding variation, pictured opposite.

¾ cup sugar
¼ cup cornstarch
3 cups milk
4 beaten egg yolks
3 tablespoons butter
    or margarine
1½ teaspoons vanilla

■ In a 1½-quart casserole stir together sugar and cornstarch. Stir in milk. Cook, uncovered, on 100% power (high) for 7 to 9 minutes or till thickened and bubbly, stirring every 2 minutes till slightly thickened, then every 30 seconds (see photo 1). Cook, uncovered, for 1 minute more.

■ Meanwhile, in a small mixing bowl beat egg yolks well with a rotary beater. Gradually stir about *1 cup* of the hot mixture into beaten egg yolks (see photo 2). Return all to the hot mixture remaining in the casserole. Cook, uncovered, on high for 2 to 3 minutes more or till edges are bubbly (see photo 3), stirring every 30 seconds. Cook, uncovered, for 30 seconds more.

■ Stir in the butter or margarine and vanilla. Serve the pudding warm or chilled. To chill, cover the surface with clear plastic wrap (see photo 4). Chill in the refrigerator without stirring. Makes 6 to 8 servings.

Low-wattage oven: For *milk-cornstarch mixture,* cook 11 to 13 minutes.

Mocha Pudding: Prepare Vanilla Pudding as above, *except* increase sugar to *1 cup.* Before cooking the milk-cornstarch mixture, stir in 3 squares (3 ounces) *unsweetened chocolate,* cut up, and 1 tablespoon *instant coffee crystals.*

Coconut Pudding: Prepare Vanilla Pudding as above, *except* stir in 1 cup *coconut* with the butter or margarine and vanilla.

Butterscotch Pudding: Prepare Vanilla Pudding as above, *except* substitute packed *brown sugar* for the sugar and increase butter or margarine to ¼ *cup.*

Citrus Pudding: Prepare Vanilla Pudding as above, *except* increase sugar to *1 cup* and cornstarch to ⅓ *cup.* Gradually stir in 1 teaspoon finely shredded *lemon or lime peel* and ⅓ cup *lemon or lime juice* with the butter or margarine and vanilla.

Maple-Nut Pudding: Prepare Vanilla Pudding as above, *except* substitute ½ cup packed *brown sugar* for the sugar and add ¼ cup *maple-flavored syrup or molasses* with the milk. Before serving, sprinkle with ¼ cup toasted chopped *pecans, walnuts, or almonds.*

1

During cooking, stir the milk-cornstarch mixture every 2 minutes until it's slightly thickened. Then stir every 30 seconds until completely thickened, as shown.

2

Gradually stir about *1 cup* of the hot mixture into the beaten egg yolks, then return all of the mixture to the cooking container. If you added the egg to the hot mixture without first warming it this way, it would cook too quickly and form flecks in the pudding.

3

After combining the hot mixture with the egg yolks, cook the pudding, uncovered, until the edges are bubbly, as shown.

4

If you chill the pudding, be sure to cover the surface with clear plastic wrap. Without the wrap, a skin would form on top of the pudding during chilling.

Meringue-Topped Pudding

Make any variation of the Vanilla Pudding or whip up a pudding mix.

Vanilla Pudding (see recipe, page 216) *or* one 6-serving-size *regular* pudding mix (see chart, page 225)
2 egg whites
½ teaspoon vanilla
¼ teaspoon cream of tartar
¼ cup sugar
1½ cups fresh fruit, cut up (optional)

■ Prepare the pudding as directed and set aside. For meringue, in a small mixer bowl combine egg whites, vanilla, and cream of tartar. Beat with an electric mixer on medium speed about 1 minute or till soft peaks form (tips curl). Gradually add sugar, beating on high speed till stiff glossy peaks form (tips stand straight) and sugar is dissolved.

■ If desired, arrange fruit in 6 microwave-safe dessert dishes. Spoon the warm pudding into the dishes. Spoon meringue atop pudding. Arrange the dishes in a circle in the microwave oven. Cook, uncovered, on 100% power (high) for 1½ to 2 minutes or till a knife inserted into meringue comes out clean (see photo 2, page 179). Serve warm or cooled. Store in the refrigerator. Makes 6 servings.

Low-wattage oven: If 6 dishes will not fit, cook 3 dishes at a time on high for 1½ to 2 minutes.

Double-Deck Parfaits

The two layers: peanutty chocolate and smooth French vanilla.

2½ cups milk
1 package 4-serving-size *regular* French vanilla pudding mix
½ cup semisweet chocolate pieces
2 tablespoons peanut butter
1 tablespoon cooking oil

■ In a 4-cup measure combine milk and pudding mix. Cook, uncovered, on 100% power (high) for 6 to 8 minutes or till slightly thickened and bubbly, stirring twice. Set aside.

■ In a 2-cup measure cook chocolate pieces, uncovered, on high for 1 to 2 minutes or till soft enough to stir smooth, stirring once during cooking (see photo 2, page 92). Stir in peanut butter, cooking oil, and *half* of the vanilla pudding mixture.

■ In 8 parfait glasses layer vanilla mixture and chocolate mixture. Cover and chill in the refrigerator till serving time. Makes 8 servings.

Low-wattage oven: For *milk mixture,* cook on high for 10 to 12 minutes.

> **Double-Deck Pops:** Spoon about *3 tablespoons* of the chocolate pudding mixture into eight 3-ounce paper cups. Add a scant *¼ cup* vanilla pudding mixture to each cup. Cover paper cups with foil. Insert a wooden stick through the foil into the center of each pop. Freeze about 4 hours or till set. Let stand for 10 to 15 minutes before serving. Remove foil and paper cups.

Mocha Mousse

Our taste panel rated this outstanding. (Pictured on pages 214–215.)

½ cup semisweet chocolate
    pieces
2 tablespoons water
1 tablespoon sugar
1½ teaspoons instant coffee
    crystals
2 slightly beaten egg yolks
½ teaspoon vanilla
2 egg whites
⅛ teaspoon cream of tartar
2 tablespoons sugar
½ cup whipping cream
    Unsweetened whipped cream
    Chocolate curls (optional)

■ In a 2-cup measure combine chocolate, water, 1 tablespoon sugar, and coffee. Cook, uncovered, on 100% power (high) for 1 to 2 minutes or till mixture is hot and chocolate is soft enough to stir smooth (see photo 2, page 92). Stir once during cooking. Gradually stir all of the hot mixture into egg yolks (see photo 2, page 217). Stir in vanilla. Beat with a rotary beater for 1 minute. Cool slightly, about 5 minutes, stirring occasionally.

■ In a small mixer bowl combine egg whites and cream of tartar. Beat till soft peaks form (tips curl). Gradually add 2 tablespoons sugar, beating till stiff peaks form (tips stand straight). Fold about *one-third* of the egg whites into cooled mixture. Fold mixture into remaining whites.

■ Beat ½ cup whipping cream till soft peaks form. Fold into mixture. Spoon into 4 or 5 dessert dishes. Cover. Chill about 3 hours or till firm. Top with whipped cream and chocolate curls, if desired. Serves 4 or 5.

Pumpkin Custards

⅔ cup canned pumpkin or
    mashed winter squash
¼ cup sugar
½ teaspoon ground cinnamon
⅛ teaspoon ground ginger
    Dash ground cloves
1 cup milk
2 eggs
2 egg yolks
½ teaspoon finely shredded
    orange peel
½ teaspoon vanilla
1½ cups water
    Whipped cream (optional)
    Chopped walnuts (optional)

■ In a 2-cup measure combine pumpkin, sugar, cinnamon, ginger, and cloves. Stir in milk. Cook, uncovered, on 100% power (high) for 2 to 4 minutes or till steaming and foamy but not boiling (about 160°) (see photo 1, page 221), stirring twice during cooking.

■ Meanwhile, in a bowl beat eggs and egg yolks well with a rotary beater. Gradually stir all of the hot pumpkin mixture into beaten eggs. Stir in orange peel and vanilla. Place four 6-ounce custard cups in an 8x8x2-inch baking dish. Pour egg mixture into custard cups.

■ In the same 2-cup measure heat water, uncovered, on high for 3 to 5 minutes or till boiling. Pour the boiling water into the baking dish around the custard cups (see photo 2, page 221).

■ Cook, uncovered, on high for 3 minutes, giving the baking dish a quarter-turn every minute (see photo 3, page 221). After 3 minutes, rotate the custard cups (see photo 4, page 221). Cook, uncovered, on high for 30 seconds to 3 minutes more or till edges are set but center still quivers. After 30 seconds, check for doneness every 15 seconds, turning custards as necessary. Remove each custard as it is done.

■ Let stand, uncovered, on a wire rack for at least 20 minutes (see photo 5, page 221). Serve warm or chilled (see photo 6, page 221). If desired, top with whipped cream and chopped walnuts. Makes 4 servings.

Low-wattage oven: Not recommended.

Cooking individual custards

Baked Custards

Satiny-smooth old-time custards with a new time: 16 minutes.

1½ cups milk
⅓ cup sugar
3 eggs
1 teaspoon vanilla
1½ cups water
   Ground nutmeg (optional)
   Chocolate curls *or* finely
      shredded orange peel
      (optional)

■ In a 2-cup measure combine milk and sugar. Cook, uncovered, on 100% power (high) for 3 to 5 minutes or till steaming and foamy but not boiling (about 180°) (see photo 1), stirring once during cooking.

■ Meanwhile, in a medium mixing bowl beat eggs well with a rotary beater. Gradually stir all of the hot mixture into beaten eggs. Stir in vanilla. Arrange four 6-ounce custard cups in an 8x8x2-inch baking dish. Pour custard mixture into custard cups.

■ In the same 2-cup measure heat water, uncovered, on high for 3 to 5 minutes or till boiling. Pour the boiling water into the baking dish around the custard cups (see photo 2).

■ Cook, uncovered, on high for 3 minutes, giving the baking dish a quarter-turn every minute (see photo 3). After 3 minutes, rotate the custard cups so the sides that were facing the center of the baking dish now face the edges (see photo 4).

■ Cook, uncovered, on high for 1 to 3 minutes more or till edges are set but center still quivers. After 1 minute, check for doneness every 15 seconds, turning custards as necessary. Remove each custard when done.

■ If desired, sprinkle custards with nutmeg. Let stand, uncovered, on a wire rack at least 15 minutes (see photo 5). Serve warm or chilled (see photo 6). If desired, unmold onto 4 dessert plates and garnish with chocolate curls or shredded orange peel. Makes 4 servings.

Low-wattage oven: Not recommended.

Baked Coffee Custards: Prepare Baked Custards as above, *except* stir 1 tablespoon *instant coffee crystals or instant flavored coffee powder* into the milk mixture before cooking.

Baked Chocolate Custards: Prepare Baked Custards as above, *except* increase sugar to ½ *cup* and combine sugar with 1 tablespoon *unsweetened cocoa powder* before adding to milk.

Spiced Baked Custards: Prepare Baked Custards as above, *except* stir ½ teaspoon ground *cinnamon or* ¼ teaspoon ground *cardamom or ginger* into the milk mixture before cooking.

1
In a cup measure heat the milk mixture, uncovered, until it's steaming and foamy but not boiling. If you have a temperature probe, use it to program your oven to stop when the mixture reaches the right temperature.

2
Pour the boiling water into the baking dish around the filled custard cups. The water helps the custards cook more evenly.

3
Cook the custards, uncovered, on high power, giving the baking dish a quarter-turn every minute of cooking.

4
After 3 minutes of cooking, rotate the custard cups in the baking dish so the sides that were facing the center now face the baking-dish edges. This helps the delicate custards cook more evenly. When checking for doneness, turn the custard cups as necessary.

5
When a custard's edges are set but its center still quivers, remove it from the oven. Let the almost-set custards stand on a wire rack to finish cooking. After standing, your baked custards should look like custard number 1, pictured above. Custard number 2 is overdone and custard number 3 is underdone.

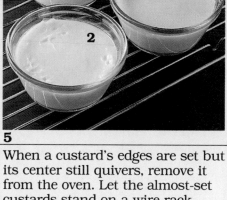

6
When you spoon into a perfectly cooked custard after the standing time, it should have a smooth, delicate texture and hold a cut edge, as shown.

Rice Pudding

Quick-cooking rice is the secret to this recipe's speed.

1½ cups milk
⅔ cup quick-cooking rice
¼ cup sugar
2 tablespoons butter *or* margarine
2 eggs
¼ cup raisins *or* other chopped dried fruit
½ teaspoon vanilla
¼ teaspoon ground cinnamon, ginger, *or* cardamom
1½ cups water

■ In a 1-quart casserole combine milk, uncooked rice, sugar, and butter or margarine. Cook, uncovered, on 100% power (high) for 3 to 5 minutes or just to boiling, stirring once to dissolve sugar.

■ In a mixing bowl beat eggs well. Gradually stir *1 cup* of the hot mixture into beaten eggs (see photo 2, page 217). Return all to the casserole. Stir in raisins, vanilla, and cinnamon, ginger, or cardamom.

■ Meanwhile, in a 4-cup measure heat water, uncovered, on high for 3 to 5 minutes or till boiling. Place the filled casserole in an 8x8x2-inch baking dish. Pour the boiling water into the baking dish around the casserole (see photo 2, page 221).

■ Cook, uncovered, on 50% power (medium) for 8 to 10 minutes or till done, stirring after 4 minutes. When the pudding is done, a knife inserted 1 inch from the edge will come out clean, though the top may still appear wet (see photo 2, opposite). Let stand, covered, on a wire rack for 15 minutes (see photos 5 and 6, page 221). Makes 4 servings.

Low-wattage oven: Not recommended.

Fluffy Tapioca Pudding

¼ cup sugar
2 tablespoons quick-cooking tapioca
2 cups milk
2 egg yolks
1 teaspoon vanilla
2 egg whites

■ In a 1½-quart casserole combine sugar and tapioca. Stir in milk and let stand for 5 minutes. Cook, uncovered, on 100% power (high) for 5 to 7 minutes or just to boiling, stirring once to dissolve sugar.

■ In a mixing bowl beat egg yolks well. Gradually stir *1 cup* of the hot mixture into beaten yolks (see photo 2, page 217). Return mixture to the casserole. Cook, uncovered, on high for 1 to 2 minutes or till bubbly (see photo 3, page 217), stirring every 30 seconds. Stir in vanilla. Let stand, uncovered, on a wire rack for 15 minutes (mixture will be thick).

■ In a small mixer bowl beat egg whites with an electric mixer till stiff peaks form (tips stand straight). Fold *1 cup* of the tapioca mixture into egg whites, then fold into remaining tapioca mixture, leaving fluffs of egg white. Cover and chill till serving time. Makes 4 servings.

> **Fluffy Pineapple-Tapioca Pudding:** Prepare Fluffy Tapioca Pudding as above, *except* stir one drained 8¼-ounce can *crushed pineapple* into tapioca mixture before adding it to egg whites.

Bread Pudding

Pictured on pages 214–215.

1 12-ounce can (1½ cups) evaporated milk *or* 1½ cups milk
¼ cup sugar
3 eggs
3 slices day-old bread, cubed (2¼ cups)
½ teaspoon vanilla
⅛ teaspoon ground nutmeg, cardamom, cinnamon, *or* ginger
¼ cup raisins *or* mixed dried fruit bits

■ In a 1-quart casserole combine milk and sugar. Cook, uncovered, on 100% power (high) for 3 to 5 minutes or just to boiling, stirring once to dissolve sugar.

■ In a mixing bowl beat eggs well. Gradually stir about *1 cup* of the hot mixture into eggs (see photo 2, page 217). Return all to casserole. Stir in bread cubes, vanilla, and nutmeg, cardamom, cinnamon, or ginger.

■ Cook the egg-bread mixture, covered, on 50% power (medium) for 1½ minutes. Stir in raisins or fruit (see photo 1, below). Cook, uncovered, on medium for 3 to 5 minutes more or till done, giving the dish a half-turn once. When the pudding is done, a knife inserted 1 inch from the edge will come out clean, though the top may still appear wet (see photo 2, below). Let stand, covered, on a wire rack for 15 minutes before serving (see photos 5 and 6, page 221). Makes 4 servings.

Low-wattage oven: For *egg-bread mixture,* cook on high for 1½ minutes. Stir in fruit. Cook on 30% power (defrost) for 6 to 8 minutes.

1

Stir the raisins or fruit into the egg-bread mixture after heating it for 1½ minutes. Stirring when the bread pudding is warm but not set helps it heat more evenly, without destroying its texture.

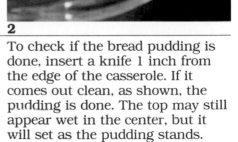

2

To check if the bread pudding is done, insert a knife 1 inch from the edge of the casserole. If it comes out clean, as shown, the pudding is done. The top may still appear wet in the center, but it will set as the pudding stands.

Creamy Cheesecake Ring

Unmold the cheesecake quickly by dipping the mold into warm water before turning the dessert out. (Pictured on pages 214–215.)

2 tablespoons finely crushed graham crackers (1 or 2 squares)
1 cup milk
½ teaspoon ground ginger
3 8-ounce packages cream cheese, cut up
1 4½-ounce package custard dessert mix
¼ cup sugar
1½ teaspoons finely shredded lemon peel
    Fresh nectarine *or* peach slices (optional)
    Mint sprigs *or* lemon leaves (optional)
    Pick-a-Fruit Sauce (see recipe, page 230) (optional)

■ Generously butter a 6-cup ring mold. Coat the mold with crushed graham crackers (see photo 2, page 77). Set aside. In a 2-cup measure combine milk and ginger. Cook, uncovered, on 100% power (high) for 2½ to 3½ minutes or till steaming and foamy but not boiling (about 180°) (see photo 1, page 221), stirring once. Set aside.

■ In a 2-quart casserole cook cream cheese, uncovered, on high for 1½ to 3 minutes or till softened, stirring once (see photo 1, below). Stir in custard mix, sugar, and lemon peel. Gradually stir in milk mixture. Cook, uncovered, on high for 3 to 5 minutes or till thickened, stirring every minute. Cook, uncovered, for 1½ minutes more.

■ Spoon mixture into the prepared mold (see photo 2, below). Cover the surface with clear plastic wrap (see photo 4, page 217). Chill in the refrigerator for 4 hours or overnight. Unmold onto a serving platter. If desired, garnish with fruit slices and mint or lemon leaves, then spoon Pick-a-Fruit Sauce over the top (see photo 3, below). Makes 12 servings.

1
Soften cream cheese quickly using the high setting on your microwave oven. Stir once during softening. Then stir in the custard mix, sugar, and lemon peel.

2
Pour the warm cheese mixture into the crumb-coated mold. To prevent a skin from forming, cover the surface with clear plastic wrap before chilling.

3
After unmolding the cheesecake, fill the center with sliced nectarines. Then spoon the fruit sauce over the whole cheesecake or, if you like, over each serving.

Making Pudding and Custard Mixes

In a 4-cup measure combine any flavor regular **pudding** or **custard** dessert mix and milk. Cook, uncovered, on 100% power (high) for time specified or till mixture boils, stirring every 2 minutes. The custard will thicken as it chills.

Regular Mix	Milk	Cooking time
4-serving-size package	2 cups	4 to 6 minutes*
6-serving-size package	3 cups	7 to 9 minutes*

*Note: Timings are for 600- to 700-watt microwave ovens and may be longer in low-wattage ovens.

Nutrition Analysis

	Number of servings	Calories	Protein (g)	Carbohydrate (g)	Fat (g)	Sodium (mg)	Potassium (mg)	Protein	Vitamin A	Vitamin C	Thiamine	Riboflavin	Niacin	Calcium	Iron
			Per Serving					Percent U.S. RDA Per Serving							
Baked Chocolate Custards (p. 220)	4	218	8	30	8	107	197	12	6	2	4	15	1	13	6
Baked Coffee Custards (p. 220)	4	183	8	22	8	97	215	12	6	2	4	15	2	13	5
Baked Custards (p. 220)	4	182	8	21	8	97	188	12	6	2	4	15	0	13	5
Bread Pudding (p. 223)	4	317	13	40	12	256	425	20	9	3	11	27	5	29	10
Butterscotch Pudding (p. 216)	6	310	6	37	16	152	292	9	13	3	5	15	1	19	9
Citrus Pudding (p. 216)	6	328	6	46	14	124	215	9	12	10	5	14	1	17	4
Coconut Pudding (p. 216)	6	350	6	42	18	158	239	10	12	3	5	15	1	17	5
Creamy Cheesecake Ring (p. 224)	12	271	5	18	21	215	106	8	17	1	1	9	1	7	4
Double-Deck Parfaits (p. 218)	8	186	4	22	11	112	189	7	2	2	2	8	4	10	3
Double-Deck Pops (p. 218)	8	186	4	22	11	112	189	7	2	2	2	8	4	10	3
Fluffy Pineapple-Tapioca Pudding (p. 222)	4	196	7	26	7	90	290	11	7	10	8	17	1	17	4
Fluffy Tapioca Pudding (p. 222)	4	177	7	21	7	89	216	11	7	3	4	16	1	16	3
Maple-Nut Pudding (p. 216)	6	325	6	37	17	131	302	10	12	3	9	15	1	20	9
Meringue-Topped Pudding (p. 218)	6	324	7	44	14	141	212	11	12	3	5	16	1	17	4
Mocha Mousse (p. 219)	4	286	5	23	21	41	131	7	12	0	2	8	1	4	6
Mocha Pudding (p. 216)	6	387	7	50	20	125	303	11	12	3	5	16	2	17	8
Pumpkin Custards (p. 219)	4	173	7	19	8	71	219	11	186	5	5	14	1	11	10
Rice Pudding (p. 222)	4	283	8	37	12	139	242	12	10	3	9	14	4	13	7
Spiced Baked Custards (p. 220)	4	182	8	21	8	97	188	12	6	2	4	15	0	13	5
Vanilla Pudding (p. 216)	6	287	6	35	14	124	197	9	12	3	5	14	1	16	4

SAUCES

Whip up super fast and easy sauces in your microwave oven. Once you've used our stir-and-heat sensations to dress up pork, poultry, pasta, fish, fruit, vegetables, ice cream, and cake, you may never go back to your conventional saucepans.

Sauces: sweet or savory
Our sauces offer a little something for every cook. You can concoct our simple dessert toppings by melting a few ingredients together. Or, you can try your hand at our classic sauces for spooning over meats, poultry, and fish.

We wanted our sauces to have something extra, so we dreamed up all sorts of flavor variations for you to taste. Our white sauce alone has four versions.

Sauce-cooking savvy
Because large amounts take a long time to cook in the microwave oven, our sauce recipes all make less than 3 cups and fit perfectly into either 2- or 4-cup glass measures.

You'll find a glass measure is just the thing for sauce cookery. You can mix and cook in it, then use the handle and spout for easy pouring. In most cases, we call for a glass measure with about twice the volume of the sauce. That way, the mixture has room to bubble up without spilling over.

If you do notice your sauce bubbling up, you can easily stop it from going over the top. Just open the microwave oven door and stir. Stirring from the center to the edges helps the sauce mixture heat evenly.

Chocolate Topping
(see recipe, page 232)

Citrus Sauce
(see recipe, page 231)

Praline Topping
(see recipe, page 232)

Pineapple-Rum-Raisin Sauce
(see recipe, page 231)

Pick-a-Fruit Sauce
(see recipe, page 230)

Thickening a sauce

White Sauce

A recipe no cook can be without! (See Cheese Sauce version, opposite.)

2 tablespoons butter *or* margarine
2 tablespoons all-purpose flour
⅛ teaspoon salt
Dash pepper
1 cup milk

■ In a 2-cup measure cook butter or margarine, uncovered, on 100% power (high) for 40 to 50 seconds or till melted. Stir in flour, salt, and pepper till combined (see photo 1). Add milk all at once. Stir to combine.

■ Cook, uncovered, on high for 3 to 5 minutes or till thickened and bubbly, stirring every minute till the sauce starts to thicken (see photo 2), then stirring every 30 seconds (see photo 3). Cook, uncovered, for 30 seconds more. Serve the sauce over fish, poultry, or vegetables. Makes about 1 cup (8 servings).

Cheese Sauce: Prepare White Sauce as above, *except* omit the salt and stir in 1 cup shredded *cheese* (4 ounces) after thickening. (Choose from *cheddar, Swiss, American, Havarti, Monterey Jack, Muenster, or brick cheese.*) Stir till cheese is melted (see photo 4). Serve over vegetables, fish, chicken, or eggs (see large photo).

Herbed White Sauce: Prepare White Sauce as above, *except* stir in 1½ teaspoons snipped *fresh herb or* ½ teaspoon crushed *dried herb* with flour. (Choose from *basil, dill, tarragon, thyme, or oregano.* Or, use 1 tablespoon *fresh parsley or chives or* 1 teaspoon *dried parsley or chives.*) Serve over chicken, vegetables, or fish.

Spiced White Sauce: Prepare White Sauce as above, *except* stir in ¼ teaspoon ground *spice* with the flour. (Choose from *cinnamon, cardamom, nutmeg, ginger, fennel seed, caraway seed, or aniseed.*) Serve over lamb, pork, beef, or vegetables.

Wine Sauce: Prepare White Sauce as above, *except* stir in 2 tablespoons *dry white wine, dry sherry, or dry marsala* after thickening. Serve over fish, pork, or chicken.

Doubled White Sauce: Prepare White Sauce as directed, *except* double all of the ingredients and use a 4-cup measure. Cook the butter or margarine on high for 45 to 60 seconds. Cook the sauce on high for 6 to 8 minutes. Makes 2¼ cups (18 servings).

Low-wattage oven: For *Doubled White Sauce,* cook the sauce on high for 16 to 19 minutes, stirring every 2 minutes till slightly thickened, then every 30 seconds.

1
Stir the flour and pepper into the melted butter or margarine. Mix the dry ingredients and butter well so the white sauce won't lump when you add the milk.

2
Cook the white sauce, uncovered, until it's slightly thickened, as shown. During this time you should stir the mixture every minute. Be sure to scrape the corners as you stir.

3
Cook the slightly thickened sauce till thickened and bubbly, as shown. During this time you should stir every 30 seconds to keep lumps from forming and the mixture from boiling over.

4
For the cheese sauce, you won't need to cook the mixture to melt the cheese. Just add the shredded cheese and stir till it's melted, as shown above. Then pour the sauce over fish, chicken, eggs, or vegetables, as shown at right.

Chunky Tomato Sauce

Use your kitchen shears to snip the tomatoes right in the can.

½ cup chopped onion
½ cup chopped carrot, celery,
    green pepper, *or* zucchini
2 cloves garlic, minced
1 teaspoon dried oregano
    or basil, crushed
1 16-ounce can tomatoes
1 6-ounce can tomato paste
½ teaspoon sugar
    Few drops bottled hot
    pepper sauce (optional)

■ In a 1½-quart casserole combine onion; chopped carrot, celery, green pepper, or zucchini; garlic; oregano or basil; and 2 tablespoons *water*. Cook, covered, on 100% power (high) for 4 to 6 minutes or till tender.

■ Cut up tomatoes. Stir *undrained* tomatoes, tomato paste, sugar, and hot pepper sauce (if desired) into the vegetable mixture. Cook, covered, on high for 3 to 5 minutes or till boiling, stirring once. Cook, covered, on 50% power (medium) for 10 minutes, stirring once. Serve over meat, fish, eggs, pasta, or poultry. Makes about 2½ cups sauce (10 servings).

Low-wattage oven: Cook on high for 5 minutes after boiling.

Spiced Applesauce

Serve with pork or over ice cream or pound cake.

6 medium apples (2 pounds)
¼ to ⅓ cup sugar
¼ cup cranberry juice cocktail
    or water
¼ teaspoon ground cinnamon,
    dash ground cloves, *or* one
    1-inch piece of fresh
    gingerroot, peeled

■ Peel, quarter, and core apples. Set aside. In a 2-quart casserole combine sugar, juice or water, and cinnamon, cloves, or gingerroot. Add apples. Toss gently to coat. Cook, covered, on 100% power (high) for 7 to 9 minutes or till tender, stirring every 3 minutes. If using ginger, remove it. For smooth applesauce, mash with a potato masher. Serve warm or chilled. Makes 2 cups (4 to 6 servings).

Low-wattage oven: Cook on high for 10 to 12 minutes.

Pick-a-Fruit Sauce

See the strawberry sauce, pages 215 and 227; the raspberry, page 224.

½ teaspoon finely shredded
    orange peel
¼ cup orange juice
1 tablespoon cornstarch
¼ teaspoon ground cinnamon
    Desired fruit*

■ See photos, page 229. In a 4-cup measure combine peel, juice, cornstarch, and cinnamon. Stir in *undrained* fruit. Cook, uncovered, on 100% power (high) 3 to 5 minutes or till thickened and bubbly, stirring every minute till slightly thickened, then every 30 seconds. Cook for 1 minute more. Serve over cake or ice cream. Makes 1½ cups (6 servings).

*Fruit options: 1 partially thawed 10-ounce package frozen red raspberries, strawberries, *or* peach slices (in quick-thaw pouch); *or* one 8- to 8¾-ounce can unpeeled apricot halves, pitted light sweet cherries, fruit cocktail, peach *or* pear slices, *or* crushed pineapple.

Citrus Sauce

Pictured on pages 226–227.

½ teaspoon finely shredded
   orange peel (optional)
¾ cup orange, grapefruit,
   or unsweetened pineapple
   juice
¼ cup packed brown sugar
1 tablespoon cornstarch
   Orange peel strips (optional)

■ In a 2-cup measure combine shredded orange peel (if desired), juice, brown sugar, and cornstarch. Cook, uncovered, on 100% power (high) for 2 to 3 minutes or till thickened and bubbly, stirring every minute till slightly thickened, then every 30 seconds (see photos 2 and 3, page 229). Serve warm over sponge cake, gingerbread, or bread pudding. Garnish with peel strips, if desired. Makes 1 cup (4 servings)

Lemon or Lime Sauce: Prepare Citrus Sauce as above, *except* increase brown sugar to ⅓ *cup,* substitute ½ teaspoon finely shredded *lemon or lime peel* for the orange peel, and substitute ⅓ cup *lemon or lime juice* and ⅓ cup *water* for the juice.

Pineapple-Rum-Raisin Sauce

Pictured on pages 226–227.

2 tablespoons raisins
2 tablespoons rum
1 8¼-ounce can pineapple
   chunks
2 tablespoons brown sugar
1 tablespoon butter *or*
   margarine
2 teaspoons cornstarch

■ In a small bowl combine raisins and rum. Set aside. Drain pineapple chunks, reserving ⅓ *cup* of the syrup. Set pineapple chunks aside. In a 2-cup measure combine reserved syrup, brown sugar, butter or margarine, and cornstarch. Cook, uncovered, on 100% power (high) for 1 to 2 minutes or till thickened and bubbly, stirring every minute till sauce starts to thicken, then every 30 seconds (see photos 2 and 3, page 229).

■ Stir in raisins, rum, and pineapple chunks. Cook, uncovered, on high about 1 minute more or till heated through. Serve over ice cream or cake. Makes 1¼ cups (5 servings).

Marshmallow-Chocolate Sauce

For parfaits, layer ice cream and peanuts with the chocolate sauce.

1 cup tiny marshmallows
1 6-ounce package (1 cup)
   semisweet chocolate *or*
   butterscotch-flavored
   pieces
¼ cup milk

■ In a 4-cup measure combine marshmallows, chocolate or butterscotch pieces, and milk. Cook, uncovered, on 100% power (high) for 1 to 2 minutes or till mixture is hot and marshmallows and pieces are soft enough to stir smooth, stirring once during cooking (see photo 2, page 92). Serve warm over ice cream or cake slices. Makes 1 cup (8 servings).

Chocolate Topping

Pictured on pages 226–227.

1 6-ounce package (1 cup) semisweet chocolate pieces
¼ cup milk
¼ cup light corn syrup
2 teaspoons desired liqueur (optional)

■ In a 2-cup measure cook chocolate, uncovered, on 100% power (high) for 1½ to 2½ minutes or till soft enough to stir smooth, stirring once (see photo 2, page 92). Stir in milk and syrup. Cook, uncovered, on high for 1 to 2 minutes more or till warm. Stir till smooth. Stir in liqueur, if desired. Serve over ice cream. Makes about 1 cup (8 servings).

Mocha Topping: Prepare Chocolate Topping as above, *except* stir in 2 teaspoons *instant coffee crystals* with the milk and corn syrup.

Peanut Butter 'n' Chocolate Topping: Prepare Chocolate Topping as above, *except* stir in ¼ cup *creamy peanut butter* with the milk and corn syrup.

Minty Chocolate Topping: Prepare Chocolate Topping as above, *except* stir in 10 crushed *colored butter mints* with milk and syrup.

Nutty Chocolate Topping: Prepare Chocolate Topping as above, *except* stir in 2 tablespoons chopped *nuts* with milk and syrup.

Butterscotch Topping

See the Praline Topping variation on pages 226–227.

½ cup packed brown sugar
2 tablespoons butter *or* margarine
2 tablespoons milk
½ teaspoon vanilla

■ In a 2-cup measure combine brown sugar, butter or margarine, and milk. Cook, uncovered, on 100% power (high) 1 to 2 minutes or till sugar is dissolved and mixture is heated through, stirring every 30 seconds. Stir in vanilla. Serve over ice cream. Makes about ½ cup (4 servings).

Praline Topping: Prepare Butterscotch Topping as above, *except* stir in 2 tablespoons toasted chopped *pecans* with the vanilla.

Coconut Topping: Prepare topping as above, *except* add ¼ cup *coconut* and 2 tablespoons chopped *walnuts* with the vanilla.

Quick Caramel Topping

As easy as unwrapping caramels.

25 vanilla *or* chocolate caramels
2 tablespoons water

■ In a 4-cup measure cook caramels and water, uncovered, on 100% power (high) for 2 to 3 minutes or till soft enough to stir smooth, stirring once (see photo 1, page 92). Top ice cream. Makes ¾ cup (6 servings).

Nutrition Analysis

	Number of servings	Per Serving						Percent U.S. RDA Per Serving							
		Calories	Protein (g)	Carbohydrate (g)	Fat (g)	Sodium (mg)	Potassium (mg)	Protein	Vitamin A	Vitamin C	Thiamine	Riboflavin	Niacin	Calcium	Iron
Butterscotch Topping (p. 232)	4	158	0	27	6	71	108	0	5	0	0	1	0	3	5
Cheese Sauce (p. 228)	8	109	5	3	9	132	63	7	6	1	2	6	1	14	1
Chocolate Topping (p. 232)	8	142	1	20	8	11	81	2	0	0	0	2	1	2	5
Chunky Tomato Sauce (p. 230)	10	31	1	7	0	211	297	2	48	26	4	3	5	3	5
Citrus Sauce (p. 231)	4	80	0	20	0	5	136	1	1	30	2	1	1	2	3
Coconut Topping (p. 232)	4	206	1	30	10	84	143	2	5	0	1	1	1	4	6
Doubled White Sauce (p. 228)	18	46	1	3	4	68	43	2	3	1	1	3	1	3	1
Herbed White Sauce (p. 228)	8	53	1	3	4	77	58	2	4	1	2	3	1	4	1
Lemon or Lime Sauce (p. 231)	4	81	0	21	0	6	88	0	0	16	0	0	0	2	3
Marshmallow-Chocolate Sauce (p. 231)	8	131	1	17	8	6	81	2	0	0	0	2	1	2	4
Minty Chocolate Topping (p. 232)	8	160	1	25	8	22	81	2	0	0	0	2	1	2	6
Mocha Topping (p. 232)	8	142	1	20	8	11	81	2	0	0	0	2	1	2	5
Nutty Chocolate Topping (p. 232)	8	154	1	21	9	11	90	2	0	0	1	2	1	2	6
Peanut Butter 'n' Chocolate Topping (p. 232)	8	190	3	21	12	49	136	5	0	0	1	2	6	2	6
Pick-a-Fruit Sauce (p. 230)	6	58	0	15	0	1	74	1	1	15	1	1	1	1	2
Pineapple-Rum-Raisin Sauce (p. 231)	5	84	0	13	2	26	106	1	2	6	3	1	1	1	3
Praline Topping (p. 232)	4	183	1	28	9	71	122	1	5	0	2	1	0	4	6
Quick Caramel Topping (p. 232)	6	155	2	30	4	88	75	2	0	0	1	4	0	6	3
Spiced Applesauce (p. 230)	4	168	0	44	1	1	224	0	2	24	2	1	1	1	1
Spiced White Sauce (p. 228)	8	53	1	3	4	77	58	2	4	1	2	3	1	4	1
White Sauce (p. 228)	8	52	1	3	4	77	49	2	3	1	2	3	1	4	1
Wine Sauce (p. 228)	8	56	1	3	4	77	58	2	4	1	2	3	1	4	1

SOUPS AND STEWS

Microwave soups and stews can be hearty or light, homey or elegant, chunky or smooth.

But best of all, they can be quick. Take a look at the recipes in this chapter and see for yourself.

Soup's on!
If you've mastered boiling water in the microwave oven, then you're on your way toward making soups and stews. Simply combine the ingredients, then cook and stir until everything is done and the mixture is hot. Some of our recipes need thickening, but don't worry. We'll guide you through the extra step without a hitch.

Stewing power
We found that soups and stews cook fastest in small amounts on high power, so we scaled our recipes to serve two to four people and cooked most on high. Soups or stews that contain less-tender

Zesty Tomato Soup
(see recipe, page 241)

Creamed Leek Soup
(see recipe, page 242)

Gingered Vegetable-
Chicken Soup
(see recipe, page 240)

to bubble up but not over. And, because many of our recipes need covering, we chose casseroles with microwave-safe lids.

About the only other equipment you'll need is a blender or a food processor to make recipes like our Creamed Leek Soup.

meats, however, cook best on medium-high. The lower power and longer cooking help tenderize the meat and blend the flavors.

Microwave soup pots
As we selected cooking containers, we made sure each was large enough to allow the soup or stew

Taking the chill off
When it comes to reheating chilled or frozen soups, your microwave can't be beaten. For one or two servings, you can heat the mixture in individual bowls or mugs. The warmed bowls will help keep the soup hot and you won't have to wash extra dishes.

Polish Sausage Soup
(see recipe, page 238)

Simmering a stew

Lamb Stew with Minted Dumplings

Lamb and mint, stew and dumplings are natural go-togethers.

2 tablespoons butter *or* margarine
1 pound boneless lamb, trimmed and cut into ½-inch cubes
1 large onion, coarsely chopped (1 cup)
2 cloves garlic, minced
1 cup beef broth
½ cup dry white wine
3 medium carrots, cut into ¼-inch slices (1½ cups)
1 stalk celery, sliced ½ inch thick (½ cup)
½ teaspoon dried rosemary *or* thyme, crushed
¼ teaspoon salt
¼ teaspoon pepper
1 bay leaf
¼ cup cold water
2 tablespoons cornstarch
1 cup packaged biscuit mix
2 teaspoons dried parsley flakes
½ teaspoon dried mint, crushed
⅓ cup milk

■ In a 2-quart casserole cook butter or margarine, uncovered, on 100% power (high) for 40 to 50 seconds or till melted. Add lamb, onion, and garlic. Cook, covered, on high for 6 to 8 minutes or till lamb is no longer pink, stirring once.

■ Stir beef broth and wine into lamb mixture (see photo 1). Add carrots, celery, rosemary or thyme, salt, pepper, and bay leaf. Cook, covered, on high for 5 minutes or till boiling. Stir. Cook, covered, on 70% power (medium-high) for 15 to 20 minutes or till meat and vegetables are tender, stirring once.

■ Combine cold water and cornstarch (see photo 2). Stir cornstarch mixture into hot mixture. Cook, uncovered, on high for 2 to 3 minutes or till thickened and bubbly, stirring every minute till slightly thickened, then every 30 seconds (see photo 3). Remove bay leaf.

■ In a small mixing bowl stir together biscuit mix, parsley, and mint. Make a well in the center. Add milk all at once. Stir gently with a fork till just moistened. Drop from a tablespoon onto hot mixture in 8 mounds around the edges of the casserole (see photo 4).

■ Cook, uncovered, on high for 3 to 5 minutes or till dumplings are done, giving the dish a half-turn once. When done, the dumplings will no longer be doughy. To test for doneness, scratch the slightly wet surface with a wooden toothpick. The dumpling should be cooked underneath (see photo 5). Makes 4 main-dish servings.

Low-wattage oven: For *meat-vegetable mixture,* cook on high instead of medium-high and stir twice.

1

When the lamb has lost its pink color, add the beef broth and wine, as shown. Then stir in the carrots, celery, rosemary or thyme, salt, pepper, and bay leaf.

2

Stir together cold water and cornstarch, blending well. Make sure the water is cold; otherwise the cornstarch will lump during heating. Stir the cornstarch mixture into the hot mixture after simmering. The stew will look cloudy at first, then turn clear as it cooks and thickens.

3

Cook, uncovered, till the stew is clear, thickened, and bubbly, stirring every minute till slightly thickened, then every 30 seconds till thickened.

4

With 2 tablespoons, drop the dumpling dough onto the hot mixture, using the second spoon to push the dough off the first. Form 8 mounds around the edges of the casserole, leaving the center open. The ring formation allows the dumplings to cook evenly.

5

The dumplings won't brown, but you can tell when they're done by scratching the slightly wet surface with a toothpick. When done, the dumplings will look cooked just beneath the surface.

Beef and Barley Soup

Barley thickens this beef and vegetable soup.

1½ cups sliced mushrooms
½ cup coarsely chopped onion
½ cup sliced celery
¼ cup water
1 small clove garlic, minced
¾ pound beef stew meat, cut into ½-inch cubes
2 cups water
1 8-ounce can tomato sauce
1 7½-ounce can tomatoes, cut up
2 teaspoons instant beef bouillon granules
1 teaspoon dried basil, crushed
1 teaspoon Worcestershire sauce
⅛ teaspoon pepper
⅓ cup quick-cooking barley

■ In a 3-quart casserole combine mushrooms, onion, celery, ¼ cup water, and garlic. Cook, covered, on 100% power (high) for 3 to 5 minutes or till vegetables are tender, stirring once.

■ Add beef, 2 cups water, tomato sauce, *undrained* tomatoes, bouillon granules, basil, Worcestershire sauce, and pepper. Cook, covered, on high for 12 to 16 minutes or till boiling, stirring twice.

■ Stir barley into hot mixture. Cook, covered, on 70% power (medium-high) for 20 to 25 minutes or till meat and barley are tender, stirring 3 times. Makes 4 main-dish servings.

Low-wattage oven: For *barley mixture,* cook on high, not medium-high.

Polish Sausage Soup

Pictured on pages 234–235 and on the cover.

1½ cups water
½ cup elbow macaroni
1 medium onion, chopped (½ cup)
½ cup chopped green pepper
1 clove garlic, minced
2 teaspoons Worcestershire sauce
1 teaspoon instant beef bouillon granules
½ teaspoon dried basil, crushed
¼ teaspoon pepper
1 small zucchini, halved lengthwise and sliced
1 16-ounce can tomatoes, cut up
1 8-ounce can tomato sauce
1 pound fully cooked Polish sausage, sliced ¼ inch thick

■ In a 2-quart casserole combine water, macaroni, onion, green pepper, garlic, Worcestershire sauce, bouillon granules, basil, and pepper. Cover and cook on 100% power (high) for 10 to 12 minutes or till macaroni is tender, stirring twice. *Do not drain.*

■ Stir in sliced zucchini, *undrained* tomatoes, and tomato sauce. Cook, covered, on high for 7 to 9 minutes or till zucchini is crisp-tender, stirring once.

■ Stir in Polish sausage. Cook, covered, on high for 2 to 3 minutes more or till heated through, stirring once. Makes 4 main-dish servings.

Easy Cassoulet

Here's a quick takeoff on the classic French sausage-and-bean stew.

3 slices bacon
1 pound ground lamb
1 medium onion, chopped
    (½ cup)
1 clove garlic, minced
½ pound fully cooked Polish
    sausage, sliced ½ inch
    thick
1 15-ounce can great northern
    beans
1 8-ounce can tomato sauce
1 tablespoon chili sauce
½ teaspoon dried thyme,
    crushed
½ teaspoon instant beef
    bouillon granules
¼ teaspoon pepper
1 bay leaf

■ In a 1½-quart casserole arrange bacon slices. Cover with paper towels. Cook on 100% power (high) for 2 to 3 minutes or till crisp (see photo 1, page 191). Remove bacon, reserving drippings in casserole. Drain bacon on paper towels. Crumble bacon and set aside.

■ In the same casserole crumble lamb. Add onion and garlic. Cook, covered, on high for 4 to 7 minutes or till meat is no longer pink, stirring once. Drain off fat.

■ Stir in Polish sausage, *undrained* beans, tomato sauce, chili sauce, thyme, bouillon granules, pepper, and bay leaf. Cook, covered, on high for 9 to 12 minutes or till heated through, stirring twice.

■ Before serving, remove bay leaf. Sprinkle crumbled bacon on top. Makes 4 main-dish servings.

Turkey Chili Soup

For extra zing, spike this chunky soup with hot pepper sauce.

½ pound ground raw turkey
1 medium onion, chopped
    (½ cup)
¼ cup chopped green pepper
1 teaspoon chili powder
1 8-ounce can red kidney
    beans, drained
1 8-ounce can tomato sauce
1 7½-ounce can tomatoes,
    cut up
2 tablespoons catsup
½ teaspoon dried oregano,
    crushed
    Shredded cheddar cheese
    (optional)

■ In a 1½-quart casserole combine ground turkey, onion, green pepper, and chili powder. Cook, covered, on 100% power (high) for 4 to 6 minutes or till meat is no longer pink, stirring twice to break up meat.

■ Stir in kidney beans, tomato sauce, *undrained* tomatoes, catsup, and oregano. Cook, covered, on high for 7 to 10 minutes or till heated through, stirring once. Sprinkle each serving with shredded cheese, if desired. Makes 3 main-dish servings.

Gingered Vegetable-Chicken Soup

A quick fix-up for two. (Pictured on pages 234–235.)

1 14½-ounce can chicken broth
1 tablespoon dry sherry
¼ teaspoon ground ginger
1 cup loose-pack frozen mixed vegetables
1 cup cubed cooked chicken

■ In a 1½-quart casserole combine chicken broth, sherry, and ginger. Cook, covered, on 100% power (high) for 4 to 6 minutes or till boiling. Stir in vegetables and chicken. Cook, covered, on high for 3 to 5 minutes or till vegetables are crisp-tender and chicken is heated through, stirring once. Makes 2 main-dish servings.

Low-wattage oven: For *broth mixture,* cook on high for 9 to 11 minutes. For *soup,* cook on high for 6 to 8 minutes.

Dilled Fish Chowder

For an easy supper, serve this creamy chowder with a salad and rolls.

½ pound fresh *or* frozen fish fillets (cod, haddock, *or* orange roughy)
2 slices bacon
¼ cup sliced green onion
1 clove garlic, minced
1 medium potato, peeled and cut into ½-inch cubes (about 1 cup)
⅓ cup water
¼ cup chopped celery
1 tablespoon snipped parsley
1 teaspoon instant chicken bouillon granules
½ teaspoon dried dillweed
1¼ cups milk
2 tablespoons all-purpose flour
¼ teaspoon pepper

■ Thaw fish, if frozen (see photo 1, page 111). Cut into ¾-inch cubes. In a 1½-quart casserole place bacon. Cover with paper towels. Cook on 100% power (high) for 1½ to 2½ minutes or till crisp (see photo 1, page 191). Remove bacon, reserving drippings. Drain bacon on paper towels. Crumble bacon and set aside.

■ Add green onion and garlic to reserved drippings. Cook, uncovered, on high for 1 to 2 minutes or till green onion is tender.

■ Stir in potato, water, celery, parsley, chicken bouillon granules, and dillweed. Cover and cook on high for 4 to 6 minutes or till vegetables are almost tender, stirring once. Add fish. Cook, covered, on high for 3 to 5 minutes or till fish flakes with a fork.

■ Stir together milk, flour, and pepper. Stir into soup mixture. Cook, uncovered, on high for 4 to 6 minutes or till slightly thickened and bubbly, stirring every minute. Cook, uncovered, for 1 minute more, stirring once. Sprinkle crumbled bacon over each serving. Makes 2 main-dish servings.

Manhattan Clam Chowder

Tomatoes turn Manhattan clam chowder a distinctive red—a contrast to its cream-colored cousin, New England clam chowder.

1 slice bacon
1 small potato, peeled and cut into ½-inch cubes (¾ cup)
¼ cup chopped onion
¼ cup chopped celery
1 7½-ounce can tomatoes, cut up
1 6½-ounce can minced clams
1 6-ounce can tomato juice
1 small bay leaf
⅛ teaspoon dried thyme, crushed
⅛ teaspoon pepper
Snipped parsley (optional)

■ In a 1½-quart casserole place bacon. Cover with paper towels and cook on 100% power (high) for 1 to 2 minutes or till crisp (see photo 1, page 191). Remove bacon, reserving drippings. Drain bacon on paper towels. Crumble bacon and set aside.

■ Add potato, onion, and celery to reserved drippings. Cook, covered, on high for 4 to 6 minutes or till vegetables are tender, stirring once.

■ Stir in *undrained* tomatoes, *undrained* clams, tomato juice, bay leaf, thyme, and pepper. Cook, uncovered, on high for 3 to 5 minutes or till heated through, stirring once. Remove bay leaf. Stir in crumbled bacon. Garnish with parsley, if desired. Makes 3 side-dish servings.

Zesty Tomato Soup

Worcestershire + radish + lemon = zest! (Pictured on pages 234–235.)

1½ cups chicken *or* beef broth
1 10¾-ounce can condensed tomato soup
2 large radishes, shredded
1 teaspoon snipped fresh dill *or* ¼ teaspoon dried dillweed
1 teaspoon Worcestershire sauce
¼ teaspoon pepper
2 slices lemon, halved

■ In a 4-cup measure combine chicken or beef broth, condensed tomato soup, shredded radishes, fresh or dried dill, Worcestershire sauce, and pepper. Cook, uncovered, on 100% power (high) for 7 to 9 minutes or till heated through, stirring once.

■ Pour soup into 4 small soup bowls. Garnish each serving with a lemon slice half. Makes 4 side-dish servings.

TIP Topping Soup Off

Top off soup with something fun that adds flavor and texture. For flavor, try citrus slices, fresh herbs, crumbled bacon, or shredded cheese. For crunch, float oyster crackers, croutons, or popcorn.

Creamed Leek Soup

Use process cheese for a velvety soup. (Pictured on pages 234–235.)

4 medium leeks (¾ pound)
1 tablespoon water
2 tablespoons butter *or* margarine
2 tablespoons all-purpose flour
½ teaspoon instant chicken bouillon granules
⅛ teaspoon ground nutmeg
⅛ teaspoon pepper
2 cups milk
1 cup shredded process Swiss cheese (4 ounces)
Snipped chives (optional)

■ Clean and thinly slice leeks (see photo 1, below). You should have about 2½ cups. In a 1½-quart casserole combine leeks and water. Cook, covered, on 100% power (high) for 3 to 5 minutes or till tender. Add *undrained* leeks to a food processor or blender container. Cover and process or blend till mixture is nearly smooth (see photo 2, below).

■ For soup base, in the same casserole cook butter or margarine on high for 40 to 50 seconds or till melted. Stir in flour, bouillon granules, nutmeg, and pepper (see photo 1, page 229). Stir in milk. Cook, uncovered, on high for 6 to 8 minutes or till slightly thickened and bubbly, stirring every minute till thickening starts, then every 30 seconds (see photos 2 and 3, page 229).

■ Add cheese. Stir till melted (see photo 4, page 229). Add pureed leeks (see photo 3, below). Cook, uncovered, on high for 1 to 2 minutes or till heated through. Top with chives, if desired. Makes 4 side-dish servings.

Low-wattage oven: For *soup base,* cook on high for 8 to 10 minutes. For *soup,* cook on high for 2 to 3 minutes.

1

With a sharp knife, thinly slice the cleaned leeks. Then measure to see if you have 2½ cups. If not, slice another leek.

2

Place the undrained cooked leeks in a food processor or blender container. Cover and process or blend until the mixture is nearly smooth, as shown.

3

Add the pureed leeks to the cheesy soup base. Stir well to distribute. The leeks help to thicken and flavor the soup.

Scandinavian Fruit Soup

Serve as a first course or a dessert.

1   12-ounce can apricot nectar
2   teaspoons quick-cooking
      tapioca
1   cup mixed dried fruit
      (apricots, apples, pears,
      and prunes)
1½ cups water
¼   cup raisins
1   to 2 inches stick cinnamon
¼   teaspoon ground nutmeg
¼   cup currant jelly
      Whipped cream (optional)

■ In a 2-cup measure combine apricot nectar and tapioca. Let stand for 5 minutes.

■ Meanwhile, cut dried fruit into bite-size pieces, discarding prune pits. In a 2-quart casserole combine cut fruit, water, raisins, cinnamon, and nutmeg. Cook, covered, on 100% power (high) for 3 to 5 minutes or till fruit is almost tender, stirring once.

■ Stir nectar mixture and currant jelly into fruit mixture. Cook, covered, on 70% power (medium-high) for 7 to 10 minutes or till tapioca is clear and fruit is tender, stirring twice (see photo, page 131). Remove stick cinnamon. Serve warm or chilled. Dollop with whipped cream, if desired. Makes 4 side-dish servings.

Nutrition Analysis

	Number of servings	Calories	Protein (g)	Carbohydrate (g)	Fat (g)	Sodium (mg)	Potassium (mg)	Protein	Vitamin A	Vitamin C	Thiamine	Riboflavin	Niacin	Calcium	Iron
Beef and Barley Soup (p. 238)	4	235	21	23	6	531	760	33	19	27	10	18	29	5	22
Creamed Leek Soup (p. 242)	4	303	14	22	18	256	376	21	14	20	8	20	3	47	12
Dilled Fish Chowder (p. 240)	2	343	30	32	10	478	1066	46	7	26	17	21	22	22	8
Easy Cassoulet (p. 239)	4	449	32	22	26	1073	885	49	13	21	37	20	35	7	26
Gingered Vegetable-Chicken Soup (p. 240)	2	216	26	14	5	731	543	40	93	11	11	11	56	4	12
Lamb Stew with Minted Dumplings (p. 236)	4	395	21	35	17	853	532	32	310	16	21	20	28	8	16
Manhattan Clam Chowder (p. 241)	3	111	8	16	2	721	559	12	17	31	8	7	11	7	20
Polish Sausage Soup (p. 238)	4	493	21	27	33	1592	965	32	29	59	55	18	33	7	21
Scandinavian Fruit Soup (p. 243)	4	209	1	54	0	13	457	2	32	85	1	2	2	2	8
Turkey Chili Soup (p. 239)	3	186	23	19	3	761	972	36	34	86	33	27	40	7	20
Zesty Tomato Soup (p. 241)	4	69	3	11	2	828	256	5	9	50	4	3	10	2	8

VEGETABLES

Your microwave oven is just about the best vegetable cooker around. Vegetables not only cook quickly in the microwave, but they also retain their valuable nutrients and natural color.

A cut above
Vegetables micro-cook more evenly if all the pieces are the same size. To avoid having one potato cook faster than another, choose whole potatoes that are of equal size. For cut-up vegetables, cube, slice, or chop them into even-size pieces.

Making arrangements
Because foods in the center of a dish cook slower than foods at the edges, place the tenderest parts of your vegetables toward the middle. That way, delicate asparagus tips or broccoli flowerets will be cooked just right at the same time the less-tender stems are done.

For even cooking, remember to move less-cooked pieces from the center to the edges periodically during cooking. Don't worry, though, about trying to figure out when rearranging is necessary. Our recipes tell you.

Letting off steam
Some whole vegetables with skins, such as potatoes and squash, can pop when you micro-cook them.

Nacho Potato Slices
(see recipe, page 260)

That's why it's important to prick the skins with a fork before cooking. The tiny holes let steam escape as the vegetables cook.

Although you don't want steam to build up inside vegetables, you do want steam to cook them on the outside. For that reason, cover vegetables with a microwave-safe lid or vented clear plastic wrap to trap steam and speed cooking.

Cooking on high
It's easy to remember which button to press when you're cooking vegetables. As a rule, just use high power.

When are they done?
Most vegetables are ready to eat when they're crisp-tender. That means the vegetables are tender but still slightly firm to the bite.

Peas, corn, potatoes, and some beans, however, should be cooked until completely tender to get rid of their starchy flavor. You can judge tenderness by poking vegetables with a fork.

Herbed Garlic Broccoli
(see recipe, page 249)

Creamy Peas and Carrots
(see recipe, page 260)

Steaming asparagus

Cheesy Asparagus Spears

¾ pound fresh asparagus *or* one 10-ounce package frozen asparagus spears
2 tablespoons water
½ cup cream-style cottage cheese, drained
¼ cup shredded cheddar cheese (1 ounce)
1 tablespoon sliced green onion
⅛ teaspoon pepper
  Several dashes bottled hot pepper sauce
1 teaspoon butter *or* margarine
2 tablespoons fine dry bread crumbs

■ Wash fresh asparagus and break off tough ends (see photo 1). In a 10x6x2-inch baking dish arrange fresh or frozen spears with tips toward center. Add water (see photo 2). Cover with vented clear plastic wrap. Cook on 100% power (high) for 7 to 9 minutes or till tender, rearranging asparagus once by switching center spears with those on the edges.

■ Meanwhile, in a small mixing bowl combine cottage cheese, cheddar cheese, green onion, pepper, and hot pepper sauce. Set aside. In a custard cup cook butter or margarine, uncovered, on high for 20 to 30 seconds or till melted. Stir in bread crumbs and set aside.

■ Drain asparagus (see photo 3). In the same baking dish arrange asparagus spears with tips toward edges. Spoon cheese mixture atop. Sprinkle with crumb mixture (see photo 4). Cook, uncovered, on high for 1 to 2 minutes or till cheddar cheese is melted, giving the dish a half-turn once. Serve immediately (see large photo). Makes 4 servings.

TIP **Buying Fresh Asparagus**

Look for fresh asparagus from mid-February through June. The season's best asparagus has firm, straight stalks with compact, closed tips. Avoid asparagus with wilted stalks and loose tips, signs that indicate toughness and stringiness.

To keep asparagus fresh in your refrigerator for one to two days, first wrap the stem ends in moist paper towels. Then place the whole stalks in a plastic bag to store.

1
Break off the woody base of each fresh asparagus spear where it snaps easily. You'll be left with the tender part of the stem and tip.

2
Arrange the asparagus spears in the baking dish with the tips facing the center. That way, the delicate tips won't overcook before the stems are done. Then spoon the water over the vegetables. You just need a little for steaming.

3
When the spears are tender, drain the water from the baking dish. By using as little water as possible for cooking, you're draining away fewer nutrients.

4
With the asparagus tips toward the edges, spoon the cheese mixture over the cooked spears, leaving the tips uncovered. Sprinkle the crumb mixture over the cheese, as shown above. Heat just to melt the cheese, then serve, as shown at right.

Savory Three-Bean Bake

Cook the bacon, then mix, heat, and serve—all in the same dish.

6 slices bacon
2 medium onions, sliced and separated into rings
1 16-ounce can baked beans
1 16-ounce can butter beans, drained
1 8½-ounce can lima beans, drained
¼ cup packed brown sugar
¼ cup chili sauce
3 tablespoons vinegar
1 tablespoon prepared mustard

■ In a 2-quart casserole arrange bacon. Cover with paper towels to prevent spattering. Cook on 100% power (high) for 4 to 6 minutes or till crisp (see photo 1, page 191). Remove bacon from the dish, reserving 1 tablespoon drippings. Drain on paper towels. Crumble and set aside.

■ Add onion rings to reserved drippings. Cook, covered, on high for 3 to 5 minutes or till onion is tender, stirring once. Drain well.

■ In the same casserole combine bacon, onion rings, *undrained* baked beans, drained butter beans, drained lima beans, brown sugar, chili sauce, vinegar, and mustard. Cook, uncovered, on high for 11 to 13 minutes or till heated through, stirring once. Makes 6 servings.

Low-wattage oven: For *bacon,* cook on high for 6 to 7 minutes.

Creamy Beans and Mushrooms

1 cup chopped celery
1 medium onion, chopped (½ cup)
¼ cup water
1 16-ounce package frozen cut green beans
1 7¾-ounce can semicondensed cream of mushroom soup
½ cup shredded American cheese (2 ounces)
1 4-ounce can mushroom stems and pieces, drained
¼ cup plain yogurt
Dash pepper

■ In a 2-quart casserole combine celery, onion, and water. Cook, covered, on 100% power (high) for 4 to 6 minutes or till vegetables are crisp-tender, stirring once. Stir in green beans. Cook, covered, on high for 8 to 10 minutes or till beans are crisp-tender, stirring once. Drain.

■ In a mixing bowl stir together semicondensed soup, shredded cheese, mushrooms, yogurt, and pepper. Stir into bean mixture. Cook, covered, on high for 2 to 3 minutes or till hot, stirring once. Makes 6 servings.

Low-wattage oven: For *soup mixture,* cook on high for 3 to 5 minutes.

Piquant Green Beans

2 slices bacon
1 teaspoon Dijon-style
   mustard
1 teaspoon Worcestershire
   sauce
4 drops bottled hot pepper
   sauce
1 9-ounce package frozen
   French-style green beans

■ In a 1-quart casserole arrange bacon. Cover with paper towels. Cook on 100% power (high) for 1½ to 2½ minutes or till crisp (see photo 1, page 191). Drain on paper towels, reserving 2 tablespoons drippings. In a small mixing bowl combine reserved bacon drippings, mustard, Worcestershire sauce, and hot pepper sauce. Set aside.

■ In the same casserole cook beans, covered, on high for 5 to 7 minutes or till crisp-tender, stirring once. Drain and return to the casserole. Pour mustard mixture over beans and toss to coat. Cook, uncovered, on high for 30 to 60 seconds or till heated through. Crumble bacon and sprinkle on top. Makes 3 servings.

Low-wattage oven: For *bacon,* cook on high for 2½ to 3½ minutes.

Cranberry-Sauced Beets

¼ cup frozen cranberry juice
   concentrate, thawed
2 tablespoons water
2 teaspoons cornstarch
¼ teaspoon finely shredded
   orange peel
   Dash salt
1 16-ounce can julienne
   beets, drained

■ In a 1-quart casserole combine cranberry juice concentrate, water, cornstarch, orange peel, and salt. Cook, uncovered, on 100% power (high) for 1 to 2 minutes or till thickened and bubbly, stirring every 30 seconds.

■ Stir beets into hot mixture. Cover with waxed paper. Cook on high for 2 to 3 minutes or till heated through, stirring once. Makes 3 servings.

Herbed Garlic Broccoli

See the mixed-vegetable option on pages 244–245.

1 10-ounce package frozen cut
   broccoli *or* 2 cups loose-
   pack frozen mixed
   vegetables
1 tablespoon butter *or*
   margarine
1 small clove garlic, minced
¼ teaspoon dried basil,
   crushed

■ In a 1-quart casserole cook broccoli or mixed vegetables, covered, on 100% power (high) for 4 to 6 minutes or till heated through, stirring once to break apart. Drain. Return broccoli to the casserole.

■ Add butter or margarine, garlic, basil, and a dash *pepper.* Cook, covered, on high for 2 to 4 minutes or till broccoli is crisp-tender. Toss gently to coat. Makes 4 servings.

Brussels Sprouts Italian

Gingered Broccoli Pilaf

¼ cup long grain rice
1 10-ounce package frozen
   cut broccoli
1 medium onion, chopped
   (½ cup)
2 tablespoons butter *or*
   margarine
1 clove garlic, minced
1 cup sliced fresh mushrooms
2 small tomatoes, peeled
   and chopped (⅔ cup)
¼ teaspoon salt
¼ teaspoon ground turmeric
¼ teaspoon ground ginger
¼ teaspoon ground cumin
   Dash ground red pepper
¼ cup plain yogurt

■ Cook rice according to the package directions. Meanwhile, in a 2-quart casserole cook frozen broccoli, covered, on 100% power (high) for 6 to 8 minutes or till crisp-tender, stirring once. Drain well and set aside.

■ In the same casserole combine onion, butter or margarine, and garlic. Cook, covered, on high for 2 minutes. Add mushrooms. Cook, covered, for 2 to 3 minutes more or till onion is tender.

■ Add cooked rice, broccoli, tomatoes, salt, turmeric, ginger, cumin, and red pepper. Stir in yogurt. Cook, uncovered, on high for 2 to 3 minutes or till heated through, stirring once. *Do not boil.* Makes 4 to 6 servings.

Brussels Sprouts Italian

To cook fresh brussels sprouts, see the directions on page 264.

1 10-ounce package (2 cups)
   frozen brussels sprouts
1 medium onion, cut into
   12 wedges
2 tablespoons Italian salad
   dressing
½ cup cherry tomatoes, halved

■ Hold frozen brussels sprouts under cold running water to separate. Cut large brussels sprouts in half. In a 1-quart casserole combine brussels sprouts, onion wedges, and salad dressing. Cook, covered, on 100% power (high) for 8 to 10 minutes or till tender, stirring once.

■ Stir in cherry tomato halves. Cook, covered, on high for 30 to 60 seconds more or till tomatoes are heated through. Makes 4 servings.

Low-wattage oven: For *sprouts,* cook on high for 11 to 13 minutes.

Chinese Cabbage
In Cheese Sauce

Chinese cabbage, Napa cabbage, and celery cabbage all describe the same vegetable.

2 slices bacon
1 medium head Chinese
   cabbage, coarsely chopped
   (6 cups)
2 tablespoons water
2 tablespoons sliced green
   onion
1 tablespoon all-purpose flour
¼ teaspoon dried dillweed
⅛ teaspoon salt
¾ cup milk
1 slice process Swiss cheese,
   cut into pieces

■ In a 1-quart casserole arrange bacon slices. Cover with paper towels. Cook on 100% power (high) for 1½ to 2½ minutes or till crisp (see photo 1, page 191). Remove bacon from the casserole, reserving 1 tablespoon drippings. Drain bacon on paper towels. Crumble and set aside.

■ In a 2-quart casserole place cabbage. Add water. Cover and cook on high for 2 to 4 minutes or till cabbage is crisp-tender. Drain cabbage well. Return cabbage to the casserole and set aside.

■ For sauce, in the 1-quart casserole cook green onion in reserved drippings, covered, on high for 1 to 2 minutes or till tender. Stir in flour, dillweed, and salt (see photo 1, page 229). Stir in milk. Cook, uncovered, on high for 3 to 5 minutes or till thickened and bubbly, stirring every minute till slightly thickened, then every 30 seconds (see photos 2 and 3, page 229). Cook for 30 seconds more. Add Swiss cheese. Stir till melted (see photo 4, page 229). Stir sauce into cabbage. Sprinkle crumbled bacon on top. Makes 4 servings.

Low-wattage oven: For *bacon,* cook on high for 2½ to 3½ minutes. For *cabbage,* cook on high for 5 to 7 minutes.

Cabbage in Chunky
Tomato Sauce

1 small head cabbage, cut
   into 4 wedges (1½ pounds)
2 tablespoons water
⅓ cup chopped onion
⅓ cup chopped green pepper
1 tablespoon olive *or*
   cooking oil
1 8-ounce can tomato sauce
¼ cup snipped parsley
2 tablespoons dry red wine
¼ teaspoon salt
⅛ teaspoon pepper
   Dash ground red pepper
   Grated Parmesan *or* Romano
   cheese

■ In an 8x8x2-inch baking dish combine cabbage and water. Cover with vented clear plastic wrap. Cook on 100% power (high) for 10 to 12 minutes or till cabbage is tender, giving the dish a half-turn and turning wedges over once. Drain well. Return cabbage to the dish and set aside.

■ For sauce, in a 2-cup measure combine onion, green pepper, and olive or cooking oil. Cook, covered, on high for 2 to 3 minutes or till vegetables are tender, stirring once.

■ Stir in tomato sauce, parsley, wine, salt, pepper, and ground red pepper. Cook, uncovered, on high for 1½ to 3 minutes or till boiling, stirring once. Pour over cabbage wedges. Sprinkle with Parmesan or Romano cheese. Makes 4 servings.

Orange-Glazed Carrots

Brown sugar and orange juice make a glossy caramel-colored glaze.

4 *or* 5 medium carrots
2 tablespoons water
2 tablespoons orange juice
2 teaspoons brown sugar
½ teaspoon cornstarch
  Dash salt
1 tablespoon butter *or*
  margarine
  Parsley sprigs (optional)

■ Bias-slice carrots into ½-inch pieces. (You should have 1½ cups.) In a 1-quart casserole combine carrots and water. Cook, covered, on 100% power (high) for 5 to 7 minutes or till crisp-tender. Drain and set aside.

■ For glaze, in a 1-cup measure combine orange juice, brown sugar, cornstarch, and salt. Cook, uncovered, on high for 30 seconds to 1½ minutes or till thickened and bubbly, stirring every 30 seconds. Add butter or margarine, then stir till melted. Pour over carrots. Toss to coat. If desired, garnish with parsley. Makes 3 servings.

Nutmeg-Carrot Puree

1½ pounds carrots, sliced
    (about 4 cups)
2 tablespoons water
¼ cup light cream *or* whipping
    cream
⅛ teaspoon salt
⅛ teaspoon ground nutmeg
    Dash pepper
1 egg
    Snipped parsley (optional)

■ In a 1½-quart casserole combine carrots and water. Cook, covered, on 100% power (high) for 14 to 16 minutes or till very tender, stirring twice. Drain. Place carrots in a blender container or food processor bowl. Cover and blend or process till smooth.

■ Add cream, salt, nutmeg, and pepper. Cover and blend till combined. Add egg and blend till combined. Spoon mixture into four 6-ounce custard cups. Cook, uncovered, on high for 1 to 2 minutes or till heated through. If desired, garnish with snipped parsley. Makes 4 servings.

Low-wattage oven: For *carrots,* cook on high 20 to 22 minutes. For *mixture in cups,* cook on high 3 minutes, rearranging after 2 minutes.

Curried Cauliflower

1 small onion, cut into wedges
2 tablespoons butter *or*
  margarine
1 clove garlic, minced
½ teaspoon curry powder
½ teaspoon grated gingerroot
¼ teaspoon salt
⅛ teaspoon pepper
4 cups cauliflower flowerets
1 tablespoon diced pimiento

■ In a 1½-quart casserole combine onion, butter or margarine, garlic, curry, gingerroot, salt, and pepper. Cook, covered, on 100% power (high) for 2 to 4 minutes or till onion is crisp-tender, stirring once.

■ Add cauliflower flowerets. Cook, covered, on high for 5 to 7 minutes or till cauliflower is crisp-tender, stirring once. Stir in diced pimiento. Makes 4 to 6 servings.

Low-wattage oven: For *onion mixture,* cook on high for 4 to 6 minutes. For *cauliflower mixture,* cook on high for 8 to 10 minutes.

Calico Cabbage Rolls

As you can see in photo 1, the texture of savoy cabbage adds a new wrinkle to this side-dish version of cabbage rolls.

⅓ cup long grain rice
1 8-ounce can tomato sauce
2 tablespoons chopped onion
2 tablespoons chopped celery
2 tablespoons finely chopped carrot
⅛ teaspoon dried basil, crushed
3 tablespoons grated Romano *or* Parmesan cheese
2 tablespoons snipped parsley
4 medium savoy *or* green cabbage leaves
Grated Romano *or* Parmesan cheese (optional)

■ Cook rice according to package directions. Meanwhile, for sauce, in a 2-cup measure combine tomato sauce, onion, celery, carrot, and basil. Cook, covered, on 100% power (high) for 5 to 7 minutes or till vegetables are crisp-tender, stirring once. Set aside.

■ For filling, in a small mixing bowl combine 3 tablespoons Romano or Parmesan cheese and parsley. Stir in cooked rice. Set aside.

■ Using a sharp knife, cut along both sides of the large center vein of each cabbage leaf and remove the vein, keeping the leaf in 1 piece (see photo 1). Rinse leaves and place in a 10x6x2-inch baking dish.

■ Cover the dish with vented clear plastic wrap. Cook on high for 5 to 7 minutes or till tender, rearranging once (see photo 2). Drain.

■ Place about ⅓ cup of the rice filling on *each* leaf. Fold in sides. Starting at an unfolded edge, roll up each leaf, making sure the folded sides are tucked into the roll (see photo 3).

■ Arrange rolls, seam side down, in the same 10x6x2-inch baking dish (see photo 4). Pour tomato sauce over cabbage rolls. Cook, covered, on high for 3 to 5 minutes or till filling is heated through, giving the baking dish a half-turn once.

■ If desired, serve the stuffed cabbage rolls and sauce with additional Romano or Parmesan cheese (see large photo). Makes 4 servings.

1

Use a sharp knife to cut along both sides of the large center vein of each savoy or green cabbage leaf. Remove the vein, keeping the leaf in one piece.

2

While cooking the cabbage, gently rearrange the leaves once so they will cook more evenly. The cabbage leaves are ready when they are limp enough to bend without breaking.

3

After you fold the sides of each leaf over the filling, start at an unfolded edge and roll the leaf to form a cabbage bundle, tucking in the sides to enclose the filling as you roll.

4

Arrange the filled cabbage rolls, seam side down, in the 10x6x2-inch baking dish, leaving some space between each roll, as shown above. After cooking, serve the cabbage rolls as a side dish with meat. Top with sauce and additional Romano or Parmesan, if desired, as shown at right.

Corn-Stuffed Green Peppers

Also try sweet red peppers for the edible bowls.

2 large green peppers
¼ cup dairy sour cream
1 teaspoon cornstarch
2 tablespoons milk
¼ teaspoon salt
⅛ teaspoon dried thyme, crushed
   Dash pepper
1 12-ounce can whole kernel corn with sweet peppers
1 4-ounce can mushroom stems and pieces, drained
1 tablespoon butter *or* margarine
1 small tomato, chopped

■ Cut green peppers in half lengthwise. Discard seeds and membranes. In an 8x8x2-inch baking dish arrange peppers, cut side down (see small photo). Cover with vented clear plastic wrap. Cook on 100% power (high) for 5 to 7 minutes or till crisp-tender. Drain. Set aside.

■ For filling, in a 1-quart casserole stir together sour cream and cornstarch. Stir in milk, salt, thyme, and pepper. Add *undrained* corn, drained mushrooms, and butter or margarine. Cook, uncovered, on high for 5 to 7 minutes or till thickened and bubbly, stirring every 2 minutes.

■ Invert cooked pepper halves in dish. Fill with corn mixture (see large photo). Cook, uncovered, on high for 2 to 3 minutes or till heated through. Sprinkle chopped tomato on top. Makes 4 servings.

Arrange the green pepper halves, cut side down, in the baking dish, as shown above. Cover with vented clear plastic wrap to cook. After cooking, invert the peppers and spoon in the warm corn filling, as shown at right. Heat through, then sprinkle with chopped tomato.

Fiesta Corn

¼ cup chopped onion
1 tablespoon butter *or* margarine
½ teaspoon chili powder
1 8¾-ounce can cream-style corn
1 8¾-ounce can whole kernel corn, drained
½ cup coarsely crushed taco-flavored tortilla chips
1 4-ounce can green chili peppers, rinsed, seeded, and chopped
2 tablespoons chopped pimiento
½ cup broken taco-flavored tortilla chips

■ In a 1-quart casserole combine onion, butter or margarine, and chili powder. Cook, covered, on 100% power (high) for 2 to 3 minutes or till onion is tender, stirring once.

■ Stir in cream-style corn, whole kernel corn, ½ cup crushed tortilla chips, chili peppers, and pimiento. Mix well. Cook, covered, on high for 4 to 6 minutes or till heated through, stirring once. Sprinkle ½ cup broken tortilla chips around the edges of the casserole. Makes 4 servings.

Cheesy Ratatouille

An Italian-style stewed vegetable mixture (pronounced ra-ta-TOO-ee).

2 slices bacon
1 small eggplant, peeled and cut into ½-inch cubes (3 cups)
1 large zucchini, halved lengthwise and sliced ½ inch thick (2 cups)
1 medium onion, chopped (½ cup)
1 clove garlic, minced
¼ cup water
2 tablespoons all-purpose flour
1 teaspoon dried basil, crushed
½ teaspoon salt
¼ teaspoon pepper
1 16-ounce can tomatoes, cut up
½ cup shredded process Swiss cheese (2 ounces)

■ In a 2-quart casserole arrange bacon. Cover with paper towels. Cook on 100% power (high) for 1½ to 2½ minutes or till crisp (see photo 1, page 191). Remove and drain on paper towels, reserving 2 tablespoons drippings in the casserole. Crumble bacon and set aside.

■ To reserved drippings add eggplant, zucchini, onion, and garlic. Cook, covered, on high for 7 to 9 minutes or till tender, stirring twice.

■ In a small mixing bowl combine water, flour, basil, salt, and pepper. Stir into vegetable mixture. Stir in *undrained* tomatoes. Cook, uncovered, on high for 5 to 7 minutes or till thickened and bubbly, stirring twice.

■ Sprinkle with shredded cheese. Cover and let stand for 1 to 2 minutes or till cheese is melted. Sprinkle with bacon. Makes 6 to 8 servings.

Low-wattage oven: For *bacon,* cook on high for 2½ to 3½ minutes. For *flour-vegetable mixture,* cook on high for 10 to 12 minutes.

Stuffing potatoes

Cheesy Stuffed Potatoes

A new version of an old favorite.

4 medium baking potatoes
(6 to 8 ounces each)
1 3-ounce package cream
cheese with chives
¼ teaspoon onion salt
⅛ teaspoon pepper
Dash garlic powder
Milk (optional)
¼ cup shredded cheddar
cheese (1 ounce)

■ Scrub potatoes. Prick several times with a fork (see photo 1). Arrange potatoes on a microwave-safe plate (see photo 2). Cook, uncovered, on 100% power (high) for 14 to 17 minutes or till tender, rearranging once. Let stand for 5 minutes.

■ Meanwhile, place cream cheese in a small microwave-safe mixing bowl. Cook, uncovered, on high for 15 to 30 seconds or till softened. Stir in onion salt, pepper, and garlic powder. Set aside.

■ Cut a lengthwise slice from the top of each baked potato. Remove the skin from the top slice and put the pulp into a small mixer bowl. Scoop the pulp from each potato, leaving ¼-inch-thick shells (see photo 3). Add the pulp to the mixer bowl. Set the potato shells aside.

■ Add the cheese mixture to the potato pulp. Beat with an electric mixer on medium speed till smooth, adding milk, if necessary, for desired consistency (see photo 4).

■ Spoon *one-fourth* of the potato filling into *each* potato shell (see photo 5). Arrange stuffed potatoes on a plate. Cook, uncovered, on high for 4 to 6 minutes or till heated through, giving the dish a half-turn once. Sprinkle shredded cheese on top (see photo 6). Cook, uncovered, for 30 to 60 seconds more or till cheese is melted. Makes 4 servings.

TIP Tip-Top Potato Toppings

Here's a custom-made mix-and-match potato side dish. Just cook some potatoes (see recipe, above, and chart, page 265). Then cut the cooked potatoes in half lengthwise. Score the cut surfaces with a crisscross pattern of ⅛-inch-deep cuts.

Now choose the toppings that best suit your menu and your taste buds. Try butter and Parmesan cheese, creamy salad dressings, sour cream, yogurt, salsa, or shredded cheese. Let your imagination be your guide and dream up your own combinations.

1

Keep the potatoes from exploding in your oven by pricking their skins with a fork before cooking. The holes let the steam escape gradually.

2

Arrange the potatoes spoke-style on a microwave-safe plate. Rearrange them once during cooking so they'll cook evenly.

3

Scoop the pulp from each potato, leaving ¼-inch-thick potato shells. The shells will make sturdy edible containers for the cheesy potato-pulp filling.

4

While beating the filling mixture, add milk, if necessary, to make the filling fluffy and easy to spoon. Be sure to add only a little at a time. It's easier to add more milk to get the right consistency than it is to remove some if you overdo.

5

Use two spoons to spoon some of the whipped potato filling into each potato shell. Push the filling off the first spoon with the back of the second spoon. You should have enough filling to pile it high in each shell.

6

After the stuffed potatoes are heated through, sprinkle them with shredded cheese. Then cook a little more to melt the cheese.

Nacho Potato Slices

For real zing, top with hot-style taco sauce. (Pictured on pages 244–245.)

2 medium potatoes (about 12
   ounces total)
2 tablespoons thinly sliced
   green onion
2 tablespoons finely chopped
   green pepper
¼ cup bottled taco, barbecue,
   or spaghetti sauce
⅓ cup shredded American
   cheese

■ Scrub potatoes. Trim ends. Cut potatoes into ⅜-inch-thick slices. In an 8x8x2-inch baking dish arrange potato slices, putting smaller slices in the center. Sprinkle with green onion and green pepper.

■ Cover with vented clear plastic wrap. Cook on 100% power (high) for 7 to 10 minutes or till tender, giving the dish a half-turn once. Drizzle sauce over slices. Sprinkle with shredded cheese. Cook, uncovered, for 30 to 60 seconds more or till cheese is melted. Makes 4 servings.

Creamy Peas And Carrots

Pictured on pages 244–245.

1 10-ounce package frozen
   peas and carrots
½ cup milk
1 tablespoon all-purpose flour
¼ teaspoon dried dillweed
⅛ teaspoon lemon pepper

■ In a 1-quart casserole cook frozen peas and carrots, covered, on 100% power (high) for 5 to 7 minutes or till tender, stirring once. Drain. Return vegetables to the casserole and cover to keep warm.

■ For sauce, in a 2-cup measure combine milk, flour, dillweed, and lemon pepper. Cook, uncovered, for 1 to 2 minutes or till thickened and bubbly, stirring every 30 seconds. Stir into vegetables. Makes 4 servings.

Pea Puree

1 10-ounce package frozen
   peas
⅓ cup dairy sour cream
2 parsley sprigs
1 teaspoon finely shredded
   orange peel
   Finely shredded orange peel
   (optional)
   Fresh mint leaves (optional)

■ In a 1-quart casserole cook frozen peas, covered, on 100% power (high) for 5 to 7 minutes or till tender, stirring once. Drain well.

■ In a blender container or food processor bowl combine peas, sour cream, parsley, and 1 teaspoon orange peel. Cover and blend till smooth.

■ In the same casserole cook pea puree, covered, on 50% power (medium) for 2 to 4 minutes or till heated through, stirring once. *Do not boil.* Spoon pea puree onto individual plates. If desired, garnish with additional shredded orange peel and fresh mint leaves. Makes 3 servings.

Low-wattage oven: For *pea puree,* cook on high for 1 to 2 minutes.

Savory Stuffed Onions

You won't shed a tear when you eat this onion dish. As they cook, onions change from pungent to sweet and mild. (Pictured on page 262.)

4 large onions (2 pounds)
3 slices bacon
½ cup herb-seasoned stuffing mix
1 small apple, cored and chopped (½ cup)
⅓ cup shredded cheddar cheese
1 tablespoon chicken broth *or* water
⅛ teaspoon celery seed

■ Cut a thin slice from the bottom and top of each onion. Peel onions. To hollow, make deep slashes (about ¾ of the way down) in a grid pattern in each onion center, cutting to, but not through, the outer edges. Scoop out the centers, leaving ¼-inch-thick shells (see photo 3, page 259). Chop onion centers and measure 1 cup. Set aside. (Cover and store the remaining chopped onion in the refrigerator for another use.)

■ For filling, in a 1-quart casserole arrange bacon. Cover with paper towels. Cook on 100% power (high) for 2 to 3 minutes or till crisp (see photo 1, page 191). Remove bacon, reserving 2 tablespoons drippings in the casserole. Drain bacon on paper towels. Crumble and set aside.

■ Add the 1 cup chopped onion to reserved drippings. Cook, covered, on high for 3 to 5 minutes or till tender, stirring once. Stir in bacon, stuffing mix, apple, cheese, chicken broth or water, and celery seed.

■ Spoon *one-fourth* of the filling into *each* onion shell (see photo 5, page 259). Arrange stuffed onions in an 8x8x2-inch baking dish. Cover with waxed paper. Cook on high for 7 to 9 minutes or till tender, giving the dish a quarter-turn twice. Makes 4 servings.

Low-wattage oven: For *bacon*, cook on high 4 to 5 minutes. For *chopped onion*, cook 7 to 9 minutes. For *stuffed onions*, cook 18 to 20 minutes.

Nutty Curried Spinach

8 cups torn fresh spinach *or* one 10-ounce package frozen chopped spinach
⅓ cup sliced green onion
1 clove garlic, minced
1 tablespoon olive *or* cooking oil
2 teaspoons vinegar
½ teaspoon sugar
½ teaspoon curry powder
¼ teaspoon dry mustard
Dash salt
Dash pepper
2 tablespoons coarsely chopped peanuts

■ In a 1½-quart casserole combine fresh or frozen spinach, green onion, and garlic. (If using fresh spinach, add 2 tablespoons *water.*) Cook, covered, on 100% power (high) till vegetables are tender, stirring once. Allow 3 to 4 minutes for fresh spinach and 6 to 8 minutes for frozen. Drain spinach mixture well and return to the casserole.

■ Meanwhile, in a small mixing bowl stir together olive or cooking oil, vinegar, sugar, curry powder, dry mustard, salt, and pepper.

■ Pour curry mixture over spinach mixture in the casserole. Cook, covered, on high for 30 to 60 seconds or till heated through. Sprinkle with peanuts. Makes 3 or 4 servings.

Low-wattage oven: For *frozen spinach,* cook on high for 8 to 10 minutes.

Savory Stuffed Onions
(see recipe, page 261)

Spinach- and
Cheese-Stuffed Tomatoes

Spinach- and Cheese-Stuffed Tomatoes

Want easy-to-serve side dishes for a cookout? Micro-cook these and Savory Stuffed Onions while your meat is grilling. (Pictured opposite.)

6 medium tomatoes
1 10-ounce package frozen chopped spinach
¾ cup cream-style cottage cheese with chives, drained
¼ cup grated Parmesan cheese
3 tablespoons fine dry bread crumbs
½ teaspoon dried basil, crushed

■ Cut stem ends from tomatoes. Scoop out and discard pulp, leaving ¼-inch-thick shells (see photo 3, page 259). Salt lightly, invert, and drain. For filling, in a 10x6x2-inch baking dish cover spinach with vented clear plastic wrap. Cook on 100% power (high) 6 to 8 minutes, stirring once. Drain. Stir in cottage cheese, Parmesan, crumbs, basil, and dash *pepper*.

■ Spoon *one-sixth* of the filling into *each* tomato shell (see photo 5, page 259). Arrange in the same dish. Cook, uncovered, on high for 3 to 4 minutes or till warm, giving the dish a half-turn once. Makes 6 servings.

Low-wattage oven: For *spinach*, cook on high for 8 to 10 minutes.

Cinnamon-Glazed Squash

An old-fashioned favorite to make in minutes.

1 medium acorn squash (about 1 pound)
2 tablespoons brown sugar
2 tablespoons dark corn syrup
2 tablespoons butter *or* margarine
⅛ teaspoon ground cinnamon

■ Quarter squash lengthwise. Scoop out seeds and discard. Arrange in an 8x8x2-inch baking dish. Cover with vented clear plastic wrap. Cook on 100% power (high) for 6 to 9 minutes or till done, giving the dish a half-turn once. In a 1-cup measure combine sugar, corn syrup, butter, and cinnamon. Cook, uncovered, on high for 1 to 2 minutes or till butter is melted. Stir to blend. Sprinkle squash with salt and pepper. Spoon sugar mixture over top. Cook, covered, for 30 seconds more. Serves 4.

Low-wattage oven: For *squash*, cook on high for 11 to 13 minutes.

Zucchini with Pimiento

Got a bumper crop of zucchini? Put it to a deliciously good use.

1 pound zucchini *or* crookneck squash
½ cup chopped onion
1 4-ounce can diced green chili peppers, drained
1 3-ounce package cream cheese, cut up
1 2-ounce jar sliced pimiento, drained and chopped

■ Cut squash into ¼-inch-thick slices. In a 1½-quart casserole combine squash, onion, and 2 tablespoons *water*. Cook, covered, on 100% power (high) for 7 to 9 minutes or till crisp-tender, stirring once. Drain.

■ Stir chili peppers, cream cheese, pimiento, ¼ teaspoon *salt*, and ⅛ teaspoon *pepper* into squash. Cook, covered, on high for 2 to 3 minutes or till cheese is softened, stirring twice. Stir in 1 tablespoon *milk*, if necessary, for desired consistency. Makes 6 servings.

Cooking Fresh Vegetables

For **whole vegetables,** wash and prick skin. For **vegetable pieces,** wash, trim, and peel, as necessary. Cut into ¼-inch slices, ½-inch cubes, 3- to 4-inch lengths, or other uniformly sized pieces.

In a baking dish or casserole combine vegetables with 2 tablespoons *water.* Cover with a microwave-safe lid or vented clear plastic wrap. (For **whole potatoes,** arrange on a plate in spoke fashion, omitting water and the cover.)

Cook on 100% power (high) for the time shown or till tender or crisp-tender, stirring or rearranging once. Drain. (Let potatoes stand for 5 minutes to finish cooking.)

Vegetable	Amount	Cooking time
Acorn squash halves	Two 8-ounce halves	6 to 9 minutes*
Artichokes	One 10-ounce	5 to 7 minutes
	Two 10-ounce	6 to 8 minutes*
Asparagus cuts	½ pound (1½ cups)	5 to 7 minutes
	1 pound (3 cups)	6 to 8 minutes*
Asparagus spears	½ pound	4 to 6 minutes*
	1 pound	7 to 9 minutes*
Beans, green (whole or cut)	½ pound (1½ cups)	10 to 12 minutes
	1 pound (3 cups)	16 to 19 minutes
Broccoli, ½-inch cuts	1 pound	5 to 7 minutes*
Broccoli spears	1 pound	6 to 8 minutes*
Brussels sprouts (large sprouts, halved)	½ pound (2 cups)	3 to 5 minutes
	1 pound (4 cups)	6 to 8 minutes
Butternut squash halves	Two 2-ounce halves	10 to 13 minutes
Cabbage, shredded	1 pound (5 cups)	10 to 12 minutes
Cabbage wedges	1½ pounds (6 wedges)	10 to 12 minutes
Carrot, ¼-inch slices	1 pound (3 cups)	7 to 9 minutes*
Cauliflower flowerets	½ pound (3 cups)	5 to 7 minutes
Celery, chopped	1 cup	5 to 7 minutes
Celery, ½-inch slices	2 cups	5 to 7 minutes
Corn on the cob	One 7-ounce ear	3 to 5 minutes
	Two 7-ounce ears	5 to 7 minutes
	Four 7-ounce ears	9 to 11 minutes
Eggplant, ¾-inch cubes	1 medium (5 cups)	5 to 7 minutes*
Leeks, whole	½ pound (3 medium)	3 to 5 minutes

Note: Timings are for 600- to 700-watt microwave ovens and may be longer in low-wattage ovens.

Cooking Fresh Vegetables *(continued)*

Vegetable	Amount	Cooking time
Mushrooms, ¼-inch slices	½ pound (3 cups)	2½ to 3½ minutes
Onions, chopped	¼ cup	1 to 1½ minutes
	⅓ cup	1½ to 2½ minutes
	½ cup	2 to 3 minutes
	1 cup	3 to 5 minutes
Onions, quartered	1 pound (4 medium)	8 to 10 minutes
Onions, ¼-inch rings	½ pound (2 medium)	3 to 5 minutes
Parsnips, ¼-inch slices	½ pound (1½ cups)	4 to 6 minutes
Pea pods	6 ounces (2½ cups)	3 to 5 minutes
Peas, shelled	2 cups	6 to 8 minutes
Peppers, green, chopped	¼ cup	30 to 60 seconds
	⅓ cup	1 to 1½ minutes
	½ cup	1½ to 2 minutes
	1 cup	3 to 5 minutes
Peppers, green, halved	2 large (4 halves)	5 to 7 minutes
Potatoes, ¼-inch slices	5 medium (5 cups)	11 to 14 minutes
Potatoes, 1-inch cubes	5 medium (4 cups)	11 to 14 minutes
Potatoes, quartered	5 medium (4 cups)	12 to 15 minutes
Potatoes, whole	One 6- to 8-ounce	5 to 7 minutes
	Two 6- to 8-ounce	8 to 10 minutes
	Four 6- to 8-ounce	14 to 17 minutes
Rutabaga, ½-inch cubes	1 pound (4 cups)	11 to 13 minutes*
Spinach leaves	1 pound (12 cups)	7 to 9 minutes
Tomato, ½-inch slices	4 medium	3 to 5 minutes
Zucchini, ¼-inch slices	1 pound (4 cups)	7 to 9 minutes

Note: Timings are for 600- to 700-watt microwave ovens and may be longer in low-wattage ovens.

Cooking Frozen Vegetables

For **frozen vegetables,** cook according to the package's microwave directions or follow these guidelines. In a baking dish or casserole place vegetables. Do not add water, *except:* to carrot, cauliflower, and mixed vegetables, add 2 tablespoons water; to lima beans, add ¼ cup water.

Cover with a microwave-safe lid or vented clear plastic wrap. Cook on 100% power (high) for the specified time, stirring or rearranging once. Drain.

Vegetable	Amount	Cooking time
Artichoke hearts	One 9-ounce package	7 to 9 minutes
Asparagus cuts	One 8-ounce package	5 to 7 minutes
Asparagus spears	One 10-ounce package	7 to 9 minutes
Beans, green, cut	One 9-ounce package	5 to 7 minutes
Beans, lima	One 10-ounce package	8 to 10 minutes
Broccoli, ½-inch cuts	One 10-ounce package	6 to 8 minutes
Broccoli spears	One 10-ounce package	7 to 9 minutes
Brussels sprouts (large sprouts, halved)	One 10-ounce package	8 to 10 minutes*
Butternut squash, mashed	One 10-ounce package	7 to 9 minutes
Carrot, crinkle cut	One 10-ounce package	7 to 9 minutes*
Cauliflower flowerets	One 8-ounce package	7 to 9 minutes
Corn, whole kernel	One 10-ounce package	6 to 9 minutes
Corn on the cob	One 8-ounce ear	3 to 6 minutes
	Two 8-ounce ears	6 to 8 minutes
	Four 8-ounce ears	12 to 15 minutes
Mixed vegetables	One 10-ounce package	7 to 9 minutes*
Pea pods	One 6-ounce package	3 to 5 minutes
Peas, shelled	One 10-ounce package	5 to 7 minutes
Peppers, green, chopped	½ cup	2 to 3 minutes
Spinach leaves	One 10-ounce package	6 to 8 minutes*

Note: Timings are for 600- to 700-watt microwave ovens and may be longer in low-wattage ovens.

Nutrition Analysis

		Per Serving						Percent U.S. RDA Per Serving							
	Number of servings	Calories	Protein (g)	Carbohydrate (g)	Fat (g)	Sodium (mg)	Potassium (mg)	Protein	Vitamin A	Vitamin C	Thiamine	Riboflavin	Niacin	Calcium	Iron
Brussels Sprouts Italian (p. 251)	4	77	3	9	4	72	334	5	16	67	6	6	3	3	5
Cabbage in Chunky Tomato Sauce (p. 252)	4	102	3	14	4	534	625	5	20	108	8	5	6	10	10
Calico Cabbage Rolls (p. 254)	4	64	3	10	2	437	287	5	35	17	4	3	5	9	5
Cheesy Asparagus Spears (p. 246)	4	96	8	6	5	193	267	12	17	29	7	10	5	9	4
Cheesy Ratatouille (p. 257)	6	108	6	15	4	497	568	9	16	22	13	6	8	14	9
Cheesy Stuffed Potatoes (p. 258)	4	202	8	22	10	223	737	12	8	23	3	8	9	12	32
Chinese Cabbage in Cheese Sauce (p. 252)	4	120	5	6	9	303	286	8	42	37	5	10	4	18	4
Cinnamon-Glazed Squash (p. 263)	4	141	1	23	6	104	323	1	10	11	8	0	3	4	7
Corn-Stuffed Green Peppers (p. 256)	4	169	4	24	7	577	405	6	27	134	10	9	10	4	10
Cranberry-Sauced Beets (p. 249)	3	83	1	21	0	288	151	1	0	47	1	3	1	2	10
Creamy Beans and Mushrooms (p. 248)	6	117	5	12	6	530	305	8	10	15	8	9	5	13	6
Creamy Peas and Carrots (p. 260)	4	60	3	10	1	6	160	5	109	7	12	6	5	5	4
Curried Cauliflower (p. 253)	4	82	2	6	6	209	391	4	6	88	5	3	3	4	4
Fiesta Corn (p. 257)	4	208	4	34	8	478	203	6	13	73	3	5	8	2	4
Gingered Broccoli Pilaf (p. 251)	4	141	5	18	6	223	347	7	37	40	9	11	8	7	7
Herbed Garlic Broccoli (p. 249)	4	44	2	4	3	45	120	3	26	29	2	3	1	4	2
Nacho Potato Slices (p. 260)	4	93	4	12	3	244	415	7	4	19	2	4	5	9	16
Nutmeg-Carrot Puree (p. 253)	4	102	3	13	5	133	429	5	689	13	9	8	6	5	5
Nutty Curried Spinach (p. 261)	3	120	6	9	8	187	905	9	197	50	9	17	10	16	24
Orange-Glazed Carrots (p. 253)	3	93	1	14	4	118	341	2	543	15	6	3	5	3	3
Pea Puree (p. 260)	3	124	5	14	6	89	200	8	19	15	16	7	6	6	9
Piquant Green Beans (p. 249)	3	62	3	7	3	187	184	5	8	15	8	5	4	4	5
Savory Stuffed Onions (p. 261)	4	234	7	21	14	393	219	11	2	12	9	6	6	11	6
Savory Three-Bean Bake (p. 248)	6	268	12	42	6	729	586	19	6	12	14	5	8	9	21
Spinach- and Cheese-Stuffed Tomatoes (p. 263)	6	77	7	7	3	272	210	11	66	12	4	9	3	14	5
Zucchini with Pimiento (p. 263)	6	72	2	5	5	136	244	4	15	57	5	4	3	4	4

BEYOND MICROWAVE BASICS

This section is brimming with extras to help you micro-cook more efficiently. You'll find information on micro-cooking entire meals, converting recipes, coping with high altitudes, planning nutritious menus, and storing, freezing, and defrosting foods. What's more, there's a mini-chapter of handy microwave cooking tips you'll want at your fingertips.

Micro-cooking meals
Cut the time you spend preparing meals by using your microwave oven as much as possible. You can use it for individual cooking tasks, whole recipes, or even entire meals. Turn to page 270 to find out how to cook meals faster.

Nutrition and the microwave
Microwave cooking is nutrition-conscious cooking, because it preserves precious vitamins and minerals. That's why at the end of every chapter we list each recipe's nutrition analysis. On page 271, we explain how we calculated the nutrient amounts and how you can use the information to plan a balanced diet for your family.

Converting recipes
Many of our letters come from readers wanting microwave directions for a traditional family recipe. They want the familiar look and flavor along with the microwave's convenience and speed. All of that is possible when you follow our hints for adapting recipes on pages 272 and 273.

High-altitude microwave cooking

Because our Test Kitchen is located fairly close to sea level, our recipe timings and ingredient proportions work best at low altitudes. But we didn't forget those of you who live in the mountains, where low air pressure affects the way many foods cook.

To learn how altitude affects our microwave recipes, we sent some of them to Colorado for additional testing. Fortunately, we found that most of them needed no changes. You'll find our recommendations for high-altitude adjustments on pages 274 and 275.

Freezing, storing, and defrosting

Today's heat-and-eat life-style means food often hits the freezer before it hits the table, with an appearance by the microwave oven in between. If that combination sounds familiar, you need to know how best to store foods. Check our storage chart and information on pages 276 and 277.

Microwave hints

Following this chapter, you'll find a collection of speedy microwave tricks we came up with during recipe testing. We started experimenting with appetizers and meats, then tried vegetables, fruits, rice, breads, and desserts. We perfected timings for toasting nuts, melting butter, and softening cheese. These helpful and convenient tips start on page 278. Microwave cooking has never been so easy.

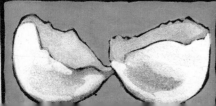

Make it a microwave meal

When the dinner countdown begins, turn to your microwave oven. It can do all sorts of recipe steps, prepare whole recipes, or even cook an entire meal.

For starters, use your microwave for little jobs as you're preparing meals. By using your microwave oven and conventional appliances for the tasks they do best, you'll pare your kitchen time. The tips starting on page 278 show you lots of microwave shortcuts to use in cooking.

Once you're in the habit of including your microwave in meal preparation, try cooking one or two of our speedy microwave-only recipes. You may even consider cooking your whole meal in the microwave oven.

Microwave-only meals

Occasionally, preparing an entire meal in your microwave makes sense, whether you cook the foods in stages or all at once. When foods vary greatly in size, shape, and quantity, cook each item separately. Here's how to design a cooking sequence that guarantees each dish is ready when you want:

■ First, prepare foods to be served chilled or at room temperature, or those that can be chilled and reheated before serving.

■ Then cook foods that need standing time before serving.

■ Next, while other foods stand, cook any quick-cooking foods or reheat any made-ahead dishes.

■ Finally, before serving, warm last-minute items such as rolls, or foods that have cooled too much during standing.

One-plate meals

You can also prepare an all-microwave meal by placing single servings of each menu item on individual plates, then reheating each plate. If one food takes less time to cook than another, add it later. For example, heat your entrée till slightly warm, then add the vegetables. Warm your bread during the last few seconds.

To make sure everything heats evenly, arrange pieces with the thicker portions facing the outside and put thinner or less-dense foods near the center. During cooking, rotate the dish or rearrange pieces for even cooking. If you notice that a food is done early, remove it or cover it with a small piece of foil to prevent further cooking. (First check your owner's manual to be sure you can use foil in your oven.)

Bi-level cooking

If your oven comes with a rack, you can cook several dishes at once. This is the trickiest way to make an all-microwave meal, because cooking times vary with the types and amounts of foods. For directions on cooking your specific menu, refer to your microwave owner's manual. Here are some general pointers on cooking with a rack:

■ First, see if you will save time. To estimate the total microwave-cooking time, simply add the times of all the menu items together. Compare that figure to the conventional-cooking time.

■ Make sure the dishes will all fit into the microwave oven at once.

■ To best use your microwave oven's cooking pattern, arrange the menu items the way your owner's manual suggests.

■ Check foods often as they cook, rearranging if necessary.

■ Remove and cover each dish when it's done, keeping it warm until everything else is ready.

Nutrition and the microwave

Microwave meals may be speedy, but that doesn't mean you have to sacrifice good nutrition. The microwave oven can provide the variety of foods you need for a balanced diet. As an adult, you should eat daily: four servings each of vegetables or fruit and bread or cereal, and two servings each of milk or cheese and meat, fish, poultry, or dried beans.

Planning to eat right
To make sure your meals are nutritious, follow these seven meal-planning steps:

1. Select a main dish featuring meat, fish, poultry, or dried beans.

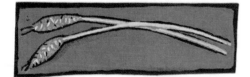

2. Add a bread or cereal.

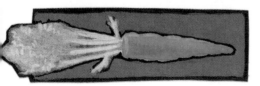

3. Choose a hot or cold vegetable.
4. Toss in a hot or cold salad.
5. Add a dessert. Remember that a light dessert is best after a heavy meal. Fruits make a good dessert, as do milk-based selections, such as puddings or custards.

6. Choose a beverage. (Keep in mind your need for two servings of milk each day.)

7. Add extra fats such as butter and sweets in moderation to suit your family's tastes.

Microwaves save nutrients
The microwave oven offers a nutrition plus. Some foods, particularly fruits and vegetables, retain more nutrients when micro-cooked than when conventionally cooked, because in the microwave they cook faster and need less water. That means there's less time for the heat to destroy valuable vitamins and minerals, and less chance that the water will wash away those all-important nutrients.

Using our nutrition information
To help you keep track of the calories, protein, fat, cholesterol, sodium, vitamins, and minerals you eat each day, we've included a nutrition analysis for each recipe at the end of every chapter. You'll find the calorie count and the nutrient amount by gram weight per serving. You can also check the vitamin and mineral contents, which are given in percentages of the United States Recommended Daily Allowances (U.S. RDAs). The U.S. RDAs are standards set by the federal Food and Drug Administration. We based our nutritional values on the United States Department of Agriculture's Handbook Number 8.

Put nutrition analysis to work
To figure out how a recipe fits into your daily food plan, look at the nutrients each recipe provides. Then compare those figures to these simple guidelines, based on the daily nutrition needs of females, 23 to 50 years old:
    calories—2,000
    protein—45 to 65 grams
    fat—85 grams
    cholesterol—300 milligrams
    sodium—1,100 to 3,300
      milligrams
In general, males and teenagers need more calories.

Our method for tallying
We used the following guidelines to figure the nutrition analysis of each recipe:
■ When ingredient options appear in a recipe, the first ingredient choice was used for the analysis.
■ Optional ingredients were omitted in the nutrition analyses.
■ The nutrition analyses for recipes calling for fresh ingredients were calculated using the measurements for raw fruits, vegetables, and meats.
■ If a recipe has a serving range ("Makes 6 to 8 servings"), the nutrition analysis was calculated using the first figure.

Converting recipes

Do you have a favorite conventional recipe you'd like to micro-cook? Making the necessary adjustments is easy if you use a similar recipe in this book as your pattern (one that calls for the same amounts and types of main ingredients).

For example, if you want to convert a casserole based on one pound of ground beef, look for a microwave recipe with the same amount of meat.

Read the tips on these two pages and, with a little practice, you'll soon be able to judge which of your conventional recipes will cook well in the microwave oven. You'll also learn how to choose the best size dish, change ingredients or ingredient proportions, select cooking times and power levels, and incorporate microwave-cooking techniques.

Selecting recipes to convert

For best results, choose recipes with foods that cook well in moist heat, such as chicken, fish, ground meat, vegetables, and fruits. Other good choices are sauces, soups, scrambled- or poached-egg dishes, quick breads, snack cakes, melt-and-stir candies, and beverages.

Adapting ingredient proportions

Most conventional recipes need only minor ingredient changes before being cooked in the microwave oven.
■ For all foods, make sure pieces are as equal in shape and size as possible. Fat attracts microwaves, so trim visible fat from meats.
■ For beverages, soups, vegetables, fruits, and main dishes, decrease or eliminate any fat used to prevent sticking; the microwave's moist heat will help keep foods from sticking to the pan or drying.

■ You can also reduce the liquid used to cook these foods, because micro-cooking forces less evaporation than conventional cooking. Decreasing the liquid by about one-third will prevent soupy results and shorten the cooking time. Check your recipe often during cooking and add more liquid if it seems dry.
■ Adapting baked products and candies can be trickier. First try the recipes with the conventional proportions. If a baked product seems tough, try it again with an additional tablespoon of fat. If that doesn't work, eliminate an egg and add ¼ cup more liquid. (Do not try this adjustment if the recipe has only one egg.)
■ Don't tamper with the delicate balance of ingredients in candy recipes. If a candy fails in the microwave the first time you try it, return to the conventional cooking directions.

Choosing the right container

Use a microwave-safe dish and try a slightly larger size than the conventional recipe specifies. This allows extra room for the food to bubble up as it micro-cooks, and plenty of "splash space" for stirring. As a rule, choose a dish twice the volume of the food.

To spread the heat from the steam, cover any recipes that you usually cover during conventional cooking. If your dish has no cover, substitute vented microwave-safe plastic wrap. Cover meats and poultry loosely with waxed paper to prevent spattering. Cover high-fat or crumb-coated foods with microwave-safe paper towels to absorb grease or moisture. Do not cover cakes, cookies, breads, or any recipes that require frequent stirring during cooking.

Choosing cooking times

Check similar microwave recipes to choose cooking times and power levels. Remember to adjust for differences in the food's starting temperature and the amount of liquid or fat. When in doubt, be cautious; choose a shorter cooking time or a lower power level. You can always micro-cook an underdone food a little longer.

If you can't find a similar microwave recipe, try cutting the time to one-fourth or one-third of the conventional cooking time. Test for doneness frequently. If the food needs more cooking time, add it little by little.

Picking power levels

Generally, choose high or 100% power. It works well for most foods, including soups, beverages, fruits, vegetables, fish, ground meat, and poultry. Use medium-high or 70% power for simmering stews, medium or 50% power for baking breads and cakes and cooking less-tender meats, and medium-low or 30% power for defrosting. To quickly proof yeast dough, use low or 10% power.

If your recipe calls for convenience foods, look on the package for suggested microwave timings and power levels. Many products carry such information or offer it on request.

Adapting cooking techniques

For even micro-cooking, you may need to stir or rearrange food. To know when, watch your recipe as it cooks. When one spot bubbles or cooks before the rest, stir or rearrange the food.

For a food with a large surface area, watch the edges; they may cook before the center. If you can use metal in your oven (check your owner's manual), shield the cooked edges with small pieces of aluminum foil. Or, remove the food from the microwave oven before it is completely cooked. Then let it stand a few minutes so its own heat will cook the center.

Special converting tips

■ Stick to small amounts to preserve the microwave's timesaving advantage.
■ For a crusty look on baked items, coat greased pans with ground nuts or crumbs.
■ For egg-based mixtures that shouldn't be stirred during cooking, heat the milk mixture before adding eggs.

■ Add cheese and other toppings near the end of cooking to keep the top from becoming tough or soggy.
■ When adding liquid to meats, avoid flour coatings; they'll get soggy.

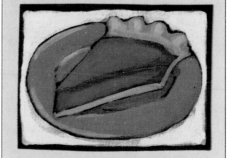

■ For fruit pies, cook the single crust and filling separately so the crust won't steam and get soggy.
■ Use quick-cooking rice instead of long grain rice.
■ Heat sandwich fillings alone, without the bread.

High-altitude microwave cooking

Do you live in an area from western Nebraska to the mountains of California, between the Canadian border and Tucson or El Paso? Then you've probably noticed the influence high altitude has on your cooking. Slight changes become noticeable at 2,500 feet above sea level; the changes are even more dramatic above 5,000 feet. Fortunately, microwave cooking at high

for each 1,000 feet above sea level. Because of this lower temperature, you may need to increase the cooking time for foods cooked in liquid, such as vegetables, rice, stews, and candy. (Use a water test for candy; see pages 84 and 85.)

But for altitudes above 7,500 feet, cooking may actually speed up. At such high elevations, the low air pressure influences cooking times more than the low boiling point. Low air pressure means faster evaporation, more drying, and, in many cases, faster cooking. So, if you're above 7,500

Foods tend to cool faster at higher altitudes. If your recipe cools too much while standing, reheat it quickly in the microwave before serving.

Suggestions for cooking at 5,000 to 6,500 feet
Unfortunately, there are no formulas for adjusting all of your high-altitude cooking to match sea-level results. You'll need to experiment. The guidelines below, though, will give you a head start. Keep notes on any changes you make in our recipes, and remember, accurate measurements are very important.

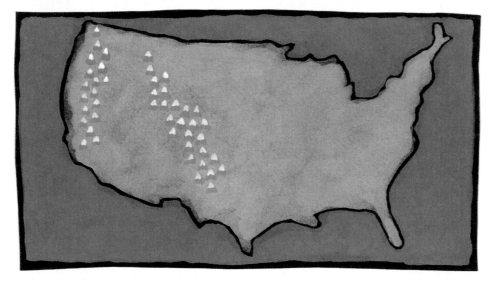

■ *Vegetables*
Follow our directions on pages 264 to 266 with the following adjustments. For *fresh vegetables,* prick whole vegetables all over. Add an extra 2 tablespoons water to beans or carrots. If the vegetables are not done after the suggested cooking time, continue cooking and check every minute.

If you want *frozen vegetables* to be crisp-tender, decrease the suggested cooking time by 1 minute. If you prefer tender vegetables, add 1 to 2 tablespoons water and increase the cooking time by 1 to 3 minutes.

altitudes needs fewer recipe adjustments than conventional cooking requires at such heights.

The high-altitude difference
Because the air is thinner at high altitudes, foods that puff, rise, or foam often expand more. That means you'll need slightly larger containers for beverage, sauce, soup, cereal, candy, cake, and bread recipes.

Another high-altitude cooking phenomenon is that water boils at a lower temperature. At 5,000 feet, water boils at 202° instead of the sea-level 212°. The boiling temperature, in fact, drops by 2°

feet, carefully watch food during cooking and check our recipes for doneness *before* our suggested minimum timings.

To compensate for the faster evaporation above 5,000 feet, add an extra tablespoon of liquid to meats and other nonbaked products and cover them tightly. Tightly wrap all baked goods *immediately* after cooling to keep them moist.

■ *Meats, fish, poultry*
Most meats and fish cook in about the same time at high altitudes as at sea level, but there are a few exceptions. Less-tender cuts of beef that cook in liquid will take 5 to 15 minutes longer. If a meat recipe cooks first for 5 minutes on high before dropping to medium, increase the time on high to 10 minutes. Cooking ground meat till no pink remains may take you an additional 1 to 2 minutes. Poultry may need 5 to 9 minutes more.

■ Baked products

Baking in a conventional oven always has been a challenge for high-altitude cooks, but microwave-baked goods may not need any changes. First try our recipes as written. If that fails, try again following these suggestions.

For *quick breads,* use the next size larger loaf dish, or plan on an extra 1 or 2 muffins. If your first loaf is too dry or compact, add an extra 1 to 2 tablespoons liquid to the batter the next time. If it is coarse or bitter tasting, reduce the baking powder by ¼ teaspoon for every teaspoon baking powder (for example, use 1½ teaspoons instead of 2). Do not change the amount of baking soda.

If the bread is too tender, cut the sugar by 2 tablespoons for every cup sugar. If it's oily and heavy, decrease the oil by 2 tablespoons for every cup oil.

For *yeast breads,* use about ½ cup less flour. You should use enough flour to make the dough smooth and elastic when kneading. The microwave rising time will be 1 to 2 minutes less than the time given in this book.

■ Cakes

To allow for higher rising, use high-sided baking dishes. For heavy cake batters, fill the dish half full; for light batters, fill one-third full. Increase the first baking time (on medium) by 2 minutes.

If your first cake is too dry or compact, increase the liquid in your next try by 1 to 2 table-spoons. If the cake is overly moist, increase the flour by 1 to 2 tablespoons. If it's coarse or bitter flavored, decrease the baking powder ¼ teaspoon for each teaspoon baking powder (for example, use 1½ teaspoons instead of 2). Do not change the level of baking soda.

When a cake is too tender, decrease the sugar 2 to 3 tablespoons for every cup sugar. And be sure to use large eggs instead of medium ones. For beaten egg whites, use cold eggs, and slightly underbeat them to soft, instead of stiff, peaks.

For *pudding cakes,* use the next larger size baking dish and add an extra 2 tablespoons liquid to the pudding mixture.

For *packaged mixes,* look for high-altitude microwave directions. If there are none, base your timing on the manufacturers' microwave directions and follow their conventional high-altitude adjustments for ingredient amounts. Or, contact the food manufacturer for specific high-altitude microwave directions.

■ Beverages and sauces

With the lower boiling point, beverages and other liquids bubble up more often. You'll need to stir them more frequently to keep them from boiling over.

For starch-thickened sauces, don't count on bubbling to tell you when a sauce is properly thickened. Check the sauce carefully to make sure it is thick enough. If it's not thickened after the suggested cooking time, continue cooking and check every 30 seconds.

If your sauce does not thicken after the extended cooking time, try increasing the flour by 1 teaspoon for every tablespoon flour or the cornstarch by ¾ teaspoon for every tablespoon cornstarch. (The low boiling points found at 7,500 feet and higher may not be hot enough to thicken cornstarch-based sauces, so try substituting double the amount of flour for the cornstarch.)

■ Cereals

Because cereals may bubble over, use larger bowls with plates underneath. For quick-cooking rice, increase the water by 1 tablespoon for each serving. Cook the rice for 1 to 2 minutes more before letting it stand.

Maximum Storage Times

Food		Refrigerator	Freezer
Meat	Beef	3 to 5 days	6 to 12 months
	Pork	3 to 5 days	4 to 8 months
	Ground meats	1 to 2 days	3 to 4 months
	Ham	7 days	1 to 2 months
	Bacon	7 days	1 month
	Frankfurters	7 days	1 to 2 months
	Fresh pork sausage	1 to 2 days	1 to 2 months
	Luncheon meats	3 to 5 days	1 to 2 months
	Lamb	3 to 5 days	6 to 9 months
	Veal	3 to 5 days	4 to 8 months
	Variety meats	1 to 2 days	3 to 4 months
	Cooked meats	3 to 4 days	2 to 3 months
Poultry	Chicken, whole	1 to 2 days	12 months
	Chicken, pieces	1 to 2 days	9 months
	Turkey, pieces	1 to 2 days	6 months
	Poultry, cooked	3 to 4 days	1 month
Fish	Fat fish	1 to 2 days	4 months
	Lean fish	1 to 2 days	8 months
Eggs	Whole eggs	4 weeks	9 to 12 months*
	Egg whites	7 days	9 to 12 months
	Egg yolks	2 to 3 days	9 to 12 months
Dairy	Hard cheese	Several months	6 months
	Soft cheese	2 weeks	4 months
	Cottage cheese	5 days	Do not freeze
	Butter	7 days	3 to 6 months

Note: To freeze whole eggs, break and stir together.

Storing food for microwave cooking

Busy cooks used to avoid frozen foods because they would forget to thaw the foods ahead. Then the microwave oven appeared, making fast work of defrosting frozen food. Today, microwave reheating and defrosting have become so easy that you can now chill or freeze more foods than ever. Check the chart at left to see how long chilled and frozen foods will keep. Then read on for specific storing instructions. When it's time to thaw, turn to the charts in the recipe chapters.

Preparing food for storage
■ *Meat and poultry:* Refrigerate meat and poultry in the original packaging. To freeze, remove the packaging and wrap the food tightly in moisture- and vaporproof material. (Freeze meat and poultry in the original packaging for up to two weeks without rewrapping.) Freeze cooked poultry without any liquid.
■ *Fish:* Tightly wrap fresh fish in moisture- and vaporproof material before freezing or refrigerating.
■ *Eggs:* Refrigerate eggs in the covered egg carton. To freeze, break and stir eggs. For ⅓ cup whole eggs (two whole) or ¼ cup yolks (four yolks), add ⅛ teaspoon salt or 1½ teaspoons sugar. (Whites need no additions.) Store in freezer containers. Use within 24 hours of thawing. Take added salt or sugar into account.
■ *Dairy products:* Store cheese and butter in the refrigerator or freezer. Do not freeze milk, cream, buttermilk, sour cream, yogurt, mayonnaise, or cottage cheese.
■ *Sauces, soups, and stews:* Flour-thickened mixtures may break down during freezing. To freeze, substitute half as much cornstarch for the flour.

The deep freeze

For optimum freezing and storage, make sure your freezer is set at 0° or lower. Limit the amount of food you freeze at one time; adding too much fresh food at once will make the freezer temperature rise too high. Within a 24-hour period, freeze only two to three pounds of food for every cubic foot of freezer space. And, when you add food to the freezer, separate the packages until they're solidly frozen. This allows cold air to circulate.

Before freezing, quickly cool hot foods in shallow containers of ice. Because small amounts freeze better than large amounts, package foods in small portions. Follow the directions below for wrapping, sealing, and labeling, and refer to the chart, opposite, for maximum storage times.

■ *Wrapping:* Use freezer containers, or wrap foods in moisture- and vaporproof materials such as freezer paper or heavy-duty plastic wrap. For extra convenience, choose containers that can later go directly from your freezer to the microwave oven. Do not use waxed paper, nontempered glass, or containers not specifically labeled as freezer safe or microwave safe. And avoid using metal containers or foil for foods high in acid (like tomatoes); the acid reacts with the metal to create off-flavors.

To wrap for freezing, place the food in the center of the freezer paper or plastic wrap. Bring the edges of the wrap together over the food as illustrated at right. Fold the wrap down to the food in folds about 1 inch deep. Press the wrap closely to the food to force out air. Next, push out air as you shape the ends into points. Fold the ends snugly to the center of the package to lock out air. Seal with freezer tape.

To save freezer space and allow dishes to be reused, line containers with freezer paper or plastic wrap, leaving long ends. Fill, cover, and place the container in the freezer. When frozen, remove the food from the container by the long ends of the paper or plastic. Wrap, seal, label, and return to the freezer. When you're ready to thaw and reheat, unwrap the frozen food and return it to the original baking dish for a perfect fit.

■ *Sealing:* Sealing food tightly is just as important as using the right kind of container or wrap. Seal in as little air as possible. If necessary, use freezer tape to make a tight seal. Liquid or semi-liquid foods, such as soups and stews, are an exception. They will expand when frozen, so leave about ½ inch of space below the rim of the freezer container.

■ *Labeling:* Label every package with the recipe title or type of food; number of servings, quantity, or weight; date frozen; maximum freezing time; and any other preparation directions (such as microwave thawing time).

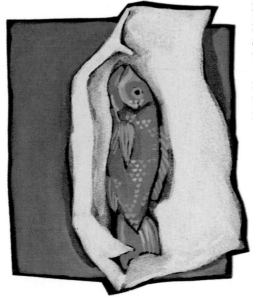

To label packages, use a wax crayon, ballpoint pen, waterproof marking pen, or colored pencil. Write directly on the package or use adhesive or tie-on labels. Labeling will remind you to use your oldest packages first.

Defrosting

When it's time to thaw your frozen food, remove any metal and foil packaging. Vent the microwave-safe container or packaging to allow steam to escape. Then follow the microwave defrosting directions we've given throughout the book (see index for pages).

During thawing, stir or turn the food to break up the frozen chunks and even the thawing. If some parts thaw before others, shield them from the microwaves with foil. (First check your owner's manual to see if you can use foil in your microwave oven.)

Make sure the food is completely defrosted before micro-cooking. Otherwise, you'll have thawed parts cooking faster than still-frozen parts. To see if the food is properly thawed, touch it with your finger. It should be cool yet pliable. The edges should be uncooked and the center slightly icy. You may need to let large amounts stand for a while to thoroughly defrost.

After thawing, cook or chill foods immediately. Do not refreeze thawed food, unless you cook it first and then refreeze it.

Microwave Hints

Need to melt butter for a sauce or toast nuts for a topping? Look no further than this handy reference for all sorts of practical and easy microwave hints. We tested these tips in 600- to 700-watt ovens, so if your oven has fewer watts, you may need to add to the cooking time. (See pages 6 and 9 for wattage information.)

Reheating appetizers: When warm appetizers cool on the serving table, pop them and their microwave-safe container into the microwave oven. Heat, uncovered, on 100% power (high), checking every 30 seconds and rearranging or stirring as necessary.

Making quick canapés: Arrange bread or toast pieces or crackers on a microwave-safe plate lined with paper towels. Top with desired spread. Cook 7 to 9 appetizers at a time, uncovered, on 100% power (high) about 20 seconds or till spread is hot.

Crisping snacks: Spread 1 cup stale or soft chips, crackers, or other snacks in a shallow baking dish. Cook, uncovered, on 100% power (high) for 30 to 45 seconds. Let stand for 2 to 3 minutes. The snacks will crisp as they stand.

Cooking ground meat: Crumble 1 pound ground meat into a 1½-quart casserole. Cook, covered, on 100% power (high) till no pink remains, stirring once or twice. Allow 4 to 6 minutes for beef, 5 to 7 minutes for turkey, and 6 to 8 minutes for pork. Drain off fat.

Cooking bacon: Place bacon on a microwave-safe rack or a plate lined with paper towels. Cover with paper towels. Cook on 100% power (high) till done. Allow 1½ to 2 minutes for 2 slices, 2½ to 3½ minutes for 4 slices, and 4 to 5 minutes for 6 slices.

Cooking chicken: Place 1 skinned large chicken breast (14 to 16 ounces) in a casserole. Cook, covered, on 100% power (high) for 8 to 10 minutes or till tender, turning once. When cool enough to handle, remove meat from the bones and cut up. One large chicken breast will yield 1 cup cut-up cooked chicken.

Cooking shrimp or scallops: Allow ¼ cup water for every ½ pound shrimp or scallops. In a 1½-quart casserole heat the water, uncovered, on 100% power (high) for 1 to 4 minutes or till boiling.

Meanwhile, cut any large scallops in half. Add fresh or frozen shrimp in shells or scallops to the boiling water. Cook, covered, on high till shrimp turn pink or scallops are opaque, stirring twice during cooking. Allow 2 to 4 minutes for ½ pound seafood, 2 to 5 minutes for 1 pound seafood, and 5 to 7 minutes for 1½ pounds seafood. Drain. Peel and devein shrimp before serving, if you like.

Cooking frozen vegetables: Cook frozen vegetables according to package directions. Or, place in a 1-quart casserole. Cook, covered, on 100% power (high) till tender, stirring or rearranging once. Before cooking, add 2 tablespoons water to carrot, cauliflower, or mixed vegetables.

For an 8- to 10-ounce package: allow 5 to 7 minutes for asparagus cuts, cut green beans, or peas; 6 to 8 minutes for broccoli cuts or spinach leaves; and 7 to 9 minutes for artichoke hearts, asparagus spears, broccoli spears, cauliflower flowerets, crinkle-cut carrots, or mixed vegetables. Drain.

Baking potatoes: Prick medium potatoes (6 to 8 ounces each) with a fork. Cook, uncovered, on 100% power (high) till almost tender, rearranging once. Allow 5 to 7 minutes for 1 potato, 8 to 10 minutes for 2 potatoes, and 14 to 17 minutes for 4 potatoes. Let stand for 5 minutes.

Heating canned vegetables: Drain canned vegetables, reserving 2 tablespoons liquid. Place vegetables and reserved liquid in a 1-quart casserole. Cook, covered, on 100% power (high) till heated through, stirring or rearranging once. Allow 2 to 3 minutes for an 8- to 9-ounce can of vegetables and 3 to 5 minutes for a 16-ounce can. Drain.

Cooking onion: In a 1-cup measure cook chopped onion in 1 tablespoon butter or margarine, uncovered, on 100% power (high) till tender. Allow 1 to 1½ minutes for ¼ cup onion and 2 to 3 minutes for ½ cup.

Peeling tomatoes: In a 2-cup measure heat 1 cup water, uncovered, on 100% power (high) for 2½ to 3½ minutes or till boiling. Holding tomato on a fork, dip into boiling water for 12 seconds. Run cold water over tomato. Remove the skin.

Rehydrating (plumping) dried fruit: Place fruit in a 1-quart casserole. Add an equal amount of water. Cook, covered, on 100% power (high) till boiling, stirring once. Allow 1½ to 2½ minutes for ½ cup dried currants or raisins, 2 to 3 minutes for ½ cup mixed dried fruit, 2 to 3 minutes for 1 cup dried apricots, and 3 to 5 minutes for 1 cup dried apples, currants, raisins, figs, mixed fruit, peaches, or prunes. Drain.

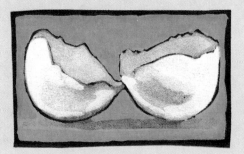

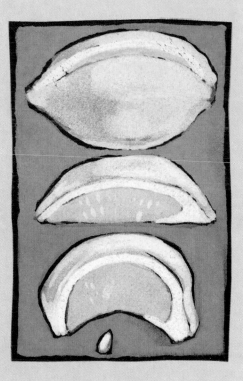

Juicing lemons: Halve or quarter 1 lemon. Heat on 100% power (high) for 30 to 45 seconds. Squeeze out juice.

Heating canned fruit: Pour undrained canned fruit into a 1-quart casserole. Cook, covered, on 100% power (high) till heated through, stirring once. Allow 1½ to 2½ minutes for an 8- to 9-ounce can of fruit and 3 to 5 minutes for a 15- to 17-ounce can.

Quick soup: In a 4-cup measure combine one 10- to 11-ounce can condensed soup and 1 can of water. Cook, uncovered, on 100% power (high) for 2½ to 3½ minutes or till heated through.

Hard-cooked egg: Break an egg into a custard cup. Prick yolk and white all over with a toothpick. Cover with vented clear plastic wrap. Cook on 100% power (high) for 30 to 60 seconds or till done. Let stand, covered, for 2 minutes. When cool, sieve, slice, or chop.

Quick-cooking rice: In a 2-cup measure combine quick-cooking rice and an equal amount of water. Cover with vented clear plastic wrap. Cook on 100% power (high) till the water is boiling. Allow 1 to 2 minutes for ¼ cup uncooked rice (1 serving) and 3 to 5 minutes for 1¼ cups uncooked rice (4 servings). Let stand, covered, for 5 minutes.

Making plain croutons: Spread 2 cups ½-inch bread cubes in a shallow baking dish. Cook, uncovered, on 100% power (high) for 2½ to 4½ minutes or till dry, stirring every 2 minutes.

Softening tortillas: Place four 6- to 7-inch flour tortillas between paper towels. Cook on 100% power (high) for 45 to 60 seconds or till softened.

Reheating muffins and rolls: Place muffins or rolls on a microwave-safe plate. Heat, uncovered, on 100% power (high) till warm. Allow 15 to 20 seconds for 1 or 2 muffins and 30 to 60 seconds for 4 muffins.

Reheating sauces: For chilled flour- or cornstarch-thickened sauces and sauces with dairy sour cream, yogurt, or egg, cook in a 1-cup measure, uncovered, on 50% power (medium) till warm, stirring every 30 seconds. Allow 30 seconds to 1½ minutes for ¼ cup and 1 to 2 minutes for ½ cup.

Heat chilled tomato- or soup-based sauces, uncovered, on 100% power (high), stirring every 30 seconds. Allow 1 to 2 minutes for ½ cup in a 1-cup measure, 3 to 4 minutes for 1 cup in a 2-cup measure, and 5½ to 7½ minutes for 2 cups in a 4-cup measure.

Heating pancake syrup: Heat, uncovered, on 100% power (high) till warm. Allow 30 to 60 seconds for ½ cup syrup in a 1-cup measure and 1 to 1½ minutes for 1 cup syrup in a 2-cup measure.

Heating ice-cream topping: Heat chilled topping, uncovered, on 100% power (high) till warm. Allow 30 to 60 seconds for ¼ cup topping in a 1-cup measure, ½ to 1½ minutes for ½ cup in a 1-cup measure, and 1 to 2 minutes for 1 cup in a 2-cup measure.

Cooking convenience piecrusts: Prepare pastry according to the package directions. Place in a 9-inch microwave-safe pie plate. Flute edges and prick bottom generously with a fork. Cook, uncovered, on 100% power (high) till surface is dry and bubbly, giving the dish a quarter-turn every 2 minutes. Allow 5 to 6 minutes for one folded refrigerated unbaked piecrust and 7 to 9 minutes for one pastry from a stick or mix. Cool before filling.

Warming fruit pie: Place 1 slice of fruit pie (⅛ of pie) on a microwave-safe plate. Heat, uncovered, on 100% power (high) for 45 to 60 seconds or till warm.

Dissolving gelatin: In a microwave-safe container combine gelatin and liquid. Let unflavored gelatin stand for 5 minutes. (Flavored gelatin does not need to stand.) Cook, uncovered, on 100% power (high) till dissolved.

For unflavored gelatin, allow 30 to 40 seconds for 1 envelope in ¼ cup water. For flavored gelatin, allow 3 to 5 minutes for one 3-ounce package in 1 cup water and 7 to 9 minutes for one 6-ounce package in 2 cups water.

Making pudding: In a 4-cup measure combine *regular* pudding mix and milk. Cook, uncovered, on 100% power (high) till boiling, stirring every 2 minutes. Allow 4 to 6 minutes for one 4-serving-size package in 2 cups milk and 7 to 9 minutes for one 6-serving-size package in 3 cups milk. Cover and chill. The pudding will thicken as it chills.

Softening ice cream: Heat 1 pint solidly frozen ice cream in a microwave-safe container, uncovered, on 100% power (high) for 15 seconds or till soft.

Toasting nuts: In a 2-cup measure cook nuts, uncovered, on 100% power (high) till toasted, stirring every minute for the first 3 minutes, then every 30 seconds. Allow 2 to 3 minutes for ½ cup pecans or almonds, 2 to 3 minutes for 1 cup almonds, 3 to 4 minutes for ½ cup raw peanuts or walnuts, 3 to 4 minutes for 1 cup pecans or coconut, and 4 to 5 minutes for 1 cup raw peanuts or walnuts.

Whole nuts may toast first on the inside, so open a few to check for doneness. At the first sign of toasting, spread whole or chopped nuts on paper towels to cool. Let them stand for at least 15 minutes. They will continue to toast as they stand.

Blanching almonds: In a 2-cup measure cook 1 cup water, uncovered, on 100% power (high) for 3 to 5 minutes or till boiling. Add ½ cup whole almonds. Cook, uncovered, on high for 1½

minutes. Drain, then rinse with cold water. When cool, slip off the almond skins.

Moistening brown sugar: In a 1-cup measure cook ½ cup water, uncovered, on 100% power (high) for 1 to 2 minutes or till boiling.

Place brown sugar in a microwave-safe container near water. Heat, uncovered, on high till softened. Allow 1½ to 2½ minutes for ½ pound brown sugar and 2 to 3 minutes for 1 pound.

Thawing frozen whipped topping: Heat topping, uncovered, on 30% power (medium-low) till softened. Allow 45 to 60 seconds for one 4-ounce container and 1 to 1½ minutes for an 8-ounce container.

Melting chocolate: Cook chocolate, uncovered, on 100% power (high) till soft enough to stir smooth, stirring every minute during cooking. (It won't seem

melted till stirred.) For squares, in a 1-cup measure, allow 1 to 2 minutes for 1 ounce (1 square) and 1½ to 2½ minutes for 2 ounces (2 squares).

For chocolate pieces, allow 1 to 2 minutes for ½ cup in a 1-cup measure, 1½ to 2½ minutes for one 6-ounce package (1 cup) in a 2-cup measure, and 2 to 3 minutes for one 12-ounce package (2 cups) in a 4-cup measure.

Melting caramels: Cook caramels, uncovered, on 100% power (high) till soft enough to stir smooth, stirring every minute during cooking. (They won't seem melted till stirred.) Allow 30 to 60 seconds for 14 caramels in a 1-cup measure, 1 to 2 minutes for 25 caramels (½ of a 14-ounce package) in a 2-cup measure, and 2½ to 3½ minutes for a 14-ounce package in a 4-cup measure.

Melting butter: Place butter or margarine in a custard cup. Cook, uncovered, on 100% power (high) till melted. Allow 40 to 50 seconds for 2 tablespoons, 45 to 60 seconds for ¼ cup, and 1 to 2 minutes for ½ cup.

Softening butter: Place ½ cup butter or margarine in a microwave-safe container. Cook, uncovered, on 10% power (low) for 1 to 1½ minutes or till softened.

Softening cream cheese: Place cream cheese in a microwave-safe container. Cook, uncovered, on 100% power (high) till softened. Allow 15 to 30 seconds for 3 ounces cream cheese and 45 to 60 seconds for 8 ounces.

Warming finger towels: Soak 4 washcloths in water. Squeeze out excess water and roll up. Heat on 100% power (high) for 2 to 3 minutes or till hot.

TECHNIQUE INDEX

A-C

Almonds, blanching, 281
Appetizers
  Arranging bite-size snacks, 34
  Bacon-wrapped nibbles, 30
  Crisping a cereal mix, 64
  Crisping snacks, 278
  Making quick canapés, 278
  Reheating appetizers, 29, 278
  Serving hot dips in cheese
    shells, 38
  Thickening a hot dip, 38
Apples for micro-cooking,
  choosing, 128
Asparagus, fresh, buying, 246
Bacon, cooking, 278
Beverages, heating, 51
Browning dish, stir-frying in, 152
Brown sugar, moistening, 281
Butter, melting, 281
Butter, softening, 281
Cabbage rolls, shaping, 254
Cakes
  Cooking a one-layer cake, 70
  Fast-cooking cupcakes, 70
  Making a ring-shaped cake, 76
Candies, easy, 92
Caramels, melting, 93, 281
Cereals, cooking, 67
Chicken
  Coating chicken pieces, 196
  Cooking chicken, 212, 278
  Cooking cut-up chicken,
    190, 212
  Cooking poultry, 212
  Cooking poultry in low-wattage
    ovens, 190
  Creating a chicken
    casserole, 208
  Defrosting poultry, 211
  Microwave-grilled chicken, 194

Chicken *(continued)*
  Quick-cooking chicken, 208
  Skinning chicken for fewer
    calories, 9
  Stuffing a chicken breast, 200
  Stuffing a whole bird, 186
Chocolate, melting, 93, 281
Cocoa, reheating, 47
Converting recipes, 272, 273
Cookies, bar, layering, 80
Cooking time, factors affecting, 18
Cookware, 16
  Cookware for caramelizing, 87
  Dish test for glass and
    ceramic cookware, 15
  Microwave-safe materials, 14
Cream cheese, softening, 34, 281
Croutons, plain, making, 280
Custard mixes, making, 225, 280
Custards, individual, cooking, 220

D-L

Defrosting, 277
Divinity, making, 88
Divinity, saving, 89
Dried fruit, rehydrating, 139, 279
Eggs
  Hard-cooked eggs, 279
  Poaching and frying eggs, 103
  Poaching eggs, 96
  Scrambling eggs, 99
Even-cooking techniques, 20
Finger towels, warming, 281
Fish
  Coating thick fillets, 114
  Cooking fish and seafood, 124
  Cooking thin fillets, 110
  Cooking whole fish, 106
  Crumbs for coating fish, 114
  Defrosting fish and seafood, 123
  Stuffing a whole fish, 106
  Thick and thin fish fillets, 110
Freezing, 277
Fruit
  Choosing apples for micro-
    cooking, 128
  Defrosting frozen fruit, 138
  Heating canned fruit, 279
  Preparing fruit cobbler, 134
  Rehydrating dried fruit,
    139, 279
  Steaming fresh fruit, 138

Fruit *(continued)*
  Steaming stuffed fruit, 128
Gelatin, dissolving, 280
Granola fix-ups, 65
High-altitude microwave
  cooking, 274
Ice cream, softening, 280
Ice-cream topping, heating, 280
Lemons, juicing, 279

M-R

Meat
  Choosing roasts for micro-
    cooking, 144
  Cooking bacon, 171, 278
  Cooking ground meat, 172, 278
  Cooking meat, 171
  Cooking pork, 146
  Cooking pork ribs, 146
  Defrosting meat, 170
  Making a ground-meat
    casserole, 164
  Meat loaf toppings, 156
  Preparing patties, 160
  Reheating meatballs, 26
  Shaping a meat loaf, 156
  Shaping filled meatballs, 26
  Simmering a pot roast, 142
  Simmering a stew, 236
Meals, microwave, making, 270
Microwave Ovens
  How microwaves work, 8
  Microwave oven features, 11
  Power levels, 12, 13
  Wattage, 6, 9
Microwave-safe materials, 14
Muffins, making, 60
Muffins, reheating, 280
Muffin toppings, 60
Nut brittle, making, 86
Nutrition and the microwave, 271
Pancake syrup, heating, 280
Pies
  Cooking an unpricked
    crust, 180
  Cooking convenience
    piecrusts, 183, 280
  Meringue topping, 179
  Preparing a pie pastry, 176
  Thawing frozen whipped
    topping, 180, 281
  Warming fruit pie, 280

RECIPE INDEX

A-B

D-G

H-M

N-P

Q-S

T-Z

Have BETTER HOMES AND
GARDENS® magazine delivered
to your door. For information,
write to:
MR. ROBERT AUSTIN
P.O. BOX 4536
DES MOINES, IA 50336